First Cats

Amazing Origins of the UK Sports Tradition

Tom Stephens

Oakleaf Publishing, Inc.

www.FirstCats.net

Published by Oakleaf Publishing, Inc., Louisville, Ky.

ISBN 0-9772683-0-6 (paper)

Cover design by Kelly O'Neill Carter

Kelly O'Neill – Artist of Life
www.my-portraits.com
1-888-8-ARTIST

All contemporary photographs by the author unless otherwise noted

For Anne

and

Ellen and Sean

Acknowledgments

This book would have forever remained a dream of mine without the support, kind words and quite a bit of hard work on the part of numerous friends and family members who volunteered to help in any way they could, lending their talents and enthusiasm to the project.

Steve Vest, publisher of *Kentucky Monthly* magazine and a friend of 30 years, spent untold hours formatting the book and providing invaluable technical advice—in addition to quite a bit of patience with an anxious author. *Kentucky Monthly* art director Kelli Schreiber was also quite helpful.

Dan Wright, who I've known since the first grade, advised me in the formation of Oakleaf Publishing Inc. and generously offered not only his accounting expertise, but also a high-energy willingness to go the extra mile in helping with marketing and sales.

Whatever quality I've been able to put into *First Cats* has been greatly enhanced by the editing of Dr. Thomas H. Appleton Jr., a good friend and mentor, whose knowledge, expertise and advice—in addition to not a little research—also did much to help me complete the project.

My sister Susan Smith proofread the entire text, giving me a reader's perspective, in addition to quite a few encouraging words—often when I needed them most. My brother-in-law Steve Belongia was always willing to answer silly computer questions—in addition to troubleshooting the various human errors I committed.

I'm also thankful for the friendly help of staff members at the University of Kentucky: Frank Stanger, Matt Harris, and Clair McCann of the Special Collections department; Tony Neely and Matt Steinke of the UK Athletics Association; Brooke Willis Ramirez of W.T. Young Library; and Sara Sjuts of UK Women's Volleyball. I would also like to acknowledge the help of Kathleen Neeley, assistant archivist at the University of Kansas.

I'm also indebted to all the fans I've known and met over the years, especially my friends Mark and Carol Hensley, Russell and Karen Moore, and Reese Graham, and my cousins Steve Smith, Harvey and Dianne Smith, Ronnie and Marion Smith and Bobby and Shirley Smith.

Thanks everyone. I am tremendously grateful.

First Cats

Contents

Preface

Because I am a lifelong student of history—in addition to a blue-bleeding Kentucky fan—friends and acquaintances are always asking me when UK started playing basketball or what are the words to the fight song, or why the school's colors are blue and white or any number of other questions.

In 2003, as the Wildcats were celebrating their first century of playing basketball, I began wondering just how our team acquired its nickname and fight song and just when it was that fans began yelling "Go Big Blue."

Fifteen months of research and writing later, I located the answers to most of the questions. They were found in newspapers, yearbooks, biographical files and many other original sources.

But this is a fan's book, which strives to tell these stories in an upbeat, readable style—the kind on the sports page. Readers will also notice some overlap in the chapters, because many pioneers of the Kentucky athletic program contributed to more than one sport. It should also be noted that this book makes no claim to be a comprehensive history of UK sports, but rather a handbook of sorts that allows Kentucky fans to answer those frequently asked questions and explore the interesting—and often amazing—origins of the school's traditions. I have also chosen to refer to campus buildings and colleges and universities by their modern names.

The experience of researching and writing *First Cats* has been a true education that makes the devotion I feel for my alma mater greater than ever.

Through the records they left behind, I've gotten a chance to meet Daddy Boles, Carl Lampert and Greg Page; Florence Offutt Stout, Alice

Courtney Pence and numerous others who spent their careers and often virtually whole lifetimes in building the UK athletic program—in addition to its mission as an institution of learning.

Almost all of us have been to a meeting or played in a pickup basketball or football game that had little or no importance or significance. UK's first basketball and football contests were very much affairs of that kind, significant not in themselves, but in what they began. The first basketball game, for example, barely rated a mention in the local newspapers and nobody even bothered to record who coached the team, if it had a coach at all. The school colors are derived from the color of a necktie a football player wore to an 1891 students' meeting. The words to the Wildcat fight song were written for a $5 prize that was never collected.

But from these events rose an athletic program that has captured the imagination of ever-loyal Kentuckians and—at times—even the nation and the world. Part of the reason we feel pride for UK athletics is because of the program's early and enduring commitment to representing the university and the state well.

May we always strive to continue the efforts of those who have gone before us, not only to further the Wildcats' unparalleled athletic excellence, but also UK's mission to educate the sons and daughters of the Commonwealth.

Tom Stephens
August 1, 2005

Introduction

A Fan's Perspective

I've heard enough UK fans talk to know that my experience is far from unique.

My Big Blue switch was thrown in January 1971, on a night my father listened to a Wildcats game on the radio as he unstrung the lights from our Christmas tree. I'm sure I wore his patience thin with questions about who was playing, why he listened and who was the man with the mellow voice telling us about it.

I remember the highlight of the experience was listening to coach Adolph Rupp's post-game show, which was part coach's show, part unintentional comedy sketch. I liked that old man, whoever he was.

It wasn't long before I knew him very well. He was the greatest basketball coach ever—and we wanted him to win every game. A few more games into the season, I knew the names of all the players too, along with their heights, weights, hometowns and scoring averages.

I listened to Cawood call those contests, acting them out on the plastic hoop in my room. I listened to games and post-games on a transistor radio—a gift from my grandmother—while lying in bed with my blanket over my head because I was supposed to be asleep. I thrilled with every win and grieved over every loss.

My first in-person look at the team was the open practices at Freedom Hall on the mornings or afternoons of the December nights they played Notre Dame. It was well known that more people attended those practices than the games of other teams that played there. Anyone who wanted one received a blue-tone mimeographed team photo, surrounded by facsimiles of the players' autographs. I studied those pages until I knew every player's face so well I would have recognized it anywhere—and I was just as proud of Tom Payne—UK basketball's first black player—as I was Larry Stamper, Ronnie Lyons or anyone else. To this day, I can point out Stan Key—now president of the UK Alumni Association—or Jim Andrews as they walk in a Rupp Arena crowd.

I couldn't believe they made coach Rupp retire.

But time went by and the old man, among other things, conducted basketball clinics with a collection of college and professional players and coaches. I attended one of these at Freedom Hall with my dad and my good friend Dan Wright. Dad awakened me very early on that Saturday morning and we arrived at the arena in plenty of time to get seats close to the floor.

The Baron soon emerged and introduced more heroes: Dan Issel, Mike Pratt and Louie Dampier, all players for the beloved Kentucky Colonels of the American Basketball Association. I sat enthralled as Rupp spoke, trying to absorb every bit of basketball wisdom he uttered. I remember a story he told about an All-American player from another school who had asked the coach how he could improve. Rupp said that's what every player should do. That type of commitment would make average players better and good players the best.

I had no trouble understanding the point. Constant effort was the way to get that blue and white uniform I was convinced I would wear someday.

After dispensing his 42 years' worth of basketball wisdom on us boys, Rupp turned the clinic over to other coaches and stood watching the next lesson. Dad told me Rupp would probably leave early and that I should try to get his autograph when he did. After a few minutes, dad said "Now," and I sprang from my seat, catching up with the old coach as he passed near a folded set of portable bleachers. Unbelievably, no other kid—or dad—in Freedom Hall had foreseen the possibility of this moment.

"Sir," I said, looking up at him, "can I have your autograph?"

"Oh, all right," Rupp replied, motioning me behind the bleachers, "but let's go over there so we don't get mawbed." I was all alone with the "Baron of Basketball," the "Man in the Brown Suit," and stood in amazement as he scribbled his name on my piece of paper and silently walked out the door.

But I was more than a fan of Adolph Rupp. I loved those Kentucky Wildcats and I started a scrapbook of press clippings from Joe Hall's first season of 1972-73. It was an interesting time to become a Kentucky fan, when the basketball team wasn't supposed to win, when it was often an unranked underdog that had to overachieve to have a chance. I vividly remember a night on the road in the SEC when virtually the entire starting five fouled out and Merion Haskins and Jerry Hale came in and pulled the game out for the Cats.

I followed Grevey, Flynn and Conner as they rose from undefeated "Kittens" into the national spotlight. I suffered through Indiana's 98-74 demolition of the team on Dec. 7, 1974, and literally banged my head on my basement ceiling while jumping for joy when Kentucky got its 92-90 revenge in the NCAA Mideast Regional the following March 22. And I saw the horrendous officiating that cost the team the 1975 national title.

I was a high school sophomore when UK won the 1978 NCAA Championship. It was such a momentous occasion that I received permission to accompany my dad and some neighbors to Bluegrass Airport to welcome the team. This was contingent upon my promise to go to school the next day no matter how tired I was. The team arrived at the terminal about 2 a.m. It was standing room only. By that I mean you couldn't sit if you wanted to. When I raised my hand to give a No. 1 sign, the space my arm had taken up was immediately filled by the guy next to me. But the next morning I showed up at Doss High School with a hot-off-the-press (it was still warm when I put it on) NCAA Champs T-shirt.

The first home game I ever saw was the night Chuck Alexsinas left the team. I sat with my back literally against one wall of Rupp Arena.

As a student a few years later, I never missed a game. Several times a season during the periodic ticket distributions, I "camped out" in a line that wound around Memorial Coliseum—on the outside—in every kind of winter weather to get the best seats possible.

But the games were wonderful. I never sat higher than 10 rows from the floor and was sometimes at the center stripe on the fifth row, absolutely the best seat a student unaffiliated with the team could get at the time. I was usually so close I could hear the on-the-court conversations, which were an education in themselves.

My only experience with a true road game came when I went to the Hall of Fame Bowl in Birmingham, Ala., in 1984. It was a completely new experience, an endless party of 10,000 or so "best friends," many of whose only association was that they wore blue and white. We drank too much, whooped too loud and staged impromptu pep rallies—complete with the boom-box-powered fight song—in the hotel courtyard. It was a blast.

When it was announced that Kentucky would play its first NCAA Tournament game in Tampa in 1983, some college friends of mine decided to drive there on their way home from a Spring break trip to Ft. Lauderdale. Arriving outside the arena with just a few dollars apiece of disposable income, they began the almost impossible task of finding tick-ets at a price they could afford. After a few minutes, a man who looked to be in his fifties approached them, asking if they needed tickets. "How much?" they asked, but the man only wanted to know if they were University of Kentucky students and if they needed tickets. "Yes," they said. The man placed a ticket in each of the students' hands. "Have a good time," he said as he walked away. "I went to UK 30 years ago." The friends walked into the arena and found their seats. They were at center court, 10 rows from the floor.

After I graduated, my friend Mark Hensley and I bought football season tickets together—mainly because basketball tickets were out of our reach. We've suffered through the losses and rejoiced at the wins for almost two decades.

Over the years, I've been accused of being a UK fanatic by any number of people who don't seem to realize that that is the meaning of the word fan. But I am by no means alone. My mother is almost unable to watch Kentucky play because of the possibility she might witness a loss. One of my friends was so upset over a former coach's betrayal of the program that she boxed up her collection of his ghost-written books and sent them back to him, along with a note explaining just what she thought of his unconcerned disloyalty. A co-worker of mine devised his own 12-step program when he decided he was taking football losses a little too hard.

Internet sites and game-day parties are filled with stories about fans wearing UK clothing being hailed with "Go Big Blue" almost anywhere in the world. As he sat contemplating Old Faithful one afternoon in 2003, my dad heard someone behind him humming a familiar tune. It was "On, On, U of K," performed by someone who had seen the back of his blue Kentucky hat.

My uncle John Colson, who works as a musician on cruise ships, relates that he has seen Wildcat merchandise all over the Caribbean, from Aruba to Jamaica and the Bahamas. Islanders, he said, often want to trade for whatever Wildcat item he might be wearing.

UK graduate and fan Wayne Breeding was traveling on a commuter bus from Tokyo to Kobe, Japan, in the late 1990s when he gazed out his window for a glimpse of the Japanese countryside. As the bus passed a small building, Breeding noticed that painted on one outside wall were the words "Wildcat Grill" in English, complete with the UK logo and an image of a Wildcat. "I just cracked up," Breeding said. "I think they just wanted to be as American as they could, so they set up a 'Wildcat Grill.'"

When Louisville's WHAS-AM became a 50,000-watt, clear channel radio station in the early 1930s, UK and its coach, Adolph Rupp, were poised to scale the heights of the basketball world. As Kentucky began to play—and beat—the elite eastern teams, WHAS' coverage turned listeners into Wildcat fans from Florida to Maine. There is a story that a group of neighbors in northern New York began congregating in a local bar to listen to the UK basketball team whenever they played. Over the years, the men turned the bar into a virtual UK shrine, with photos signed by coaches and numerous posters and other items. None of them had ever set foot in Kentucky.

My own Wildcat experience has brought me much joy and friendship. I recall watching basketball games with Russell and Karen Moore, Steve Smith, Bruce Howard, Mike Thomas and Carol McGurk. My dad and I tailgate every football season with our cousins Ronnie and Harvey Smith and their wives Marian and Diane, along with lots of friends like Jay and Judy Forman and any number of game-day acquaintances. And I've started bringing my kids to the games. My daughter knows all the words to "On, On, U of K," while my son makes a mean sound like a Wildcat.

Kentucky fans have been accused of everything from insanity to having nothing else to live for. We are not guilty. We are as proud of the Kentucky Wildcats as Green Bay residents are of their Packers or those in Beantown are of their Boston Celtics or the people of College Station are of their Aggies. No apologies are necessary and none will be given.

We simply love the Kentucky Wildcats and support them through good times and bad, win or lose, from the day we beat Illinois 6-0 in 1909 to the 1998 NCAA Championship until forever.

Football Comes to the Bluegrass

For anyone who's spent time walking its pathways, there is a timeless quality to the campus of the University of Kentucky.

Maybe it's the century-old red brick and stone buildings that dot the area around the Administration Building or the immensity of the mature trees or even the Spanish-American War cannon on the hill. Whatever the reason, the place conveys a sense of the past and a feeling of belonging.

As with many other universities of similar standing and longevity, UK's alumni develop a fondness for their school, a nostalgia based on time spent, lessons learned and perhaps the memory of a life-altering event or two.

Though it has served as Kentucky's home field only since 1973, the same thing can be said of Commonwealth Stadium. The trees are smaller, but there is a timeless quality here too, perhaps also based on time spent and lessons learned—but also barbecues attended, great plays and players remembered and the fun-loving camaraderie of supporting the Wildcats. Whether tailgating among the oak trees or watching a game in the stands, fans seem to soak up the effort and pride the Wildcats leave on the field. Win or lose, they are ever faithful, and each season brings renewed hope and the best qualities of college athletics.

It has been that way since the very beginning.

The University of Kentucky began its existence on February 22, 1865,

Though only serving as the Wildcats' home since 1973, Commonwealth Stadium is already acquiring the pleasant, tree-lined look of the rest of UK's campus.

as one of the so-called land-grant institutions founded under the Morrill Act to foster agricultural innovation and progress.

First known as the Agricultural and Mechanical College of Kentucky, the school became part of Kentucky University, traditionally known as Transylvania.

By the time the Kentucky General Assembly separated the two schools in 1878, their students had already begun playing football informally.

Under a new name, Kentucky State College, the institution moved to its present campus on South Limestone Street soon afterward. A quasi-military school, which placed particular emphasis on training civil and mechanical engineers, it was said to be undergoing a "meteoric shower of new students ..." swelling its roll to more than 250.

When the cooling autumn weather of 1881 turned the attention of the Transylvania men to football, they challenged their former schoolmates, who had come to be known as the "Cadets," to a series of three intercollegiate contests. The challenge—including the rule that players had to be under 17 years old—was accepted and the first game scheduled for Saturday, Nov. 12.

Game day dawned drizzly in central Kentucky and the *Lexington Daily Transcript* noted that the teams had "rather a slippery day" for their game that afternoon. The Cadets arrived at the "Old Fair Grounds" with 15 players. This was an acceptable number under Australian rules, upon which local football is said to have been based. They included

STATE COLLEGE ITEMS.

Col. McFarland has been too unwell to attend his classes for three days past, at the State College.

Mr. R. L. Cox, a student of the State College, is very sick. His mother arrived last night.

The following is a list of the State College boys who will play in the match game of foot-ball to-morrow: Tolbert, Clark, Bartlett, Lee, DeRoode, Seibricht, Downing, Farrell, Fyffe, Elliot, Parker, Irvine, Morgan and Downing.

Notice of the first game in UK football history-- played on Nov. 12, 1881--appeared in the *Lexington Transcript*. Kentucky State College, as it was then known, won "quite an exciting game" over Transylvania by the somewhat mysterious score of 7 1/2 to 1.

"Tolbert, Clark, Bartlett, Lee, DeRoode, Seibricht, Downing, Farrell, Fyffe, Elliot, Parker, Irvine, Morgan and Downing."

In "quite an exciting game," the Cadets triumphed by a score of 7 1/2 to 1, which is somewhat unclear because fractions weren't used in Australian football scoring. "The football club is jubilant over its success, and the boys continue to practice the art of kicking," reported the *Transcript*. "They often practice on each other's seats."

Elsewhere in the paper, a reporter predictably tried to pull competitiveness back toward academics. "If the State College and Kentucky University want to get up something more interesting than a football match, they should get up a spelling match between fifty picked men from each school. The people would take a great interest." The Transylvania correspondent conceded that a spelling contest would be popular but questioned "how many of the University boys would risk a public demonstration of their ignorance."

Athleticism prevailed, however, and the teams agreed to a return match the following Saturday, Nov. 19. Despite their loss, Transylvania reported that "the usual amount of foot-ball excitement again rages, and as a natural consequence there is an increased demand for new shirts and 'arnics.'" Transy's team members were "Clay, Davidson, Harris, Hinton, Thurgood, Rogers, McDonald, Macay, Ballou, Knight, McGarvey, Dunlap, Hunt, Phillips and Winn."

"Justice being given to all," noted a Transylvania partisan, "we can bespeak a close game for our boys." The prophesy proved correct, with KSC falling 2 to 1.

The rubber match would be on Dec. 3. The *Transcript* notice read: "There will be another match game of foot-ball between the University Club and the State College Club at the Old Fair Grounds next Saturday afternoon, beginning at 2 o'clock. Every body invited—particularly the ladies. Admission free."

"The football club is jubilant over its success, and the boys continue to practice the art of kicking. They often practice on each other's seats."

As game time neared, the newspaper again tried to drum up attendance for "that scientific and rare game, foot ball....Of course all places of business will be closed, and the entire city will turn out to enjoy this rare treat."

"These contests develop muscle wonderfully," said a *Transcript* reporter, "and if not carried too far, are admirable accomplishment for hard study. Play a fair, gentlemanly game, my hearties, but work for all that's in you."

KSC lost to its cross-town rival again, 3 1/4 to 2 1/4, ending its inaugural season with a 1-2 record.

* * *

The rivalry between KSC and Transylvania, as recalled in a 1930 *Carlisle Mercury* editorial by Warren Fisher, had its true beginnings in the 1878 squabble over which of the newly separated schools would possess the name "Kentucky." A debate between partisans in the state legislature resulted in a draw of sorts in which Transylvania would be known as Kentucky University, while the Agricultural and Mechanical College would become Kentucky State College.

3

Because KSC was intended to be the state university, however, generations of its students convinced themselves that their school had suffered an indignity and were determined to exact revenge whenever possible. One particular grievance was the words "Kentucky University" that school officials placed within a wrought iron arch above Transylvania's campus gate.

Relations between the students of the two schools, Fisher wrote, "consisted of a hearty desire to punch each other's head, upon the slightest provocation and following every athletic contest."

"It was decidedly unsafe," Fisher continued, "for one who took his educational fare within the classic corridors of Morrison Chapel to venture unattended onto the State College campus." If an offender wasn't beaten, Fisher recalled, KSC students amused themselves by "removing all garments and making truly modernistic flashlight photographs of the victim."

In 1908, when it was announced that Transylvania had abandoned its "Kentucky University" moniker, the "State student body ... came over on North Broadway and sawed the name from the iron arch...."

"If there wasn't a fight," Fisher said, "it was because we were hopelessly outnumbered."

* * *

Football of the intercollegiate brand died out for a decade until 1891, when KSC challenged Georgetown College to a contest.

The first game of KSC's football re-emergence was held on April 10, 1891, in a contest billed as the "State championship and ... the event of the season." The teams played on Transylvania's field in a struggle that was "exciting and witnessed by a large crowd." KSC won 6-2. The following school year—but still considered the same season—KSC scheduled an away game at Transylvania and a home contest against Danville's Centre College. It was a challenge game, which included $50 to guarantee the visitors' appearance.

The Transy game was cancelled after a player was injured, so the KSC partisans went back to Limestone Street and began preparing for Centre. On December 18, the night before the contest, "an enthusiastic crowd" met in the chapel. The group elected Civil Engineering professor James P. Nelson its chairman and W.S. Page, secretary. Professor J.W. Newman, noting the longstanding disagreement between the all-male Patterson Literary Society and the all-female Philosophian literary society over school colors, announced that the faculty "had decided to settle that question."

Football player Richard C. Stoll recalled that blue was suggested, and "someone on the other side of the chapel said, 'What color blue will it be?'

4

"I happened to have on a blue necktie and took it off and held it up," Stoll said. "That was the color blue which was adopted. ... The blue at the University is a peculiar color of blue, but it so happened that was the color in my necktie."

Next morning, the *Transcript* reported that state college's colors were "dark blue and light yellow. A motion was made that the colors selected be adopted, which was carried by a big majority."

The meeting-goers also adopted a "college yell," which after quite a bit of discussion—and in homage to its original Agricultural and Mechanical College moniker—turned out to be:

"Rah! Rush! Ree!
A! M!! C!!!"

Tom Shelby was granted possession of the colors, which probably took the form of blue and white streamers mounted atop a staff. "The home team is now ready for Old Centre's renowned (sons) who have won several victories of late," the *Transcript* reported the next morning. "When the sun goes down to-night we predict for our boys a great victory. This game will certainly decide the championship of the South. The two teams have never been defeated, and the friends are waiting anxiously the result."

Shelby took the school colors to the "C. S. Depot," where they were escorted to the Lexington baseball park, site of the game. "The State College boys appeal to Lexington friends to put on their colors, and witness the battle, as a large delegation of Danville people will be on hand to back their men."

The Danville Advocate noted that the 3:30 p.m. start time was decided to allow Centre's players and friends the opportunity to travel to Lexington on the "accommodation train," which left Danville that morn-

EVERYTHING READY

FOR THE GREAT GAME OF FOOT BALL THIS AFTERNOON.

The State College Boys Adopt Yell and Colors—Great Interest in the Contest.

An enthusiastic meeting of State College boys was held last night in the College chapel to arrange for the foot ball contest this afternoon, with Centre College. Prof. Nelson was elected Chairman and W. S. Page was made Secretary. Prof. Newman said there had been much trouble existing between the two literary societies over college colors, and the faculty had decided to settle that question. The State College colors will be dark blue and light yellow. A motion was made that the colors selected be adopted, which was carried by a big majority.

The next question to settle, was a college yell. Quite a number were offered, but most of them seemed too long. Dan Bryan proposed the following one which was finally adopted:

Rah! Rush! Ree!
A! M!! C!!!

The second "first game" in UK's football history was on April 10, 1891, when KSC's Cadets beat Georgetown 6-2. As they prepared for a game against Centre the following December, students met in the chapel and chose "dark blue and light yellow" as the school colors. Notice of the choice appeared in the Dec. 19, 1891 *Lexington Transcript*. The colors were changed to blue and white for the following season.

ing at 1:16 p.m. Travelers were charged $1.40 for a round-trip ticket, which the railroad company promised to reduce to $1.05 if at least 50 tickets were sold, "which will doubtless be the case."

The Advocate reported several changes in Centre's veteran lineup. "Turner, Cheek and Edwin Van Winkle will be unable to play." To take their places were "Swope, Barbour and Arthur Van Winkle, members of the Junior Eleven, and three good men." The paper said changes had also been made in the positions players would play. "Captain Berry will here after play full back entirely, as this will give him a better command of his men."

The Centre starters were "Hudson, right end; Swope, right tackle; Boyer, right guard; Allen, center guard; Willin, left guard; Barbour, left tackle; Douglass, left end; A. Van Winkle, quarter back; Cook, right half back; Hardin, left half back; Berry (Capt.) full back." KSC started Wheat, center rush; Ed Hobdy, right tackle; Colyer, right guard; Ulysses Garrard, left guard; King, tackle; Sturgil, left end; Norman, right end; John Bryan, right half back; Ferrington (Capt.), left half back; Wallis, quarter back; and Brent, full back.

"Nearly a thousand people" showed up at the baseball park to witness the contest, reportedly "the hardest fought game ever played in the State." Centre, however, didn't arrive at the train depot until 3 p.m. and by the time the visitors were ready to take the field, it was almost 4 o'clock. They were dressed in their orange and black "suits" that "showed the 'earth-earthy' nature of their favorite sport, and were considerably the worse for wear."

Centre chose "Mr. Blaine of Danville" for referee, while Dwight Harrison was the Cadets' choice at "umpire."

The visitors unleashed a mighty running game against KSC, with Douglass and Hardin "beating the record on runs and dodging." KSC's Hobdy, Brent, Wallis and Bryan slowed the onslaught, and several of their hard-hitting tackles prompted "loud and long" yells from the Lexingtonians. The *Transcript* also reported that "the young ladies seemed to enjoy the game and applauded every effort of the home team."

The squads battled until darkness, when the game was called. The score was Centre 10, KSC 0. "The home boys were placed at many disadvantages," said the *Transcript* reporter. "They had received but two weeks training, while the Centre College boys have had constant drills since September."

Still, the Lexington team impressed everyone. "Many of the best posted men say that (the) State College boys need a little more practice," said the *Transcript*. "Even the Centre College men complimented our boys by saying their efforts were magnificent."

As they left town, the visitors were also loud in their praise of the "young ladies" in the stands. Lexington, they said, was the "home of more pretty girls than all other Kentucky towns combined."

The following year, KSC changed its school colors to blue and white and enlisted Geology and Zoology professor Arthur McQuiston Miller as its football coach. Though he had never played the game, Miller's qualifications were apparently that he had attended graduate school at Princeton, then a football powerhouse. Miller, who later became the school's first dean of Arts and Sciences, handed off the team in mid-season to a real coach, John A. Thompson, who had actually played at Purdue. The team compiled a 1-2-1 record that year. Thompson also played in some games, which was not against the rules, and posted a 6-4-1 mark in 1894.

* * *

Ed Hobdy, who played right tackle for the Cadets against Centre in 1891, was captain of the 1892 team that went 2-4-1. Left guard Ulysses Garrard captained John A. Thompson's team that posted a 5-2-1 mark in 1893.

UK's first football coach was Geology and Zoology professor Arthur McQuiston Miller, whose credentials were solely based on the fact that he had attended graduate school at Princeton, one of the premier football schools in the nation. That Miller had never played the game apparently didn't matter to his players. A real coach, John A. Thompson, took over in mid-season, and the team went 1-2-1. Miller went on to become UK's first dean of Arts and Sciences.

2

The Immortals of 1898

The University of Kentucky, its fans and its coaches have been inclined to give nicknames to favorite teams.

Almost any Cat fan can rattle off the names: The Fabulous Five of 1947-48 that went 36-3 to give Adolph Rupp his first NCAA Championship; the 1957-58 Fiddlin' Five that added a third NCAA trophy to Rupp's case; the Unforgettables of 1992—participants in the "greatest college game ever played"; and the Comeback Cats, which overcame deficit after deficit to win it all in 1998 for coach Tubby Smith.

But these were all basketball teams.

UK's first labeled team was of the football variety, achievers of the only perfect pigskin record in Kentucky history. These Wildcats scored 180 points in a seven-game season; their opponents scored zero.

They were known as the Immortals of '98, and started the season as what today would be known as a club team. The school was Kentucky State College, or KSC, in those days, and its teams were known as the Cadets. Athletics was an informal affair run by elected team managers, who scheduled opponents, drummed up interest among the students, and even handled ticket sales, using profits to hire and pay coaches and other expenses.

Captains were player-coaches of a sort, providing the leadership that compelled team members to attend practice and choosing who would play in games. KSC had a fine captain in Roscoe Severs, who also played quarterback. The rest of the Immortals were C.C. "Fred" Clarke, center; Charles L. Straus, right guard; Eugene C. "Mad Anthony" Whayne, left guard; James H. Graham, left tackle; W.C. Wills, right tackle; John Willim, right end; Roy Maddox, left end; Ernest T. Lyle, right halfback; Herman Scholtz, left halfback; J. Soule Smith, fullback; and C.L. Humphrey; J. Milward Elliott; Job D. Turner; Wynne Martin; and Jack Kehoe.

KSC did have a coach, Lyman B. Eaton, but he had resigned after the previous school year and returned to his Cincinnati home. He was killed in a street-car accident soon afterward.

So the Cadets prepared for the season by themselves.

"We would go out for practice at 3 o'clock in the afternoon and practice until dark," Graham recalled. "When the light got so bad that we couldn't see the ball, we would run around the field for a while to improve our wind."

But football wasn't very popular with the faculty or administration. A motion to appropriate $200 for the 1898 season was tabled by the board of

The Immortals (front row, from left): Ernest T. Lyle, Job D. Turner, Louis Wynne Martin, John H. "Jack" Kehoe, C.C. "Fred" Clarke; (middle row): James H. Graham, Charles L. Straus, team captain Roscoe F. Severs, W. Claude Wills, Eugene C. "Mad Anthony" Whayne; and (back row): J. Soule Smith, John Willim, coach William S. "Billy" Bass, manager W.L. Bronaugh, Claude L. Humphrey, J. Milward Elliott, and Roy Maddox. Other members of the team were Herman Scholtz, Sam Hogg, A.C. Reese, and Richard "Dick" Wilson.

trustees without discussion. School president James Kennedy Patterson was against athletics altogether, saying they created "an atmosphere uncongenial to study."

"Almost as soon as college work begins, football teams are organized and begin training," Patterson lamented. "Twenty or thirty men are withdrawn for athletic exercise almost every afternoon. From the end of November until about the middle of March, when the baseball season begins, there is a comparative lull and during the interval the serious work of the year is done. I do not speak of broken noses, legs and arms, but of the time wasted, idleness encouraged and a heritage of demoralization carried over to the succeeding year."

Students did not agree, pointing out the sport's byproduct of physical fitness, as well as its tendency to end pretensions and prejudices. "Football annihilates the society dude and the cigarette worm," one wrote. "For

KSC President James Kennedy Patterson was opposed to athletics in general and football in particular. "Almost as soon as college work begins, football teams are organized and begin training," he lamented. "I do not speak of broken noses, legs and arms, but of the time wasted, idleness encouraged and a heritage of demoralization carried over to the succeeding year."

this, if for nothing else, it deserves well of the State." They found at least one ally in board of trustees member and former KSC football player Richard C. Stoll. "College athletics is of value when it hardens the muscles, puts courage in the heart, builds up esprit de corps, moulds character and insistently demands fair play," Stoll said. "It is from the friction of contact with manly characters that the sparks of truth are struck out."

But truth was illusive in the summer of 1898. It was the year of the Spanish-American War, and Lexington was playing host to thousands of soldiers encamped in nearby Loudon Park. The presence of so many young men of unquestioned athletic ability from all across the nation—at least some of whom possessing college football experience—left athletic officials on the lookout for ineligible game participants, known as "ringers."

KSC's first opponent was cross-town rival Transylvania on Oct. 1. The blue and white boys took the field at 3:05 p.m., to the "waving of college colors and the vociferous yells of enthusiastic students." It was a typical autumn afternoon in Central Kentucky, with a broiling sun and stifling humidity.

Transy arrived at 3:15 and—after being studied doubtfully by the Cadets—the charge was made that two particularly capable-looking Crimson players were unknown in Lexington and must be "ringers." Transylvania insisted the two, called "Koontz" and "Gloss," were students at Smith Business College, which was affiliated with their school, and were thus eligible to participate.

Kentucky said it would play the game under protest.

The kickoff finally took place at 3:35, with the Crimsons defending the east goal. Approximately 200 students and fans were on hand to cheer the teams, including the girls of Hamilton College, also affiliated with

10

Transylvania.

The teams were to play 20-minute halves, but, the day being "too warm for vigorous exercise," a second half of 15 minutes was played by agreement. *The Lexington Daily Leader* reporter was somewhat sparse in his descriptions, mentioning only "brilliant dashes around the ends and swift plunges through the tackles," which prompted "bursts of applause."

It is clear, however, that most of the dashes and plunges were of the blue and white variety, with Lyle scoring two 5-point touchdowns, Kehoe adding another and Smith successfully kicking the three extra points. The final score was KSC 18, Transylvania 0.

The Transylvania "students" in question were actually soldiers, a sergeant named Bloss and Oren H. Kunce, who said he was ordered by his commanding officer to play in the game. To satisfy eligibility requirements, the two had enrolled at Smith Business College on the morning of the contest and withdrew that evening.

Not content with the 18-0 showing in the first game, Severs shook up the line-up, adding five new starters for the upcoming game against the Georgetown Tigers. Sam Hogg replaced Graham at left tackle, with Humphreys instead of Wills at right tackle, Kehoe for Scholtz at left halfback, Wilson for Lyle at right halfback and Elliott in place of Smith at fullback. Williams, starter at right end for the Transy game, would share time with Wynne Martin.

The overjoyed students and faculty members looked for a way to honor their perfect team. They raised enough money to present blue turtleneck sweaters to their heroes. Upon each was sewn a white "K," the first athletic letters issued in school history.

KSC won the toss for the 3:15 game and chose the west end zone. State received the kickoff at its own 20, ending the play at the 35. The Cadets ran straight at Georgetown, knocking the visitors backward all the way down the field, until left halfback John Kehoe scored with 12 minutes to play in the first half. Elliott's kick failed, but KSC led 5-0.

Georgetown could never gain any momentum, losing the ball on downs with every possession. The Tigers were trounced 28-0. "Had State College wanted to run the score up [it] could have done so, for the Georgetown team was entirely outclassed," wrote the *Leader* reporter, who added that the Cadets' play was somewhat ragged, showing "how badly a trainer [coach] is needed."

But Kentucky manager W.L. Bronaugh faced serious problems, a catch-22 of sorts based on a lack of game attendance. The Cadets were a good team that couldn't sell tickets. They needed a coach that could generate enough excitement to attract quality teams to the schedule, which would lead to bigger crowds. But low attendance left little hope of any money to hire a coach, unless the college trustees appropriated some or funds were gathered elsewhere.

The low point occurred the next Friday, Oct. 14, when "a small crowd of soldiers and students" stood around watching KSC play a squad chosen from members of Company H of the 8th Massachusetts. In a game "utterly devoid of interest," the Cats scored after two minutes and then eight more times on long runs routinely going for 60 or 70 yards. When it was over, the score was KSC 59, 8th Massachusetts 0. But nothing had been accomplished. Kentucky was no closer to attracting a crowd than it had been the week before.

Something miraculous, however, was about to happen. Richard Stoll, the wildly popular former football fullback, prominent Lexington attorney and 22-year-old member of the KSC board of trustees, had taken an interest in the team. After Stoll served as referee in the game against the Massachusetts soldiers, the Cats somehow found the funds to hire a coach, William R. "Billy" Bass, who had graduated from the University of Cincinnati the previous year, playing on its top-notch football squad.

Bass arrived on October 24 and immediately took charge of his new team. The biggest change he implemented was with the linemen, introducing what modern coaches would call gap control.

Under Severs' leadership, the linemen took stances as close to each other as possible, "to strengthen against onslaughts." Bass, however, "placed the men apart with some distance between them, so that each stood opposite the holes in the opposite line, thus blocking more effectually these open spaces." To put his advice to a test—and gain the confidence of his players—the new coach had the second-string team try to score from first and goal.

"The new method worked like a charm," wrote a *Herald* reporter. "The second team which had hitherto succeeded in making good gains through the line of the first team, bucked in vain. It was like going against a solid wall."

Bass put his team through several hard practices in preparation for its toughest assignment yet, an October 29 match up against the powerful Louisville Athletic Club (LAC), which would also be KSC's first road game of the season. In testament to Severs' good judgment, the new coach made no changes in the starting lineup.

Louisville A.C. was a "very strong aggregation ... composed of high-class athletes, all of them heavy and experienced men," something akin to a semi-pro team. One of its members, Marvin Hart, would win boxing's heavyweight championship of the world in 1905.

No one in Lexington seemed to hold out much hope in such a men vs. boys contest. Said the *Herald* reporter: "With all their many advantages, the Louisvillians, when they get through with the plucky lads from State College, will at least know they have had a game."

Game day arrived and the Kentucky players were even more intimidated as they took the field. "There was considerable quaking of hearts by the State College lads when they gazed on the 190- and 200-pound men who were to oppose them," wrote a *Leader* reporter, pointing out that the LAC squad outweighed the Cadets by about 20 pounds per player.

A "large crowd" was on hand to witness the game. LAC won the toss and kicked the ball and Kehoe received it at the Kentucky 25, returning it 10 yards. A series of fumbles had taken up most of the first half when Martin gained 15 yards on an end-around and Kentucky was in business. Kehoe scampered for 15 more and Martin added another 20 for a first and goal. Lyle "bucked" the LAC line for the score, which stood at 5-0 after Elliott's extra point attempt failed.

KSC kicked off to start the second half, but recovered a Louisville fumble at the Wildcats' 25-yard line. Lyle ran for eight yards, followed by Kehoe, who went 10, and by Martin, who gained six. Kehoe broke free for 36 yards on another end around before being tackled at the Louisville 16. Bass called Kehoe's number again, and the fleet left end gained 15 yards, ending up at the one. Kehoe tried again and ran over the LAC center for the score. After Elliott missed another kick, the Lexingtonians owned a 10-0 lead.

According to the rules at the time, LAC kicked off and the Cadets rattled off several more long gains before Kehoe scored again and Elliott hit the extra point to give Kentucky the 15-0 win.

A crowd of cheering students surrounded the 10:40 p.m. Louisville Southern train that night when it arrived at the station, and the Immortals were greeted by distant cannon fire from the celebrating campus.

"The one-sided victory of the boys of State College was a surprise to many friends and is proof of the value of an efficient coach," a *Leader* reporter wrote. "Although Coach Bass has only been in Lexington one week, he has increased the team work of the State College eleven 50 [percent], and if he is given the proper encouragement by the students and faculty he will make the team one of the strongest in Kentucky."

"A large number of foot ball enthusiasts" came to State College field on Saturday, November 5, under threatening skies and strong winds to watch KSC play the always formidable Centre College. The game would decide the state championship and the schools' fans, at least, expected a tough fight.

KSC won the toss and chose the east goal to make Centre kick into the wind. After Reese returned the kickoff three yards, Elliott—moved from fullback to right halfback—gained 10 yards over "Harlan," Centre's right tackle. Running at Harlan again, Elliott broke off 20 more yards, then an additional two.

At second and eight, Severs handed off to A.C. Reese, and the new starting left halfback went for first down yardage through "Wilson," Centre's left tackle. Not willing to abandon a productive strategy, the KSC quarterback sent Elliott, Reese and Kehoe again and again at Harlan and Wilson,

Backup end Louis Wynne Martin's hard running against Louisville Athletic Club gained him playing time. His 95-yard touchdown in the second half against Newcastle helped ensure KSC's perfect season.

pounding them backward for gains of three, five or six yards in quick succession.

To put an end to the 13-minute drive, Elliott finally pushed across the goal line in a scrum and lay the ball down on the field. "Goodloe," the Centre quarterback, grabbed it and ran 100 yards to the Wildcat end zone, claiming a touchdown because Kentucky failed to cross the line. The officials would have none of Goodloe's pleadings and, after an Elliott extra point, the score was KSC 6, Centre 0.

By rule, Kentucky received the Centre kickoff and began another down-the-throat drive. Elliott, Reese and Turner, who was playing fullback, hit Wilson repeatedly for moderate gains to midfield. On the next play, Reese broke free for more than 40 yards. About to be tackled, Reese lateralled to Turner, who took the ball into the end zone. Centre successfully argued, however, that the play was offsides and the ball was brought back.

And so the pounding continued until a cloudburst poured a drenching rain onto the field. KSC fumbled at the Centre two-foot line and play was stopped to let the storm pass. After 20 minutes, however, the cloudburst had overwhelmed the adjacent creek and was filling the field with shoe-top-deep water. Asked if they would like to postpone the game, KSC declined. So the players marched out onto the rapidly forming mud to resume the struggle.

Centre slip-slided for one play before officials stopped the game. "The rain was rather fortunate for Centre," said the *Leader* reporter, under a headline that read "It Saved Old Centre." The teams planned to reschedule the contest, but Centre later accepted the score as final, KSC 6, Centre 0.

Kentucky paid a price for the game, however, losing Whayne and Turner to injuries. Bass switched his left guard, tackle and halfback with his right, adding Jones to the lineup at right guard to replace Whayne and Smith for Turner at fullback.

Next up was another soldiers' team, the 160th Indiana, whose months of drilling on nearby fields had left them "hardened ... so that they can stand almost any amount of the most vigorous exercise without showing any signs of tiring."

As with any other aspect of life, the soldiers saw the contest as a wagering opportunity. "They bet around $25,000 on the game," Graham recalled. "And they weren't betting they would win, but that they could score on us."

With his linemen in the mirror-images of their usual spots and two new players in the lineup, Bass' squad couldn't match "the same dash and spirit" the growing crowds had become accustomed to seeing. Kentucky ground out only short gains against the brawny troops.

The Indiana team's defense was also disruptive, with "Piggott" dominating the enormous Straus, running over him three times during the game to force fumbles by Severs. The *Leader* reporter said it was a constant question whether the KSC line would hold and "the passing of the spheroid back to the men was made quite uncertain." What the 160th Indiana possessed on defense, however, it lacked on offense, betraying a "lack of training," according to the *Leader*. "Indeed their own awkwardness cost them many yards which should have been easily gained."

But the Cadets scored, the soldiers didn't. Kentucky got two touchdowns in the first half and one in the second, with Elliott making two extra points for a 17-0 final score. Graham remembered the game as the most difficult of the year.

The game did have two interesting features. The first was a beautiful second-half play in which Martin took the handoff and—sprung by "splendid" blocks by Turner, Elliott and Smith—scampered 95 yards for the score. The second occurred when coach Bass put himself into the game at left end.

The final chance for a team to score against KSC came on Saturday, November 19—and the chance belonged to Newcastle Athletic Club. A "very large crowd" was on hand, including many partisans for the Henry County school.

The outcome, however, wasn't in doubt past the 3 1/2-minute mark. Newcastle fumbled the Cadets' kickoff and Elliott ran for a touchdown and kicked the extra point for a 6-0 lead.

The game did have two interesting features. The first was a beautiful second-half play in which Martin took the handoff and—sprung by "splendid" blocks by Turner, Elliott and Smith—scampered 95 yards for the score. The second occurred when coach Bass put himself into the game at left end. Bass' presence on the field didn't seem to bother the officials, which included Richard Stoll, and the coach had several good gains, including a late-game touchdown.

The final score was 36-0. The Cadets had accomplished something no other team in UK history would ever match. Not only were they undefeated, they had shut out all of their opponents, piling up 32 touchdowns and a season-long score of 180-0. It made them the Immortals.

The overjoyed students and faculty members looked for a way to honor their perfect team. They raised enough money to present blue turtleneck sweaters to their heroes. Upon each was sewn a white "K," the first athletic letters issued in school history.

Unable to win funds from the trustees for themselves, the 1898 Cadets nonetheless influenced the board to build on their accomplishment by establishing an annual $150 appropriation for the football team.

Critics have often been fond of pointing out that, while KSC had a perfect record, it played against war-depleted competition. They failed to mention that the Immortals faced two teams made up of soldiers—presumably where the talent had migrated—in addition to the older, bigger and stronger Louisville Athletic Club, which included a heavyweight champion of the world. It was also true that while Kentucky was fashioning a string of shutouts en route to an undefeated season, Penn State was losing to Pennsylvania 40-0, and Ohio State suffered the indignity of a 23-5 trouncing at the hands of "Case School."

* * *

Milward Elliott, the Immortals' leading scorer, played two years for KSC, spending two seasons prior to his enrollment playing for the Lexington Athletic Club team of prep-school-age boys. While most players of his day wore no protection besides "shin guards and heavily padded pants," Elliott recalled that he was one of the first to wear headgear. After a career with the Van Deren Hardware Co. in Lexington, Elliott retired and spent his time restoring antique furniture. One of his best friends was John Willim and the two rarely missed a Kentucky home game, usually sitting together. Elliott and Willim said the Immortals' strength was its concept of team, which included "no stars" and "no jealousies."

* * *

Milward
Elliott

William R. Bass coached Kentucky one more season, going 5-2-2 in 1899. He returned to Cincinnati and lived in that city's Terrace Park suburb. Wynne Martin moved to St. Louis, J. Soule Smith to Webster Grove, Mo., and C.C. Clarke became a doctor and lived in Sorocco, N.M. E.C. Kehoe lived in Cynthiana and Whayne in Clinton. Humphrey died soon after graduation, Severs died in Hazard and Maddox became a mining engineer, but was killed in a slate fall in New Mexico in

16

William R. "Billy" Bass

the early 1900s. Job D. Turner worked at the UK Agricultural Experimental Station and was the resident expert on animal feed. Lexington resident Charles L. Straus, who played at the almost unheard of weight of 240 pounds in 1898, moved to Cincinnati, where he died in the 1930s. Reese became a dentist in eastern Kentucky and died in 1947.

* * *

UK invited the Immortals to a 50-year reunion for the November 13, 1948, homecoming game against Florida. Attending were coach Bass, along with Martin, Elliott, Smith, Graham, Clarke, Willim and Whayne. During a party hosted by the UK Alumni Association, the surviving team members were presented with blue ties, each adorned with a white "98." The next afternoon, the Immortals were treated to a 35-15 trouncing of Florida and a halftime show that featured the band members forming themselves into an "1898" shape while playing "Hail, Hail the Gang's All Here."

* * *

Immortal James H. Graham spent a highly successful career at his alma mater, eventually become dean of the College of Engineering. He also served in World War I, organizing four engineering units within the American Expeditionary Forces and repairing roads in France and occupied Germany. He was awarded the Distinguished Service Medal and French Legion of Honor for his service and ended the war as a colonel in the Army Corps of Engineers, a title he carried for the rest of his life. During World War II, he served as an adviser to the War Department's general staff.

Graham had fond memories of the Immortals and their storied season. "They were all grand fellows," he said, "and they played the game because they liked it."

University of Kentucky Special Collections

Immortal James H. Graham had a distinguished career at his alma mater, eventually becoming dean of the College of Engineering. Graham also served in the U.S. Army, retiring as a colonel. He was awarded the Distinguished Service Medal and the French Legion of Honor for his service in the Corps of Engineers in Europe during World War I and served as an adviser to the War Department's general staff during World War II.

UK's first basketball season was an outgrowth of the founding of the new School of Physical Culture in 1902. Kentucky's first home court was University Gymnasium, inside the new gym, hailed as "The Athlete's Paradise--The Invalid's Sanitarium." The men's department of the school was directed by William Walter Henry Mustaine, a native of Horse Cave and 1899 graduate of Centre College.

3

First Basketball Season

As every new academic year began, returning students to Kentucky State College noted changes to the campus, from new sidewalks to tree plantings to new construction.

The most notable change in the fall of 1902 was a just-completed red brick building—symbol of a new educational theory—that was located next to the administration building.

It was known as Alumni Hall and boasted, among other things, a varnished wooden floor and a felt-covered elevated running track—"properly concaved for speed"— along with an impressive collection of medicine balls, barbells and Indian clubs. It was a gymnasium that served as the main classroom of the brand-new School of Physical Culture.

William Walter Henry Mustaine, a native of Horse Cave and 1899 graduate of Centre College, was appointed chairman of the school's male department, while Mrs. Florence Offutt Stout, who had a degree from the Yale-affiliated "New Haven Normal School of Gymnastics" directed the female department.

Physical Culture, so the theory went, was a discipline designed to ensure students' physical abilities in the way that other departments developed mental abilities. Such development would minimize disease and, said Mustaine, "prompt the maintenance of health and the increase of physical vigor, stamina, or hardihood of our citizenship. ... If the schools and colleges are to teach any practical ethical lessons, it must be done and can only be done on their playgrounds. Classroom ethics without the practical laboratory experience of the playground is futile."

Under Stout's direction, women did calisthenics and learned gymnastics, while Mustaine's students worked out with Indian clubs, in addition to participating in gymnastics.

Added to the school's "laboratory," was "basket ball," the 11-year-old game developed as a way to maintain fitness in the winter months between football and baseball seasons. KSC was behind the times in adopting the game, having had to wait for the completion of the gymnasium.

By early 1903, it had been proposed that the students expand their basketball activities from gym classes to playing full games against students from other schools. To prepare for its inaugural season, the KSC men's team held its first practice on January 24.

The first intercollegiate basketball contest in UK history took place against Georgetown College on the frigid and snowy afternoon of Friday, Feb. 6, 1903, at Alumni Hall. At the appointed hour, Kentucky's first starting five—guards Joel White Guyn and R.H. Arnett, forwards H.J. Wurtele and Lee Andrews and center Joe Coons—took to the shiny, varnished-wood floor against the Georgetown Tigers.

It has been said that Mustaine simply took up a collection, gave his players a $3 ball and told them to begin practicing. Although he was at least figuratively the school's first coach, he left everything to the team members. After all, athletics was a means to the development of health, not an activity to be perfected.

The first intercollegiate basketball contest in UK history took place against Georgetown College on the frigid and snowy afternoon of Friday, Feb. 6, 1903, at Alumni Hall.

At the appointed hour, Kentucky's first starting five—guards Joel White Guyn and R.H. Arnett, forwards H.J. Wurtele and Lee Andrews and center Joe Coons—took to the shiny, varnished-wood floor against the Georgetown Tigers.

This photo of the 1904 Kentucky basketball team includes four of the first starting five in UK history: R.H. Arnett, Joel White Guyn and Joe Coons (from left to right) and H.J. Wurtele (at right). The other starter was Lee Andrews. Kentucky lost its first game 15-6 to Georgetown on Feb. 6, 1903.

The men dressed in tank tops and shorts with thick knee socks rolled down a few inches to facilitate movement. The leather shoes they wore were undoubtedly slick-soled and negated any quickness a player may have possessed.

It was a slow-starting affair, perhaps something like watching a YMCA game today. The ball changed hands often between the squads, and was often rolled, instead of passed, among teammates. At the end of the first half, Georgetown—in its third year of intercollegiate basketball—led 7-1. Kentucky scored five points in the second half, but surrendered 10 more, for a final score of 17-6.

KSC's second game took place on Tuesday, Feb. 17, against the Lexington YMCA on the Alumni Hall floor. Kentucky shook up its starting lineup, with Smith, at guard, and Montgomery, forward, joining Coons, Arnett and Andrews. Mustaine was one of two "umpires," while another man served under the title of referee.

The game was remembered as "exceedingly close and exciting from the first," with the result "uncertain … until the last minute had been played." More important, however, was that Kentucky had its first basketball victory, by the score of 11-10.

Next up was Transylvania, then known as Kentucky University, on the afternoon of Friday, Feb. 20, in a game that had been previously postponed due to wintry weather.

The KSC players had high hopes, since they had lost to Georgetown by 11 points, while the Tigers had beaten Transy by 14. Students crowded the running track above the floor, displaying "much enthusiasm." KSC started Montgomery and Andrews at forward, Guyn and Smith at guard and Coons at center.

As time ran out in the first half, with KSC being thrashed 14-0, "a disagreement arose," which delayed the remainder of the game "for a considerable time." But State College was beaten, tiring as the contest wore on, while Transylvania poured in 28 points "in rapid succession." The final score was a humiliating 42-2.

University of Kentucky Special Collections

William Walter Henry Mustaine, founder of UK basketball. Because he left the responsibility for managing the basketball team to student subordinates, he doesn't receive credit for being the school's first coach.

Though plans had been made for two more games apiece against the YMCA and Transylvania, KSC's first basketball season ended with a 1-3 record and hope for future success. "The game seems to be growing in favor, and supplies the interim between the foot ball and base ball seasons," wrote a *Lexington Herald* reporter.

But Kentucky had to travel a long road to basketball prominence. On February 15, 1906, the Cadets traveled to Cincinnati and were shamefully manhandled by Christ Church, 54-17. The 37-point defeat remains the eighth-worst loss in school history. KSC went 0-4 against the church team from 1906 to 1913.

It would be several years before the team had its first winning record, 5-4, in 1909. The team's first professional coach was Edwin Regur Sweetland, who arrived on campus in 1909 as football coach and athletic director. Sweetland shared coaching duties with R.E. Spahr in 1910, posting a lackluster 4-8 record. His second basketball team, the 1912 Wildcats, however, posted an undefeated 9-0 record and won the Southern Championship, the first championship season in UK basketball history.

Mustaine oversaw the male department of the School of Physical Culture—later part of the Department of Health, Physical Education and Recreation of the College of Education—until 1912. He resigned to become physical education director at the University of Montana, where he also coached the men's and women's basketball teams and the track teams, in addition to promoting physical education in high schools and playgrounds for schoolchildren.

In 1920, Mustaine left Montana to become the New York State Education Department's director of physical education. He died in 1937 of a sudden heart attack at the age of 58 and was buried in Horse Cave. His tombstone reads, "A steadfast Christian, A cultured gentleman, A distinguished educator." For many years, the Kentucky Association of Health, Physical Education and Recreation presented the William W.H. Mustaine Award for contributions to health.

University of Kentucky Special Collections

Kentucky basketball's first home court, University Gymnasium, in Alumni Hall. Built in 1902, it included a felt-covered, elevated running track "properly concaved for speed," medicine balls, barbells and Indian clubs. The running track was used for spectator seating during games. It is today a dance studio.

4

First Women's Basketball Teams

Contrary to what modern-day activists might presume, the precursor to UK's athletic program drew no distinction between the sexes.

When it was founded in 1902, Kentucky State College's School of Physical Culture included programs for both men and women. The women's department was headed by Mrs. Florence Offutt Stout—a gradu-

UK's first women's basketball team played its inaugural game against Transylvania, defeating the Crimsons 16-10 on Feb. 21, 1903, two weeks after the men's team played its first game. For this feat, the word "Champions" appeared under the team photo in that year's *Kentuckian* annual. The 1903 Team: (bottom row, from left) Miriam Naïve (later Cutler), Alice Courtney Pence (later Cannon), Nell Norwood, Fanny Redd, unknown; (middle row) Amanda Maull, unknown, ____ McConathy, Helen Jaeger, Willie Spiers (later Gardner); (back row) unknown, coach Jane Todd Watson, Jimmie Offutt, unknown, and Mary E. Clarke.

ate of the New Haven Normal School of Gymnastics, which was affiliated with Yale University. Her stated goals were "To stimulate the functioning of all bodily organs....To train the muscles so that curves may displace angles and grace banish awkwardness....To arouse the mind to superior alertness....[and] To develop character."

For their part, KSC's male undergraduates were loud in their praise of this innovation. "The ideal co-ed is not a thing of books, with stooping shoulders and studious looks," wrote a student on the yearbook staff, "but a happy medium in the combination of a good intellect and a healthy body...."

The female director could only agree. "Gymnastic training," she said, "has given our girls such suppleness and endurance that their fame is more than local."

Two weeks after the men's team played the first basketball game in school history—a 17-6 loss to Georgetown College on Feb. 6, 1903—the women's team was set to play its first game on Saturday, February 21, against Transylvania. This agreed-upon date forced the postponement of KSC's annual Cadet Ball, which illustrates the game's importance in spite of Stout's rules forbidding the presence of male students.

Co-eds clad in black culottes and socks with white blouses and black ties participated in "Military Tactics, Free Gymnastics, Apparatus, Artistic Gymnastics or Gilbert Dancing," in addition to German and Swedish gymnastics. Stout, who had continued her studies at Yale and even in Europe, also founded the swimming program at KSC, the first of its kind in the South.

Women exercised in the brand-new Alumni Hall gymnasium and began a "basket ball" team in early 1903. Though she is said to have been somewhat apprehensive about intercollegiate athletic contests, Stout was an advocate of the game as soon as she arrived on campus. "Social games like basket-ball have a definite purpose in Physical Education," she wrote in the 1901 college catalog. "Players require quickness of thought, judgment, and self-control under excitement. They learn to sacrifice self for the sake of the team as a whole," Stout continued. "Girls who have had one year's training in the gymnasium or have played the game before are permitted to [practice] for a place on the team. Fortunately we have always had excellent coaches."

Under the leadership of coach Jane Todd Watson, KSC's first women's basketball team had 14 members, including team captain Alice Courtney Pence (a graduate school student), Amanda Maull, Miriam Naive, Nell Norwood, Fanny Redd, Willie Spiers, Mary E. Clark, Helen Jaeger, Grace Conn, Bessie Shaw and Jimmie Offutt.

Two weeks after the men's team played the first basketball game in school history—a 17-6 loss to Georgetown College on Feb. 6, 1903—the women's team was set to play its first game on Saturday, February 21, against Transylvania. This agreed-upon date forced the postponement of KSC's annual Cadet Ball, which illustrates the game's importance in spite of Stout's rules forbidding the presence of male students.

"The girls have been doing excellent work under the instruction of their coach, Miss … Watson," read an account in the *Lexington Herald*, "and all are looking forward to the game with much interest….The rivalry is intense and the game is expected to be a close one."

Admission was the sizeable sum of 25 cents, which helped offset the game's expenses. Tip-off was 3 p.m. in University Gymnasium.

The starting five for Kentucky—which dressed in blue and white—was Pence, Naive, Redd, Jaeger, and Spiers. Their crimson-and-white Transylvania opponents included at least six players: Kathleen Bryan (captain), Kate Ingels, Margaret Price, Lena Hottes, "Cook" and "Miss Miller."

Ingels and Cook were the stars of their team, having scored 12 points each "in brilliant and clever style" in a warm-up intrasquad game several days earlier. But KSC was the better team, winning the contest 16-10. It was the beginning and ending of women's basketball's inaugural season.

In honor of their 1-0 record, the school yearbook included a team photo, along with the title "Champions."

The women's basketball team became a popular and important part of the student experience at KSC. "Listen! Look about you!," wrote a student in the 1906 *Kentuckian* yearbook. "Who are they that arouse enthusiasm in college life, who cheer their college brothers on to victory? Who are they that contribute the soprano to the college yells? Who are they with their vivacious spirits lend the spice, the cheer, the glow to the atmosphere of college life? Hurrah, for athletic girls. The are THE girls—the co-eds of Kentucky State College."

The campus newspaper proudly boasted that, while there were many female teams all across the country, Kentucky was the only school in the South that awarded athletic letters to women.

In 1904 one male student—Herman Scholtz of Louisville—was such a fan of the female Wildcats that he dressed in women's clothing to gain admittance to Georgetown's gym to witness a game. Thrown out by half-time, Scholtz was hauled before the faculty. School officials couldn't decide which of UK's vast list of rules Scholtz had broken. They eventually "contented themselves by reprimanding him on general principles."

In Stout's mind, however, intercollegiate basketball for women had outgrown its usefulness as a way to teach physical education. In a disagreement between her and members of the 1909-10 basketball team, the program was removed from Stout's control and placed under the management of the athletic council, where it remained for several years.

By the early 1920s, the theories regarding team sports had changed in academic circles. The New Haven Normal School of Gymnastics—Stout's alma mater—now opposed intercollegiate and even intramural athletics because of their exclusivity and the physical stress it placed upon female students. When Sarah Blanding joined the UK faculty in 1923 after receiving a degree from New Haven, she added her voice to Stout's efforts to abolish female sports.

Blanding spoke in favor of a more diversified, non-competitive program of "a game for every girl and every girl playing a game," while UK president Frank L. McVey, who had replaced Barker in 1916, said basketball had "proved to be a strenuous sport for boys and was, therefore, too strenuous for girls." Women's intercollegiate sports were abolished by the university senate on November 13, 1924.

As the new thinking took hold, women's competitive athletics programs were discontinued all over the nation and would not re-appear for almost a half-century.

* * *

Alice Courtney Pence, a daughter of physics department chairman Merry Lewis Pence, was born on September 3, 1884, in Lewisport, Hancock County, Ky.

University of Kentucky Special Collections

Alice Courtney Pence

She was a member of Alpha Gamma Delta sorority and majored in anatomy and physiology in preparation for a teaching career. Receiving a master's degree from KSC in 1904, she worked as an assistant to Dr. J.W. Pryor, dean of the anatomy department, in addition to serving as a gymnastics instructor for Stout.

Pence entered the New Haven School of Physical Culture in 1906 and made the basketball team at age 22, despite—if the *Lexington Leader* can be believed—stiff competition, "much of it semi-professional."

She made quite an impression. "Miss Alice C. Pence has played right forward," reported a New Haven newspaper. "She is the surest goal thrower that the Gymnastic School has ever had. Miss Pence is a Kentucky girl....There has never been a game in which Miss Pence has not distinguished herself and she has never committed a foul during the entire season."

The young woman graduated with honors in 1907 and got a job as a teacher of physical culture at Moorhead Normal School in Minnesota at a salary of $1,200 a year.

Pence married Arthur Earl Cannon, an optometrist, and lived for many years in Fargo, N.D.

According to autobiographical information she provided UK, Pence somewhat amazingly became a captain in the U.S. Army artillery during World War I, though a cousin recalled that her duties may have been confined to nursing. She enlisted as a lieutenant at Ft. Benjamin Harrison in Indiana in August 1917 and was discharged in Chillicothe, Ohio, in January 1919.

She died of cancer in 1934.

* * *

Florence Graham Offutt Stout was the namesake of her mother, who died when she was born in Louisville on October 26, 1878.

The child, along with her three older brothers, was taken to live on the Woodford County estate owned by her maternal grandmother, Mrs. Hyman Graham. Forbidden to join in her brothers' rough and tumble games, the young Florence participated anyway, deciding that "the punishment was offset by the fun."

Passed around among family members after her grandmother's death, the teen-ager graduated from Louisville Girl's High School before moving to the home of a "horsey set" cousin of her father on Leestown Pike near Lexington. Spending her time riding horses and attending a "whirl of parties," she found herself utterly bored. "An overdose of Kentucky social life and horse racing drove me to a career," Stout would recall.

Revealing her plans to attend college, the young woman was confronted by the negative reaction of her brothers and other family members. According to a 1941 master's thesis written about her, Stout's brothers, "who saw nothing amiss in Florence's spending thirty-five dollars for a hat, felt that money invested in higher education for a woman was a total waste." She nevertheless enrolled at the University of Chicago in preparation for attending the New Haven Normal School of Gymnastics in Connecticut.

Stout began a two-year program at New Haven in 1899. Her classes

University of Kentucky Special Collections

Florence Graham Offutt Stout was director of the female department of the School of Physical Culture and founder of UK women's basketball. Stout, a native of Louisville, grew up on a horse farm near Lexington before defying her family to pursue a career. Stout was a graduate of the New Haven Normal School of Gymnastics, affiliated with Yale University. She also founded the swimming program at UK and later became dean of women, a title she hated.

were taught by Yale University medical professors, who lectured on gymnastics techniques designed to ensure physical fitness, in addition to correcting medical deficiencies. The student took courses in biology, physiology, anatomy, psychology, physics, "anthropometry," orthopedics, first aid, special medical courses and German and Swedish gymnastics. Graduating in the spring of 1901, Stout began her teaching career as a volunteer physical education instructor at Transylvania University.

By 1901, James Kennedy Patterson was in his 32nd year as president of what was then called Kentucky State College. He was a crotchety "benevolent despot" whose word was law. Patterson held onto old ways and was slow to embrace any change, especially change that involved women or athletics. "Gymnastics," he said, "are unladylike."

Patterson was against admitting women to the school at all and after they were, in 1888, opposed allowing Belle Clement Gunn—the first female graduate—to be seated with her male counterparts during the commencement ceremony.

"To stimulate the functioning of all bodily organs....To train the muscles so that curves may displace angles and grace banish awkwardness....To arouse the mind to superior alertness....[and] To develop character."

—Florence Offutt Stout, stating the goals of women's physical education, 1902.

As school officials prepared to start the new School of Physical Culture, Patterson planned to hire a man to be the director with duties including the instruction of men and women. When an illness forced the president to miss the Dec. 10, 1901, board of trustees meeting, however, the trustees took action. They created a separate position for the instruction of women and unanimously hired Stout for the job, with an annual salary of $800.

Far from a modern critic's viewpoint that such university programs were meant for the somewhat unmotivated student, physical culture in 1901 represented a new educational theory. It was designed to produce well-rounded and healthy college graduates, to ensure students' physical abilities in the way that other departments developed mental abilities.

Stout began work on Jan. 1, 1902, and by June, she had completely won over Patterson. "The organization of the female department of Physical Culture has been quite successful and has fully justified the employment of Miss Florence Graham Offutt," Patterson wrote in a report to the board. "Her instruction seems to be based upon correct principles—her knowledge of her subject complete and her enthusiasm and energy all that could be required." The president was so pleased, in fact, that he invited her to "march with him in the commencement procession" and had her present the diplomas during the ceremony.

On Dec. 23, 1903, Offutt married Robert Lee Stout in Lexington. The groom, who was soon to become a circuit court judge, "maintained a deep interest in his wife's work and encouraged her in it." Judge Stout became a member of the KSC board of trustees in June 1904.

The School of Physical Culture became an official KSC department in 1905 and Stout was awarded the rank of professor the following school year.

At the urging of a gathering of women's groups, the board of trustees appointed her the school's first dean of women in 1908. But becoming a symbol of female social progress was not right for her. "The position of dean of women somewhat impairs the distinctive quality of my [special-ty]," she wrote in a 1910 letter to new school president Henry Stites Barker, who also happened to be her cousin.

"Demonstrated by the fact that I am now introduced for any address before the public as dean of women, rather than as physical director of women, I hereby tender my resignation," she continued. "In being relieved of the very ornamental title of dean of women, I seek a greater usefulness in physical education, which is my life work and from which fact I do not wish the attention of the public diverted."

Along with William Walter Henry Mustaine, her male counterpart in the School of Physical Culture, Stout helped organize the Kentucky Physical Education Association. The group's goal was to "promote a wide and intelligent interest in physical education by acquiring and (disseminating) knowledge concerning it, to labor for the improvement and extension of gymnastic and athletic games and pastimes in the education of children and youth, and to bring the members composing it into a closer relationship."

The campus newspaper proudly boasted that, while there were many female teams all across the country, Kentucky was the only school in the South that awarded athletic letters to women.

Stout spoke on physical education topics and became active in the Kentucky Education Association and the Southern Education Association. She spent summers taking courses at the Institution of Gymnastic Work in New York and at Yale, learning more about "classic dancing" and the teaching of swimming.

She was instrumental in changing the name of her profession from physical culture—which she termed "cheap, tawdry, and obsolete"—to physical education.

Under new president Frank L. McVey—a Yale-educated economics pro-fessor— the physical education department became part of the College of Arts and Sciences and all A&S students were required to complete "two and seven-tenths credits in physical education" to graduate. The change was made, said McVey, "in the hope that a greater emphasis may be placed upon the educational side. Plans are being worked out with a view to making its work thoroughly attractive and effective in the training of

UK Sports Information

After being abolished by the University Senate in 1924, women's varsity basketball didn't reappear at UK until 1974, when former JV coach Sue Feamster guided her newly dubbed Lady Kats to a 16-9 record. Feamster later served as women's athletic director and an assistant athletic director when the two programs were merged in 1978.

every student and in the preparation of teachers for the high school."

UK Sports Information

Sue Feamster

According to UK's 1919-20 catalog, those enrolled in the women's P.E. program learned to "cultivate high ideals, true sportsmanship, the efficiency in management of athletics in the state..." in addition to "preliminary training for physical education directors, directors of recreation systems and coaches of athletics." In this new direction, UK served as a training ground for those who would bring the message of physical education to primary and secondary schools all across the state and nation.

In the remainder of her career, Stout became a proponent of applying P.E. methods to correct such physical abnormalities as scoliosis and served as "director of medical gymnastics for posture defects" at the Appalachian School of Nursing. She was the first Kentucky member of the National

With All-American Valerie Still leading the way, Kentucky won the 1982 SEC Tournament with an 80-74 win over Tennessee that saw Lady Kat fans storm the floor. That squad made it to the second round of the NCAA Tournament. The following year, on Feb. 5, 1983, the Wildcats defeated Old Dominion, attracting the largest crowd to ever see a women's college basketball game, 10,622 (above). The team was twice ranked fourth in the nation that year.

Association of Health, Physical Education and Recreation and founded a state chapter of the organization. The group presented her with a meritorious service award in 1953.

Stout retired in 1946 and died at her Lexington home on June 12, 1958. Though it provided a proper tribute to her pioneering career, she would have hated her obituary in the *Lexington Herald*. Its headline read: "Mrs. Florence Stout, First Dean of Women at UK, Dies."

UK Sports Information

The Lady Kats' highest scoring and most famous basketball player is Valerie Still, who averaged almost 23.2 points a game over her career, establishing UK's all-time career scoring record of 2,763 points in 119 games. After playing several years in the Italian Professional League, Still returned to the United States and was a charter member and two-time most valuable player in the American Basketball League for Women. She later played for the Washington Mystics of the WNBA and served as an assistant coach of the Orlando Miracle. Her jersey was retired by UK in 2003. Her Valerie Still Foundation—a not-for-profit organization—seeks to provide encouragement to girls to develop their skills and talents.

* * *

By the 1970s, theories regarding athletics had progressed once again to allow intercollegiate sports for women. After a 50-year absence, UK fielded a women's varsity basketball team in 1974.

Sue Feamster, who had reintroduced basketball on the junior varsity level beginning in 1971, became Kentucky's first coach of the modern era. She guided that first team—almost immediately dubbed the Lady Kats—to a 16-9 record, including wins over Dayton, Bellarmine and Marshall. Feamster, who was named women's athletic director in 1974, retired from coaching two years later with an overall record of 64-39. She became assistant athletic director under Cliff Hagan when the men's and women's programs were merged in 1978.

Debbie Yow took over the team for the 1976-77 season and compiled a 79-40 record in four seasons, which featured wins against Ohio State, Georgia and Auburn. Cheered on by 4,500 fans in Memorial Coliseum, her Lady Kats upset Tennessee 66-64 on January 20, 1979. Before leaving after the 1979-80 season, Yow recruited Valerie Still, Patty Jo Hedges, Lea Wise and Lisa Collins, who would energize the program in future years.

The players' new coach Terry Hall began making hoop noise as soon as the 1980-81 season began. The Wildcats piled up nine wins in a row, before bowing 69-67 at Rutgers in overtime. The team ended the season with a record-setting mark of 25-6, capturing the imagination of UK fans and making the youthful team members household names in the process.

With All-American Still and her teammates leading the way, Kentucky won the 1982 SEC Tournament with an 80-74 win over Tennessee that saw Lady Kat fans storm the floor. That squad made it to the second round of the NCAA Tournament. The following year, on Feb. 5, 1983, the Wildcats defeated Old Dominion, attracting the largest crowd to ever see a women's college basketball game, 10,622. The team was twice ranked fourth in the nation that year.

* * *

Still averaged almost 23.2 points a game over her career, establishing UK's all-time career scoring record of 2,763 points in 119 games. After playing several years in the Italian Professional League, Still returned to the United States and was a charter member and two-time most valuable player in the American Basketball League for Women. She later played for the Washington Mystics of the WNBA and served as an assistant coach of the Orlando Miracle. Her jersey was retired by UK in 2003.

Still lives in Powell, Ohio, with her husband, former Kentucky center Rob Lock, and their son Aaron. Her Valerie Still Foundation—a not-for-profit organization—seeks to provide encouragement to girls to develop their skills and talents.

* * *

Yow went on to a highly successful career in athletics management and is currently the A.D. at the University of Maryland.

* * *

Behind the excitement generated by new coach Mickie DeMoss, UK set a school season attendance record of 72,553 in 2004-05, for an average game attendance of 5,182.

The 1909 football team, whose Oct. 9, 1909, upset of vaunted Illinois placed the program above its instate rivals and changed the school's mascot from Cadets to Wildcats. Based on comparisons with other photos in UK's collection, team members are identified as: (front row, first and second steps) Albert M. "Knot Face" Mathers, George Matt Hendrickson, William "Billy" Rodes, Richard "Dick" Webb, George Dunlap, team captain Richard Carroll Barbee, and Bryan Shanklin. On the middle row, far right, is Jefferson C. Elgin. Those on the back row include Thomas B. "Big Tom" Earle (third from left) and William "Tiny" Clarke (far right). Other players included quarterback Billy Johnston; fullback _____ Threlkeld, Campbell, Plummer and Ellis. Injured players Shelby Post and Frank Baker apparently didn't play.

5

The Original Wildcats

During the first week of September 1909, as students arrived at the State University of Kentucky, five journalism students labored in the administration building basement to produce the school year's first issue of *The Idea*, the campus newspaper.

Many subjects vied for the writers' attention, from the pros and cons of a proposed medical school to a call for new members of the glee club. But there was no doubt which subject took prominence in the mind of William George Clugston: football. Clugston's accomplice in that regard was

Robert A. Lowry, the *Idea*'s assistant business manager, who also served as manager of the football team.

Lowry secured the team's schedule, purchased pads and other equipment, and even helped organize practices.

As assistant editor and senior member of the group, Clugston's opinion prevailed, and the September 9 issue's top story carried the headline, "The Future Southern Champions in Review: Football Outlook Most Promising."

"State" or KSU, as it was called, returned a veteran team that had aspirations of claiming the mythical Southern Championship if it could defeat Tennessee and North Carolina, in addition to an otherwise respectable record. For their part, school officials were leaving little to chance, demoting third-year head coach J. White Guyn—whose tenure had been the longest in school history—to assistant and hiring Edwin Regur Sweetland, a coach of "determination and ginger" with impeccable football credentials. Sweetland, an 1899 graduate of Cornell University and standout on its football, basketball and rowing teams, had led Ohio State to a 14-7-2 record in 1904 and 1905, in addition to coaching stints at Syracuse and Colgate.

University of Kentucky Special Collections

Stoll Field was moved 50 feet east of its old spot for the 1909 season. The new location was near Winslow Street and old Maxwell Spring, with its adjacent Willow-lined lake and YMCA tennis courts.

"The prospects for an all-Southern team are better this year than they were ever before in the history of the University," said Guyn, showing no signs of hard feelings over his demotion. "With the old men back in their places and the new material that is coming in, everything possible will be done and under the excellent training of Coach Sweetland, we should be able to clean up with them all."

King Football, as it was known in the local newspapers, reigned because of the growing interest and support of the students and faculties of the member institutions of the Kentucky Intercollegiate Athletic Association. Joining State in the league were Centre College—known during this period as "Central University of Kentucky," Transylvania University and Georgetown College, in addition to also-rans Kentucky Wesleyan College and Berea College.

The KIAA executive committee was commended for establishing eligibility requirements that eliminated ringers and professionals from playing

Edwin Regur Sweetland in a uniform from his days as a star at Cornell. The first true professional coach to come to UK, his emphasis on speed over size led to the Illinois win that electrified the program. Sweetland also served as the school's first athletic director and coached the basketball team to an undefeated record in 1912 en route to its first championship outside Kentucky's borders.

in league games.

The game itself had changed dramatically since the introduction of the forward pass in 1906 and the addition of rules minimizing the violent collisions that had previously resulted in head injuries and numerous deaths among collegians. "The change is decidedly for the better," wrote Ross Creekmore in the *Lexington Leader*. "That former roughness and brutality has been eliminated to a remarkable extent. ... The game, as now played, is scientific from every point of view. Bull strength no longer triumphs as in former years, and the scientific ... player, whether light or heavy-weight, is at present the man of the hour in foot ball circles."

Scientific or not, State's 1909 players were said to be superior "in weight, speed and playing ability" than any previous team to play for the blue and white. And State's athletic association, along with Lowry, "left nothing undone in a managerial way to assist the team, which will be well equipped in every way."

By the time Sweetland arrived on campus on August 30, the team already had several practices under its belt, under the direction of team captain Richard Carroll Barbee, who played left halfback, "a tireless worker and probably the best defensive man the game ever knew in Kentucky." Barbee had captained the basketball team in 1907 as a sophomore. The squad boasted eight returning starters, including "quarter" Shelby Post; center Richard S. "Dick" Webb (also major and commander of the school's battalion of cadets); George "Old Lady" Dunlap, left tackle; Tiny Clark, guard; 1908 team captain George Matt "Henny" Hendrickson, tackle; and Bryan Shanklin, right end.

Classes began on Sept. 9, with 525 students enrolling, the "largest attendance on record," according to the *Leader*. KSU was an exciting place to be. New buildings were under construction and several older ones were being renovated, creating a pleasing collegiate atmosphere of red brick and stone buildings and growing trees. And there was a new, six-foot-wide sidewalk on South Limestone Street, "taking in the full front of the college." The campus was abuzz over the new freshman fad of head-shaving, with *Idea* reporters addressing the "bald-headed question." Also new was the mustache, "the latest thing in college freaks." Everyone was impressed at the salaries of recent graduates of the College of Mining and Engineering. Louis Francis, it was announced, had secured a job as manager of the Bell County Coal Co., earning "in the neighborhood of $2,500" a year. Ethelyn Egbert, on the other hand, "a very promising engineer of last year, (would) not resume her studies. ..."

"The outcome of the game will in all probability decide for all time the kind of schedule we will have. If we make a good showing against Illinois, enough to make up for the Michigan game, we may make schedules with better teams than we usually do."

College men and co-eds alike could sample vaudeville shows at the Hippodrome, which they termed "The Hipp," or, for a nickel, "moving pictures" at The Majestic, Princess or Bluegrass theaters. The Opera House was attracting large crowds with *The Red Mill*, a musical comedy boasting some of the nation's biggest stars, from Ethel Barrymore to Maude Adams and William Gillette. Afterward, students crowded into Putman's or Hughes & Co. for "soda water" and candy. The more worldly college man could take a streetcar to Yarid's pool and billiard parlor on East Main Street, where games could be had for 2 1/2 cents per cue with "no graft."

Football practice, meanwhile, was progressing nicely. "The squad is unusually large this year," wrote an *Idea* reporter. "There are more than forty big, husky dirt-eaters out, and Coach Sweetland is wearing a contented smile." One who was not smiling was player Frank Baker, who broke his leg in practice and would miss at least most of the season.

University of Kentucky
Special Collections

Junior tackle George
Matt Hendrickson, cap-
tain of the 1908 team,
was "universally
admired for his brilliant
playing," but didn't let
his fame go to his head.
He was considered "the
ladies' choice gridiron
hero." Hendrickson
earned a mechanical
engineering degree at

A big push was on to sell season tickets to "all of you who have not signed up and who are not 'rummies.'" (Rum-drinking was considered to be a campus problem.) Anyone purchasing a ticket became a member of the school's athletic association. The association's executive committee, consisting of student and faculty members, funded each athletic team and chose its student manager.

"It takes a lot of money to run and equip a first-class team, and every ticket sold will help that much," went the sales pitch in the *Idea*. Much was apparently made of the $5 purchase price, and sellers were anxious to alleviate any financial fears. "You know that you are going to get into all the games without worrying about the price and whether you can afford it or not," wrote one student booster. "And besides, you don't have to pay for your ticket until the end of school. All you have to do is to sign ... a card saying that at the end of the year the Athletic Association may take five dollars from the deposit you have made against any damage you may do to college property. ... Simple, is it not? Instead of paying your money to damage the college, you pay part of it to help the college."

One of the innovations introduced by Sweetland was a training table, which—the *Leader* reported—was established at 368 Rose Street, and run by Mrs. Mary Best. "Only the best players," no pun intended, were allowed, with others added "as they play better ball." The Faculty Athletic Committee decided that each football player rooming at Mrs. Best's house would be paid an extra dollar per week to pay the training table expense. As of Sept. 30, the players were Hendrickson, Dunlap, Johnston, Ellis, Webb, Barbee and Shanklin.

As the opening game with Kentucky Wesleyan approached, everyone was anxious to learn who had made the team, especially after Sweetland told his players, including nine returning starters, that performance on the field was his only consideration. One newcomer who broke into the lineup was freshman Thomas B. "Big Tom" Earle, of Hopkinsville. As for the prospects of winning the South, the coach was cautious. "We will need the hardest kind of work and the best of push to have our championship," he said. Sweetland stressed campus support for the team and urged every student to attend the final pre-season practice to give the boys a boost.

The newspapers predicted that State—bigger, stronger and faster than Wesleyan—would have little trouble winning the game. Workers prepared the new location of Stoll Field, moved 50 feet east of its old spot "to give it a better sod," and replanted the goal posts. "By Herculean efforts," the university's 240-strong battalion of cadets, under Commandant Phillip W. Corbusier (a member of the Athletic Association's Executive Committee, who apparently played a role in Sweetland's hiring), moved the grandstands to correspond with the field's new location. Students were proud of the field, situated near Winslow Street and old Maxwell Spring, with its adjacent Willow-lined lake and YMCA tennis courts.

A respectable crowd showed up at Stoll Field on Saturday, September 25, for the 3 p.m. kickoff. It was announced that Shelby Post, the popular quarterback, had a sprained ankle and would not play. He was replaced by Billy Johnston, "one of the smallest and one of the best men on the team." Some were concerned about State's backfield, which was lighter than in former years.

The referees were Georgetown College coach Robert T. Hinton and Robert Parks, a friend of Sweetland's from Syracuse, who had been helping him prepare the team for the season.

The game began under fair weather, about 65 degrees, with the sound of Parks' whistle. The *Lexington Herald* reported that the teams exchanged punts and fumbles until near the end of the half, when Wesleyan attempted a pass, which was "captured," or intercepted. By rule, Wesleyan was given possession of the ball and attempted an onside kick, which Shanklin returned for a 5-point touchdown. Barbee kicked the extra point to give Kentucky a 6-0 lead at the half. Shanklin added two more touchdowns after halftime and Barbee kicked both extra points to give State the 18-0 victory.

Everyone was satisfied with the win, including Sweetland, who was able to play several reserves in the second half. It was understood that "at no time was all of the strength of the Blue and White shown."

After a warm-up 28-0 trouncing of Berea on Oct. 2, highlighted by a Shanklin 45-yard touchdown run, State's students turned their attention to Illinois. The Illini, explained the *Leader*, were "head of the big elevens in what is known as the big Northwestern Association," precursor to the Big Ten, whose members already included Michigan, Wisconsin, Indiana, Ohio State and Minnesota.

State's 1908 team had been demolished 62-0 by Michigan at Ann Arbor, and Clugston and Lowry's boosters sought to maximize support for Sweetland's squad in an effort to overcome the memory of the disaster. A

University of Kentucky
Special Collections

Right end Bryan Shanklin, "the fastest end in Kentucky," was also the team's punter, in addition to a potent runner on occasion. His 45-yard touchdown was the highlight of a 28-0 win over Berea and his powerful punting helped prevent Illinois' desperate comeback.

special railroad car was reserved for students, under Lowry's direction. "Encouragement is what the team needs," a student wrote in the *Idea*. "This only can come from a loyal bunch of rooters. A game has been won by cheering the team hard when things looked against us. ... Let us then keep up our good reputation for noise."

The round-trip cost was "a little over fifteen dollars," much too steep for the average KSU student. Nevertheless, the push was made. "It will help a lot to hear some one rooting away up there in a foreign land. So all who can raise the cash, pile on the special coach, at a special price, and go on this special trip to see a special game."

Others presented the contest as the bellwether of the school's football future. "The outcome of the game will in all probability decide for all time the kind of schedule we will have. If we make a good showing against Illinois, enough to make up for the Michigan game, we may make schedules with better teams than we usually do."

At the compulsory chapel hour on the morning of Thursday, Oct. 7, State's students listened to rousing speeches from faculty members and coach Sweetland, urging them to travel with the team or offer any other support they could muster.

At 5 p.m. "the entire student body" assembled at the Administration Building to escort the varsity to the depot. Team members boarded a "wagonette" festooned with blue and white banners, streamers and pennants. By virtue of their victory over the sophomores in the annual "flag rush" the day before, the freshman class won the privilege of pulling the wagon, and each member in attendance grabbed his portion of a long rope tied to its tongue.

Hundreds whooped and cheered as the parade, led by the battalion band, began on Limestone Street, with upperclassmen following the wagon in senior-junior-sophomore order and "stray Preps, etc." bringing up the rear. This sight "created considerable sensation" as it made its way along Main Street, with students reciting "all the yells and songs" of their school, including "S-U-Kentucky" and "The Skyrocket."

Reaching the Queen & Crescent depot, the crowd filled its platform, while the "cheer leader" climbed to its roof, to calls of "Illinois Rah!; Illinois Ree!; K.S.U.! Ken-tuck-y!" The 15 players making up the traveling squad—on whose shoulders rested the honor of Kentucky—jumped from the wagon and boarded the special coach, hanging out of its windows to answer the cheers. They were accompanied by coach Sweetland and manager Lowry, along with Lt. Corbusier, who would serve as State's representative on the officiating crew.

As the train pulled away at 6:10 p.m., students formed a line on either side of the track, shaking hands with team members as they passed by and covering the KSU car with stickers and pennants.

By the time they made their way back to campus, the students reached a consensus that State would lose "18 or 20 to 0."

Upon their arrival at the Urbana, Ill., station—after spending the night in the sleeper car—team members gathered their belongings and filed off the train. They made their way to the Illini campus, and spent the day in double-session workouts to prepare for their David vs. Goliath struggle the next day.

Kentucky's players averaged only 160 pounds apiece, reportedly 20 pounds lighter than Illinois'. But Sweetland emphasized quickness, choosing speed over bulk and prohibiting his players from wearing pads, nose guards, or any other safety device that would add weight to their uniforms.

University of Kentucky
Special Collections

Freshman Thomas B. "Big Tom" Earle of Hopkinsville contributed mightily to the team as a tackle. The "Big Boy," said the 1909 *Kentuckian*, had "wonderful natural ability and absolute fearlessness coupled with his great strength."

In an effort to keep his players' minds off the game, the coach took them to the local opera house that evening. Several telegrams were awaiting them when they returned to their hotel. "We are with you to finish. Boys, make them know they played football," read the message from the sophomore class. The freshmen urged the players to "hold hard, hit low, do your best. We are with you. Will meet you on return. Best wishes."

As 3,000 Illinois partisans took their seats at the playing field that Saturday afternoon, they were ready for a laugher, perhaps even a bigger win than the 23-0 shutout of Millikin the week before. After all, this was the same group of Kentuckians that Michigan had utterly destroyed the previous season.

For their part, the Illinois coaches doubted the "moonshine men," as the local paper dubbed KSU, could give them much of a game. They needed a strong test to get ready for their upcoming grudge match against Chicago. To solve the problem, the coaches had the Illini varsity scrimmage the freshman team before their kickoff against Kentucky. "It is thought by some," said an Illinois partisan, "that the youngsters can put up more of a fighting game than the 'southen gemmans.'"

Sweetland himself knew it was a tall order. Stressing defense, he told his players their only chance was to keep Illinois' score low. The coach tried to motivate the team by urging them not to be intimidated by their opponents' lofty reputation. In an impassioned locker-room speech, Sweetland said Kentucky had its own reputation to build and they would be its founders. He then walked toward the field, leaving "every player … with tears in his eyes."

"Keep your head up and peg into it," Sweetland told his freshman starting right guard, Tom Earle, as game time approached. "You are big

Team captain Richard Carroll Barbee, a junior, played left halfback and was the team's extra point kicker. At 5'6" and 144 pounds, Barbee was described as a "little warrior," with "clear cut grit and determination" and a "tireless worker." He was considered "probably the best defensive man the game ever knew in Kentucky" and was captain of the basketball team as a sophomore.

enough to play against any man in America."

The officiating crew was Charles A. Fairweather and E.A. White, both of Illinois, who served as referee and umpire, respectively, and Corbusier, the head linesman and timekeeper. By agreement, the teams would play 15-minute halves.

The Illinois band struck up "My Old Kentucky Home" for their guests as the "Bluegrass boys" took the field for the 3 p.m. kickoff. Kentucky won the toss and elected to receive. Dunlap caught the Illini kick and ran it to the KSU 40-yard line. Shanklin punted the ball away on first down, a common strategy.

Illinois "elected to scrimmage," gaining a first down on running plays. When Kentucky's undersized defense began to stop the run, however, a shoving match ensued between the two groups of linemen. The "mix up" left KSU center Dick Webb with a punch in the jaw, which Lexington's *Evening Gazette* said caused him to "severely lacerate" his tongue. Webb stayed in the game. Illinois resorted to the forward pass, but was held at its 40-yard line.

After two running plays, Kentucky gained a first down at the Illini 30. Johnston took the snap, turned and handed off to Billy Rodes, his speedy 140-pound left end. Rodes banged into the Illinois line and emerged on the other side, dragging several defenders with him. Twisting and turning, the "plucky little end" finally broke free, scampering for a 30-yard touchdown with 9:35 left on the clock.

An exultant Frank Baker, his broken leg still on the mend, threw away his crutches and—the *Gazette* reported—hopped to the goal line on his good leg "almost as fast as the other men" to congratulate Rodes.

The 3,000 Illinois fans "sat dazed" as Barbee "lifted his right foot and sent the oval soaring over the goal post for the additional point," to make

Kentucky 6, Illinois 2, Oct. 9, 1909.

the score 6-0. The "Kentucky subs and cripples went wild with delight."

"Illinois came back fighting desperately" in the second half, attempting to befuddle its presumably inferior opponents with "triple forward passes, on-side kicks, line bucks and in fact everything known to football." But Sweetland's eleven was well prepared, and his defense held.

The crowd came to life, however, when a pass from Illinois quarterback Billy Bernstein was caught by right end Ted Richards, who escaped several Kentucky defenders for an apparent touchdown. The offensive team was celebrating the game-tying extra point when E.A. White—the umpire as well as a member of the Illini coaching staff—blew his whistle, declaring the play an illegal forward pass. According to the rules, a pass could be completed only behind the line of scrimmage.

Back on offense, KSU failed to gain

Johnston took the snap, turned and handed off to Billy Rodes, his speedy 140-pound left end. Rodes banged into the Illinois line and emerged on the other side, dragging several defenders with him. Twisting and turning, the "plucky little end" finally broke free, scampering for a 30-yard touchdown with 9:35 left on the clock.

Three hundred twenty-five students "by actual count" paraded through the streets in "night shirts and white caps" celebrating the win. It was, wrote student journalist W.G. Clugston, "one of the most spectacular things ever witnessed in Lexington."

ground and was backed up to its 10-yard line. The Illinois linemen broke through to block Shanklin's subsequent punt, forcing him to fall on the ball in the end zone for a safety, making the score KSU 6, Illinois 2.

But Illinois never threatened again, and Kentucky was driving at the Illini 5-yard line when time expired.

Back in Lexington late that afternoon, about 75 KSU students had finished watching the Transylvania-St. Mary's game and walked to the downtown Western Union telegraph office to inquire about the Illinois score. They were met by assistant coach J. White Guyn, already awaiting the result.

"We have the coach, and O! what a coach! We cannot praise him too much; we can never show our appreciation; we can only feel the blood tingle in our veins; we can only think of all that is great when his name is mentioned...."

—Student tribute to coach Sweetland

A telegrapher handed a telegram to Guyn and he announced the 6-2 victory. "Loud cheers of unrestrained joy burst spontaneously from the crowd," Clugston wrote in the *Herald*. News traveled quickly from student to student, and a parade was organized for 7 p.m., as the crowd dispersed to prepare for the celebration.

Re-assembling at the appointed hour, "325 students, by actual count," dressed in "night shirts and white caps" and led by members of the battalion band, marched through the "business section" of the city bearing a large banner proclaiming the news: "Kentucky State, 6; Illinois, 2." It was, wrote Clugston, "one of the most spectacular things ever witnessed in Lexington."

They stopped at the Phoenix Hotel for a "snake dance ... enlivened by many hideous shouts and yells." Anxious to share their triumph, drum-pounding band members led the throng to the all-female Campbell-Hagerman College nearby, "where the young lady supporters of the institution were serenaded" amid "loud cheers by the girls." The parade then went on to Hamilton and Sayre Colleges, the "other female institutions in that section of the city."

"Tonight in their exultation," reported the *Herald*, "the Kentuckians pay tribute to the honesty of the coach who could hardly have been blamed for failing to call back the ball after his own team had scored. ... It was a hard thing to do, but White was stubborn in his conviction that Bernstein's pass had been illegal."

The *Idea* was loud in its praise of KSU's overachieving team. "Shanklin was a surprise in the punting department, out-punting his opponent fully 20 yards. Threlkeld was a star at fullback, and gained easily through the Illinois line. Barbee and Rodes played their

Cadet Commandant Phillip Worthington Corbusier, a member of the athletic association's executive committee, served as head linesman and timekeeper for the Illinois game. Two days later, Corbusier told the frenzied student body the team had "fought like wild cats." His speech gave Kentucky a new mascot.

usual snappy game. Johnston at quarter ran the team like a general, and soon found the weak spots. Campbell and Ellis, although they were in new positions, repeatedly stopped plays through their parts of the line. Dunlap and Earl played like veterans, and no ground was gained over them. Dick Webb was always on the ball, and kept his opponent guessing all the time. Shanklin and Plummer played against ends that greatly outweighed them and broke up any number of forward passes."

The students also saw the hiring of Sweetland as a masterstroke. "We have the coach, and O! what a coach!" one wrote. "We cannot praise him too much; we can never show our appreciation; we can only feel the blood tingle in our veins; we can only think of all that is great when his name is mentioned. ..."

Another was moved to write a prose-poem of sorts: "The air is still—quiet reigns. The peaceful and dreamy silence pervades all. The sun sinks to rest behind the fleecy outlined horizon, in the warm glow of tinted clouds. All is peace. But now a slight whisper, faint and far away, is heard. Louder, Louder, it becomes. It multiplies, echoes, and re-echoes. Now it is heard from all sides. Clanging, crashing, sounding and re-sounding in its deafening peal. It is Victory! Victory Triumphant! It penetrates to all points; it is flung back from the pinnacles of the highest mountains, back from the depths of the deepest valleys. Victory! Victory! Victory!"

The "conquerors" arrived back in Lexington the next morning on the 10:30 a.m. train to a hero's welcome of screaming students and cheers that, said the *Leader*, "broke the quietude of the Sabbath morning." Escorted to campus amid a light rain—at times being carried on students' shoulders—they were greeted by a huge throng assembled on the front yard. A circular space was made in the center of the crowd, which hailed each team member—in addition to Sweetland, Lowry and Corbusier—and marched in glee around them, shaking hands and making sure "their idols got safely home with the least possible trouble and inconvenience."

After witnessing the spectacle, *Idea* writer O.E. Baird also turned to poetry:

The squad went North to fight the great—
Fought to save and saved Old State;
Made a touchdown and then they skipped,
With cheers of victory on parted lips.

Hats off!
Along the street there comes
A blare of bugles, a ruffle of drums,
And loyal hearts are beating high—
Hats off!
The boys are passing by.

Corbusier, his enthusiasm showing no sign of diminishing, told the players and students they had Sweetland to thank for their breakthrough victory. The team was "like the old Germans in battle," the tall, dark-haired commandant said, "when each man fought for his chief." The Kentucky players "fought for their coach," Corbusier yelled, his speech bringing the students to a frenzy of emotion. And then: "They fought like wild cats."

The KSU faithful were still sky high on Monday morning, Oct. 11, as they took their seats in Memorial Hall for an extended chapel period. Upon the football players' arrival, the hall exploded into applause and cheers that took 15 minutes to die down. Team members took their places in special seats on the rostrum to more cheers and congratulations from members of the faculty.

Corbusier, his enthusiasm showing no sign of diminishing, told the players and students they had Sweetland to thank for their breakthrough victory. The team was "like the old Germans in battle," the tall, dark-haired commandant said, "when each man fought for his chief." The Kentucky players "fought for their coach," Corbusier yelled, his speech bringing the students to a frenzy of emotion.

And then: "They fought like wild cats."

Corbusier's speech, covered in the local newspapers, created a sensation—and his "wild cat" soon became the subject of student doodles and a long essay on the exemplary qualities of wildcats. Two years later, the new mascot appeared for the first time in the student annual. By 1921, a real wildcat was appearing at football games, and the mascot was a permanent part of UK athletics.

KSU went on to embarrass Tennessee 17-0, and demolish Transylvania 77-0, enroute to a 9-1 record. Its loss to North Carolina A&M on Oct. 21, by a score of 15-6, cost it the Southern championship.

The North Carolina game also brought the terrible news that Sweetland had fallen ill and was hospitalized. Students wrote glowing tributes to their fallen coach. "Since Coach Sweetland has been ill, the students frequently discuss as to how he had done our university the greatest good," wrote one in the Nov. 4 *Idea*. "It is a fact known in other states that he has partially developed a superb piece of machinery out of our football team and that his name has been used as a battle-cry in all our great games; but still this is not the greatest good he has

University of Kentucky Special Collections

Sophomore center Richard Spurr "Dick" Webb, 6-feet-tall and 180 pounds, became something of a legend at Kentucky. Cadet commander of the school's military battalion, he was also known for "swiping" oysters and "covertly wiring dorm rooms with electricity upon request." He suffered a severely lacerated tongue in a "mix up" with the Illinois offensive line, but remained in the game. After graduation in 1911, Webb became an assistant coach of the basketball and football teams and, in 1921, obtained UK's first live wildcat.

done us. Is the arousing of an unheard-of university spirit and a more sportsmanlike attitude in the university of much importance? It is true that we can not keep him with us always, but let us hope that the spirit he has given us may never die."

Other students agitated to keep the coach at all costs, even if it meant taking up a collection to supplement his salary. A committee of faculty members visited him in the hospital to ask him to allow the school to match any coaching offers he might receive.

Sweetland served as UK's first athletic director the following year and coached the basketball team to a 9-0 record and the Southern champi-

William "Billy" Rodes, of Lexington and a chemistry major, scored the most important touchdown in Kentucky's early football history. Another of his nicknames was "Red Doc," which was used to distinguish him from a cousin who played for Kentucky in later years. Like his teammate and brother-in-law Richard Carroll Barbee, Rodes died of a cerebral hemorrhage in 1950.

onship in 1912, the first championship basketball season in school history. He even taught a class in coaching. But he left Kentucky, continuing his career at Miami (Ohio), West Virginia and Tulane. Sweetland compiled a 68-31-9 record and a winning percentage of .671 in his 11-year football coaching career, before retiring to his New York farm. He died on Oct. 21, 1950.

The University of Illinois went on to win national football championships in 1914, 1919, 1923, and 1927.

Upon graduation, William G. Clugston moved to Kansas and began a journalism career, eventually authoring books about politics.

Hendrickson and Shanklin—both of whom graduated with mechanical engineering degrees—were fondly remembered by the senior class of 1911. Hendrickson, it was said, was "universally admired for his brilliant playing. He is one of the few 'idols of the students' who has not lost his head over the honors his work has brought him." Shanklin was "the ladies'choice gridiron hero."

Richard Spurr "Dick" Webb—a mischievous sort known for "swiping" oysters and covertly wiring dorm rooms with electricity upon request—became an assistant coach for the basketball and football teams under Sweetland. In 1921, he obtained UK's first real mascot, establishing a tradition followed to this day.

Richard Carroll Barbee Jr. and William "Billy" Rodes became gentleman farmers in Fayette County.

Barbee graduated with a civil engineering degree in 1910 and served as a captain in the U.S. Army Air Corps during World War I, before marrying Rodes' sister Elizabeth in 1920. He became a construction engineer before retiring—on "permanent disability"—in 1938.

Barbee and Rodes died within seven months of each other in 1950—of cerebral hemorrhages—unremembered stars of a long-forgotten team: the original Kentucky Wildcats.

* * *

Cadet Commandant Phillip Worthington Corbusier (pronounced Cor-boo-seer) had an important job at Kentucky State University. He was head of the school's "Military department," which oversaw the mandatory drill of the students, excluding co-eds. The department was divided in 1908 into two battalions of three companies each. Cadet officers were required to pass exams at the end of the second school term in order to remain in their positions. Corbusier led two of his battalions in Gov. Augustus E. Willson's inaugural parade in Frankfort on Dec. 10, 1907. As was the custom for cadet commandants, Corbusier's tenure at Kentucky State University was a short three years. A member of a distinguished military family, Corbusier had been born on "Centennial Day," July 4, 1876, in San Francisco. He joined the Army during the Spanish-American War and served two tours of duty in the Philippines from 1899 to 1905. As a first lieutenant in the 14th Cavalry, Corbusier was posted at the Presidio in San Francisco until his appointment at KSU at the beginning of the 1908 school year. After leaving Kentucky, he resumed his Army career, serving in the Philippines during World War II. He died there after the war.

* * *

Writing in the *Kentucky Kernel* campus newspaper in 1920, Mrs. Ollie Cruickshank Wilson—secretary of the class of 1911—fondly recalled the deeds and school spirit of her classmates. "Dick Webb, Irish, Johnny, Butch, Dope and others are almost immortal to us," she said. "Our class has made good in every line."

As a testament to the class' success, she added, "All the girls, except one, are married."

6

Kentucky's Forrest Gump: Joel White Guyn

Upon his death on April 14, 1953, Joel White Guyn, former Lexington city engineer, was remembered as having served four years as the Wildcat football coach.

Missing from Guyn's obituary was his status as the Forrest Gump of UK sports.

Like a Kentucky version of the fictional Gump, Guyn seemed to have been present at the creation of everything in Wildcat athletics. He was a five-time letterman for what was then known as the Kentucky State College (KSC) Cadets.

At 18, he was a starting guard in the school's first-ever basketball game, played at Alumni Hall on February 6, 1903, against Georgetown College. Guyn also captained and quarterbacked the football team, leading KSC to a 9-1 record as a senior in 1904.

Graduating with a civil engineering degree, the young man landed a somewhat nepotistic job in the Lexington Public Works Department, for which his father worked as an "overseer."

Joel White Guyn seemed to be present at the creation of everything in Wildcat athletics. As a senior in 1904, Guyn was captain and quarterback of the football team that went 9-1.

But Guyn's attention turned back to football in 1906. Coach F.E. Schacht, a former star tackle for Minnesota and a medical doctor—who had compiled an impressive 15-4-1 record the previous two seasons—quit as practice neared, and the program was on its usual brink of financial ruin.

The closest thing to Schacht available was the graduated captain of the 1904 squad, and team manager A.L. Donan persuaded Guyn to take the job for no pay, on the condition that he receive permission from the public works department to take afternoons off for practices.

Upon receiving the OK, Guyn scheduled seven games and took charge of the team. He faced several daunting obstacles, not the least of which was that he would have only four returning players. But the primary challenge was a rule instituted for the coming year that no student could play in an intercollegiate game without completing one year at KSC and attaining "a recognized class standing." The youthful coach's second big problem was football itself, which was transforming itself from a potentially lethal form of rugby into the modern American mutation it was later to become.

The game would be different in 1906 than it had ever been before. To end a rapid increase in deaths associated with college football, President Theodore Roosevelt convened representatives of more than 60 schools, who agreed on new rules. They included a uniform playing time of 60 minutes, the introduction of a neutral zone between the lines and increasing the number of yards to gain in three downs from five to 10. The hand-waving signal for a fair catch also made its debut.

The biggest change, however, was the introduction of the forward pass. The blue-and-white boys would learn about this innovation the hard way.

KSC's first game was against Vanderbilt in Nashville on Oct. 6, which was somewhat interestingly officiated by two members of the University of Virginia football team. Guyn's players had barely walked onto Vanderbilt Park's "checkered field" before the Commodores lit them up with the forward pass and an early score.

"The game was witnessed by a large and appreciative crowd of lovers of the sport," reported the *Lexington Leader*, "and the brilliant plays were cheered vociferously." It was soon clear that "all the Cadets could do would be to hold the score down as low as possible." That turned out to be 28-0.

University of Kentucky Special Collections

Guyn was a starting guard for the school's first-ever basketball game on Feb. 6, 1903. During his playing career, Guyn earned six letters, five in football and one in basketball.

But Guyn's sophomore-laden squad could take something from the game, in addition to defensive experience against the pass. "The Vanderbilt team outweighed the Kentucky Cadets by twenty pounds to the man, but the plucky 'corncrackers' exhibited many brilliant plays throughout the game," wrote the *Leader* reporter. Junior Sam B. Coleman played well at right guard, while senior Louis B. Pride's performance at tackle "could hardly be improved upon."

Berea cancelled its game for the following Saturday, October 13, and Donan scheduled Eminence Athletic Club as a replacement. The new opponent was considered "a strong aggregation," having played close games against Louisville Manual Training (High) School and the Kentucky Military Institute.

Guyn spent the week teaching the forward pass and allowing a "large number of candidates" to compete for starting spots. The competition brought crowds out to practice. "The interest upon the part of the student body is alert," reported the *Leader*. "In addition to the large number of fans who are on the ground every afternoon several of the girls grace the stands with their presence." Two rising players were Stanley T. Baer, a junior right end, and sophomore quarterback Earl Stone.

The Eminence game began that Saturday at 2:45 p.m. Admission was 35 cents, though "ladies" only paid a quarter.

Joe Jackson kicked off for Eminence A.C., sending the ball bouncing toward the Cadet goal line. Kentucky right end Harry Stevenson dropped back to receive the ball. Catching it, he had just begun to move forward when he was tackled by two Eminence defenders. "In some manner in falling, his leg was twisted and one of the men who had thrown him to the ground fell upon it," the *Leader* reported. "A crunching of the bones in the leg was heard and horrified, the two men quickly took their weight off his body." Doctors said the injury was a compound fracture "just above the ankle and below where the guard protects the shin." Stevenson, 19, lay on the field unconscious and, after he was revived, "was removed to his boarding house at 387 South Broadway" by ambulance.

The game resumed and the crowd soon realized they were watching a mismatch. "The Blue and White eleven were swifter and got into the plays with greater speed than their opponents," wrote the *Leader* reporter.

"The forward pass was the stronghold of the cadets, and the brilliant work at this play won them several goals. State's line was invincible for the visitors; at no time were the cadets in danger of being scored against. The individual features of the game were a forty yard quarterback run by Stone and Stanley Baer's brilliant work in the forward pass."

—Lexington Herald, Oct. 14, 1906

But the earth-shattering feature of the game was the first pass in school history. Though UK's official records credit Stone with throwing the pass, the *Leader*'s report seems to cast doubt on the claim: "The forward pass was the stronghold of the cadets, and the brilliant work at this play won them several goals. State's line was invincible for the visitors; at no time were the cadets in danger of being scored against. The individual features of the game were a forty yard quarterback run by Stone and Stanley Baer's brilliant work in the forward pass."

Though Stone was identified as playing quarterback in the game while Baer was at left end, it wouldn't be unheard of for Baer to have thrown the passes. As late as the 1950s, quarterbacks often did much of a team's running while other players threw the passes. And while it is not certain if Kentucky's first forward pass was completed, it is certainly likely, given that eight cadets scored in the game and passes were said to have been a "stronghold" of the team and the reason for "several goals."

KSC led the game 22-0 at halftime—probably consisting of four five-point touchdowns and two extra points—and won the game 48-0. Other interesting features of this momentous game in UK history were that the umpire was the school's first football coach, Professor Arthur M. Miller,

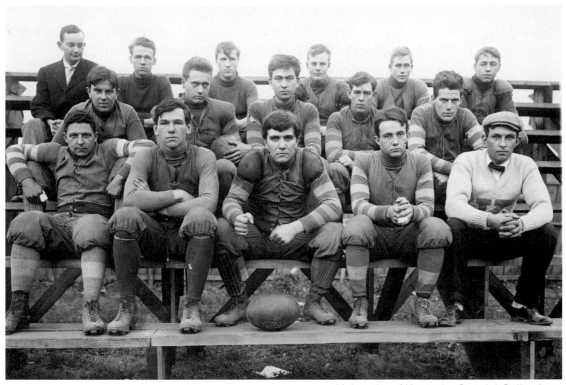

As coach of the 1906 KSC football team, Guyn (front row, far right) presided over the first forward pass in school history. Though sophomore quarterback Earl Stone was credited with the pass, contemporary accounts suggest left end Stanley T. Baer actually was the passer that day.

while one of the linesmen was George F. Brockman, a sophomore substitute on Guyn's team who had been on the traveling squad for the Vandy game.

After beating K.M.I. 16-11 on Oct. 27, Kentucky was shut out by Marietta College 16-0 at home. But Guyn's team blanked Tennessee 21-0 and Georgetown 19-0 before the Nov. 29 Thanksgiving game against Centre. This contest generated a lot of excitement, with 3,500 people showing up to watch it. KSC lost 12-6, ending its season with a winning record of 4-3.

Guyn coached two more years, compiling a 17-7-1 record—including a dazzling 9-1-1 mark in 1907—before being forced out in favor of what the local papers called an "eastern" coach. But Guyn, whose coaching career had been the longest in school history to that time, didn't complain, and graciously accepted an offer to become the new coach's assistant.

The coach was Edwin Regur Sweetland, a man of "determination and ginger" with impeccable football credentials. An 1899 graduate of Cornell University and standout on its football, basketball and rowing teams, Sweetland had led Ohio State to a 14-7-2 record in 1904 and 1905, in addition to coaching stints at Syracuse and Colgate.

KSC had officially become State University, Lexington, Kentucky by 1909. This was promptly abbreviated to KSU. The Cadets returned a veteran team that had aspirations of claiming the mythical Southern Championship if it could defeat Tennessee and North Carolina, in addition to an otherwise good record.

"The prospects for an all-Southern team are better this year than they were ever before in the history of the University," said Guyn, showing no signs of hard feelings over his demotion. "With the old men back in their places and the new material that is coming in, everything possible will be done and under the excellent training of Coach Sweetland, we should be able to clean up with them all."

Guyn was left behind for the fateful 6-0 away victory over Illinois on Oct. 9, 1909, that resulted in the team's nickname changing to Wildcats. Back in Lexington late that afternoon, about 75 KSU students had finished watching the Transylvania-St. Mary's game and walked to the downtown Western Union telegraph office to inquire about the Illinois score. They were met by Guyn, who was already awaiting the result.

Guyn coached two more years, compiling a 17-7-1 record—including a dazzling 9-1-1 mark in 1907—before being forced out in favor of what the local papers called an "eastern" coach. But Guyn, whose coaching career had been the longest in school history to that time, didn't complain, and graciously accepted an offer to become the new coach's assistant.

A telegrapher handed a telegram to Guyn and he announced the 6-2 result. "Loud cheers of unrestrained joy burst spontaneously from the crowd," wrote KSU student W.G. Clugston in the *Herald*.

Guyn returned to his job at the Lexington Public Works Department and was elected city engineer as a Democrat in 1912, a post he held for 31 years. He later served as a consulting engineer, and worked street-paving projects in numerous Kentucky cities and towns, including Olive Hill, Ravenna, Mt. Sterling, Paris and Frankfort.

He was a member of the Lexington UK Alumni Club, and helped host the group's annual homecoming reunions and dances for many years. Usually held at the Phoenix Hotel, these elaborate, highly social affairs included both teams and their coaches, along with the traveling members of the visitor's alumni organization.

Upon his retirement, Guyn built miniature houses, complete with furniture and other decorations, which he carved by hand with a penknife.

* * *

Coach F.E. Schacht, who compiled an impressive 15-4-1 record in 1904-

05, holds the distinction of being the only UK football coach who was also a medical doctor. A former star at Minnesota, Schacht was practicing medicine in Seattle when he was recruited by KSC athletic officials to coach in Lexington. Like almost anyone with any conceivable connection to that nation, Schacht was known around campus as "Germany." One of his players, Thomson R. "Tommy" Bryant, recalled his pronounced German accent, along with a propensity to save his first-team players for big games.

Bryant said the coach arose in chapel one morning and—imploring the KSC students to cheer his team to victory—said, "If you don't play, you can rut."

Coach F.E. Schacht holds the distinction of being the only UK football coach who was also a medical doctor.

7

James 'Turkey' Park and the All-Time Record

In the more than 110 years of Kentucky football, no player ever had a better game than James Park.

University of Kentucky
Special Collections

James Park's 10 touchdowns and 68 points against Earlham College on Oct. 24, 1914, remains the all-time single-game scoring record for a UK player. In all, Park set six all-time records in the game. A phenomenal athlete, the 6'2", 178-pound quarterback could pass 60 yards "with deadly precision" and had a 40-yard punting average.

Playing quarterback and kicker against Earlham College on Oct. 24, 1914, Park scored five rushing touchdowns and passed for five more, accounting for 68 of Kentucky's 81 points. He kicked eight extra points and his 19-for-27 passing day—at a time when the "forward pass" was still in its infancy—stands as the all-time pre-modern (before 1946) record in Wildcat football history. The player set six records in the game.

Park was a fine student athlete by any standard.

Born Nov. 10, 1892, in Richmond, the young man was described as "cool and quick witted" with "exemplary habits." At 6-2 and 178, he became known as Kentucky's "elongated quarterback," with a knees-and-elbows running style that may have accounted for his nickname, "Turkey."

Ahead of his time, Park could pass 50 or 60 yards "with deadly precision." He was also the team's kick return man, in addition to being its punter, with a respectable—even by today's standards—40-yard average and a long effort approaching 70. "Whenever 'Turkey' is calling signals, he has ten men working like beavers beside him," wrote a reporter in the *Idea* student newspaper. "He features with his head, but is a master at punting and passing."

Park's intellect paid big dividends for UK football, which boasted an 18-7 record during his tenure. In those early days of the forward pass, any out-of-bounds throw was awarded to the opposing team at the spot it left the playing field. Taking advantage of the rule in a 1913 game against Illinois, he began passing on fourth down, firing the ball 50 yards and sometimes farther, eliminating the possibility of a return and backing up the Illini more than if he had punted. Park's envelope-pushing forced the rule to be changed for the 1914 season.

Interestingly bearing a strong resemblance to one

of his successors, Tim Couch, Park won 10 varsity letters in his four-year career, which included being elected captain of the football and baseball teams. He was also a three-year substitute on the basketball squad. The archetypical big man on campus, Park was also a member of Phi Delta Theta fraternity, a mathematics major in the college of Arts and Sciences, senior class president, panhellenic representative, chairman of the campus YMCA and a member of the student senate. His peer-chosen motto in the 1914 *Kentuckian* was "He's some man—my Jim," along with the comment "This record is enough."

University of Kentucky
Special Collections

The archetypical big man on campus, James Park was as involved and successful academically as he was athletically. He was a member of Phi Delta Theta fraternity, a mathematics major in the college of Arts and Sciences, senior class president, panhellenic representative, chairman of the campus YMCA, and a member of the athletic committee and student senate. His peer-chosen motto in the 1914 *Kentuckian* yearbook was "He's some man—my Jim," along with the comment "This record is enough."

Park's football reputation was largely won in 1913, during a 13-7 Thanksgiving Day loss to Tennessee on a "sodden slippery" Stoll Field in Lexington. With Kentucky down 13-0 with less than a minute to play, Park took the ball from center and eluded every Volunteer defender on a "spectacular 50-yard run ... worth waiting a season to see." Elected captain of the senior-dominated 1914 team, Turkey was expected to continue his yard-gaining ways in his final campaign. He did not disappoint.

In those early days of the forward pass, any out-of-bounds throw was awarded to the opposing team at the spot it left the playing field. Taking advantage of the rule in a 1913 game against Illinois, he began passing on fourth down, firing the ball 50 yards and sometimes farther, eliminating the possibility of a return and backing up the Illini more than if he had punted. Park's envelope-pushing forced the rule to be changed for the 1914 season.

In the 87-0 warm-up opener against Wilmington that remains Kentucky's all-time biggest win, Park received a kick and repeated his feat against Tennessee, scampering through the defense for an impressive 75-yard touchdown. He also had another brilliant passing day, with "nearly all of his throws ... captured."

After another laugher against Maryville, which Kentucky won 80-0 with six touchdowns and 43 points by Cecil Tuttle, the Wildcats faced the Mississippi A&M Aggies—today's Mississippi State Bulldogs. Perhaps cowed by the blue and white's 167-0 year-to-date scoring total, A&M's players took the extreme, if not outright dishonest, measure of greasing their pants before the game.

After a quick Mississippi touchdown and Kentucky punt, "McArthur," the Aggies' left halfback, was tearing through the Kentucky line and secondary when he was met by Turkey. "Captain Park made as pretty a tackle as ever was seen in any football game," reported the *Idea*, "but was unable to hold the greasy Southerner."

Undoubtedly enraged by his opponents' unsportsmanlike tactics, Park responded with an inspired drive of "triple passes, double passes, false kicks, forward passes and a little straight football" to get the Cats within 13-6 at halftime.

After the Aggies were forced by the referees to replace their doctored pants for the second half, Turkey's passing led his team to another touchdown and a 13-13 tie with his successful extra-point kick.

After another laugher against Maryville, which Kentucky won 80-0—the Wildcats faced the Mississippi A&M Aggies— today's Mississippi State Bulldogs. Perhaps cowed by the blue and white's 167-0 year-to-date scoring total, A&M's players took the extreme, if not outright dishonest, measure of greasing their pants before the game.

"After this," reported the *Idea*, "no team on earth could hold the Wildcats." With a series of inspired runs and a defense that held, Park kicked two field goals—the last a record-setting one from the 42-yard-line with a minute remaining—to give Kentucky the 19-13 victory. Park rushed for 75 yards and passed for a touchdown in the victory and his punting average was 39.6.

Students poured from the bleachers and "for the first time in five years ... carried the Blue and White team off the field on their shoulders." The party continued that night, with 300 Wildcat faithful parading "harmlessly and joyously" through the streets of Lexington in their "night robes and pajamas."

Next up was the Earlham game, played at Stoll Field. Coach Alpha Brummage, confident his team could handle the school from Richmond, Ind., rested several of his starters for the upcoming Cincinnati game, relying on Park to make the plays.

Earlham kicked off. The ball was received at the Kentucky 40 and returned 20 yards. Set up at the Earlham 40, Park stepped back and passed to his left end, Floyd "Wrasty" Wright, who caught the ball and ran for a quick touchdown. Park kicked the extra point to make the score 7-0.

Kentucky's Fats Thompson caught an Earlham kick a few minutes later at the Kentucky 40, dodging all 11 Hoosier defenders to return it for another touchdown. Park made the point after attempt and the score was Kentucky 14, Earlham 0.

The Wildcats went up 21-0 after a "nice broken field" run and Park added the extra point.

But the team from Russellville, Ind., wasn't ready to concede defeat. After "a series of long runs," "Logan," the Earlham quarterback, kicked a field goal to put his team on the scoreboard.

Not to be outdone, Park ran for two touchdowns and added two extra points, and the Wildcats went into the locker room up 35-3. Brummage, content with the score, made wholesale substitutions for the second half, leaving Park in to quarterback virtually the entire second team.

Not skipping a beat, the "Wildcat scrubs ... all handled themselves like veterans," blocking well as Wright caught Park passes for two more scores. Turkey added two more rushing touchdowns to top off a 26-point quarter that propelled Kentucky to the rarefied tally of 62-3.

Earlham tried to answer with several "pretty runs," but the Kentucky defense stopped the drives each time.

Park ran for another touchdown in the fourth quarter to make the rout 68-3. Clark and Wright added two more 6-pointers on long runs, which—after two of Park's kicks failed—made the final score Kentucky 81, Earlham 3.

Floyd "Wrasty" Wright scored four touchdowns in UK's 81-3 win over Earlham, two on passes from Park. Wright was also a pitcher on the baseball team and, upon graduation, joined his friend on the St. Louis Browns, where he pitched from 1917-23. He appears in official Major League Baseball records as "Rasty" Wright.

With a 14-7 victory over Cincinnati the previous season, and riding an impressive 4-0 record, Kentucky was a favorite to defeat the Bearcats en route to the championship of the South. Scores of fans traveled by train to watch their team's first away game of the year. Witnessing blue sweaters filling up the stands, Pat Lyons, the UC "cheer leader," exhorted the home team's fans to get loud or they "would be outrooted on their own home grounds."

But the "Rhinelanders" had revenge for 1913 on their minds, taking it to the Wildcats, on the strength of a powerful backfield led by fullback and team captain "Teddy" Baehr. Park's punting slowed the run-happy Bearcats, but Kentucky found itself playing for a tie late in the fourth quarter.

Nothing went right. An apparent touchdown play cheered the Wildcat fans, but ended with the football "in possession of the enemy." Cincinnati won 14-7.

Kentucky was manhandled 40-6 the next week by Purdue in West Lafayette, Ind., but demolished Louisville 42-0 in that city's Manual (High School) Stadium. The last game of Park's career took place against

Tennessee in Knoxville on Nov. 26.

The Vols sent a big fullback barrelling through the Kentucky line during the game and there was no defender between him and the goal line except Park, who played safety on defense. Though he made the tackle, Turkey severely injured his pitching shoulder, and the Cats lost the game 23-6 to make their final record a somewhat respectable, though disappointing, 5-3.

The injury, however, stayed with Park, imperiling his plans to pursue his interest in baseball, his best sport. A fine pitcher with a .292 batting average, Turkey had already been scouted by several Major League Baseball teams, including Connie Mack's Philadelphia Athletics and the Cleveland Indians.

One day in St. Louis, Park was pitching in the seventh inning against the Boston Red Sox. Boston had two men on base when its manager put one of his pitchers in to pinch hit. Park prepared to make his opponents pay for the apparent blunder. He wound up, threw a fine pitch—and watched the batter whack a three-run homer to tie the game. The Boston pitcher had the first pinch-hit home run of his career. His named was George Herman "Babe" Ruth. "I can't say I'm proud of what happened," Park recalled years later. "But it put my name in Ruth's record book."

"For a while he thought he'd never be able to pitch again,..." said his son, James Park Jr. "It hurt his speed. He was a hard-ball thrower."

Slowed by the injury, Park nevertheless led his bat Cats to a winning record of 9-5, including nice victories over Illinois and Tennessee.

After graduation and being snubbed by all the major league scouts that had previously been so interested in him, Park joined the Lexington Colts, the local entry in the semi-pro Ohio State League. "It was a minor-minor league," said James Park Jr. "He was able to demonstrate that he was able to pitch." He eventually signed with the St. Louis Browns—today's Baltimore Orioles—for whom he made his Major League debut against Cleveland on Sept. 7, 1915. In that game, Park not only pitched the entire 11-inning game, but hit a two-RBI double to drive in the winning runs. Park's 2-0 record that year gave him a 1.19 earned run average. He also batted .400.

One day in St. Louis, Park was pitching in the seventh inning against the Boston Red Sox. Boston had two men on base when its manager put one of his pitchers in to pinch hit. Park prepared to make his opponents pay for the apparent blunder. He wound up, threw a fine pitch—and watched the batter whack a three-run homer to tie the game. The Boston pitcher had the first pinch-hit home run of his career. His name was George Herman "Babe" Ruth. "I can't say I'm proud of what happened," Park recalled years later. "But it put my name in Ruth's record book."

"It (the shoulder injury) may have been the best thing that ever happened to him," said his son. Browns executive Branch Rickey—a graduate of the University of Michigan law school—encouraged the young pitcher to get on with his life. "You're worth more than I'm paying you, but you ought to go back to law school." Rickey, who would later run the Brooklyn Dodgers and break Major League Baseball's color line with Jackie Robinson, gave good advice.

Back in Lexington after his second baseball season, Park attended law school while coaching the 1915-16 basketball team to an 8-6 record. He also coached the baseball team.

In all, Park played in the Pacific Coast League, for Columbus in the American Association and Oklahoma City in the Texas League. "He pitched his way through law school," said James Park Jr.

Park served in the U.S. Army Air Corps during World War I and, upon his discharge, was named athletic director at Transylvania. Continuing his law studies at UK, he was an honors graduate in 1920.

In a 52-year law career, Park continued his habit of achievement. He joined the legal practice of the legendary UK alumnus Richard C. Stoll, and served two years in the state house of representatives, two years as Fayette County attorney and 24 years as Fayette County commonwealth's attorney. A Republican, Park was a longtime chairman of the party's state central committee and its nominee for the U.S. Senate in 1944.

Park won numerous awards over the years, including the UK Centennial Medallion in 1965 as a "brilliant attorney, statesman, civic leader, and friend of the University." He died in Lexington on Dec. 17, 1970.

Courtesy of James Park Jr.

A lifetime high achiever, Park coached the UK basketball and baseball teams while simultaneously attending law school at an honors level, served in the U.S. Army Air Corps during World War I, was athletics director at Transylvania University and served as a state representative, Fayette County attorney, Fayette County commonwealth's attorney, chairman of the Republican State Central Committee and Republican nominee for the U.S. Senate. He was awarded UK's Centennial Medallion in 1965 as a "brilliant attorney, statesman, civic leader, and friend of the University."

One of his law partners, historian William H. Townsend, hailed both his manner and his achievements. "One of Mr. Park's characteristics is his utter lack of animosity," Townsend said. "I have never heard Mr. Park utter a harsh or bitter word against any human being."

Once during his career, Park prosecuted a man for murder and secured the death penalty. Before his execution, Townsend related, the condemned man sent Park a Christmas card.

8

Fight, Fight, Fight for the Blue and White

To Kentucky fans—and probably those of its SEC opponents—the melody is as familiar as "Happy Birthday" or "My Old Kentucky Home." It is "On, On, U of K," the Wildcat fight song, which served as the final puzzle piece in the early building of the Kentucky athletic program. Just as the student body needed cheers and colors with which to identify its teams, UK desperately needed a song.

University of Kentucky Special Collections

Carl Albert Lampert, a German immigrant, was the founder of UK's music department, band, philharmonic symphony and the men's glee clubs, in addition to the Central Kentucky Choral Society and the state high school music contest. Horrified that the school had no fight song for its sports teams or alma matter, Lampert wrote them himself.

The man who created it was Carl Albert Lampert, who was born in Minden, Germany, on May 13, 1874. He arrived in the United States at age 6 and the family settled in St. Louis.

Lampert grew up in a musical household, with his parents instilling a love of folk songs into their son. The youthful Lampert had an obvious musical ability, and, after graduating from Elmhurst College in Elmhurst, Ill., pursued it at the Chicago Musical College. He later earned a degree from the American Conservatory of Music.

Lampert refined his skills on the violin under celebrated teacher "Jacobsen" and joined the Chicago Symphony in 1900.

During his first year in Chicago, the young man saw a photograph of concert pianist Jeannette Phillips and decided that he loved her. He began a somewhat unorthodox courtship of Phillips, which, to his delight, resulted in their marriage within a few months.

Leaving the symphony in 1909, the Lamperts spent two years in Europe. Carl studied the works of the great composers—Bach, Wagner,

Lampert's song, which debuted in the "early spring" of 1923. No writer of lyrics, Lampert wrote "With words fitting to the swing and punch of this tune" on his composition.

Brahms and Beethoven—played in an orchestra conducted by Brahms and furthered his musical education under "Suchy."

The couple returned to the United States in 1911 and Carl Lampert accepted a job teaching string instruments and orchestral music at the University of North Dakota. While there, they became friends with the university's president, Dr. Frank LeRond McVey.

The Lamperts filled their spare time touring the country in a group called the Schumann Quintet. Such devotion to music impressed McVey, who—when he became president of the newly renamed University of Kentucky in 1917—invited Lampert to come to Lexington to start a music program.

As founder of musical education at UK, Lampert was at first both head of the department and its only instructor. Over the years, he organized or founded the university's band and philharmonic symphony and the men's and women's glee clubs, in addition to beginning the Central Kentucky Choral Society and the state high school music contest, which was often held on the UK campus.

Though starting the teaching of music at the university from scratch, Lampert was nonetheless horrified that the growing school had no fight song for its sports teams. By the spring of 1922, he had decided to solve this problem by writing a song himself. "After he had come up with a melody of sorts, he played and toyed with it, trying different versions and assorted endings," recalled Lampert's daughter Marcia. As he refined the tune on his piano at home he would ask his family members "What do you think of this, Baby?" or "Children, how does this sound?" and would receive positive or negative feedback.

Finally, the melody was finished. Lampert also had a few ideas about the lyrics, though words were not his strong suit. The first five notes, he decided, should correspond with the words "On, On, U of K," while, toward the middle of the song, they would convey "We'll fight, fight, fight for old U of K." On the top of his manuscript, the composer wrote: "With words fitting to the swing and punch of this tune."

"Prof"—as he was known to his students—then offered a $5 prize to anyone who could provide the remaining words to his creation. None came forward. But the professor had his eye on a student he thought could finish his song.

Whenever he saw Troy Perkins—a Hindman native with a penchant for writing—on campus he would hum the tune of "On, On, U of K" and tell him he needed some words for the piece. Finally, Lampert sat Perkins down in a room and said, "You're going to stay here until you write those words."

Whenever he saw Troy Perkins—a Hindman native with a penchant for writing—on campus he would hum the tune of "On, On, U of K" and tell him he needed some words for the piece. Finally, Lampert sat Perkins down in a room and said, "You're going to stay here until you write those words." A half hour later Perkins emerged with:

> *On, On, U. of K.*
> *We are right for the fight today*
> *Hold that ball and hit that line*
> *Every Wild cat star will shine*
> *We'll fight, fight, fight for the Blue and White*
> *And we'll roll to that goal Varsity*
> *And we'll kick, pass 'n' run till the battle is won*
> *And we'll bring home the Victory*

Perkins, who wrote plays and acted in them at UK's Romany Theater in addition to writing a weekly column in the *Kentucky Kernel*, handed the words to Lampert and couldn't remember if he ever got the $5 prize.

"Prof" decided to introduce his new song at an assembly early in the spring of 1923. A sizeable portion of the school's nearly 2,000 students packed into the main building's second-floor "convocation hall," receiving sheets of paper with Perkins' words to the new song printed on them.

Upon Lampert's cue, a quartet of male students began playing the song, singing as they went. Striking up the music again, the band played while the student body sang "On, On, U of K" for the first time. In the words of *Lexington Herald-Leader* reporter R. Marshall Shepherd, "the song caught on like wildfire," and was soon accepted as UK's own fight song.

It was first played "off-campus" on Nov. 17, 1923, when the Wildcat football team traveled to Atlanta to play Georgia Tech. "On, On, U of K" was received in Atlanta just as it had been in Lexington, winning fame not only for the school, but for the UK band. The "windjammers," as the *Kernel* referred to them, "took the field, and passed in review so gallantly and paraded past the stands with such a devil may care hauteur, that the people arose en masse and acclaimed them. ..."

Early in the spring of 1923— upon Lampert's cue, a quartet of male students began playing the song, singing as they went. Striking up the music again, the band played while the student body sang "On, On, U of K" for the first time. In the words of Lexington Herald-Leader *reporter R. Marshall Shepherd, "the song caught on like wildfire."*

By 1925, UK's annual staff wanted to print the words and music in that year's *Kentuckian* and found that the song hadn't been copyrighted. *Kentuckian* editors Frank H. "Herb" Carter and William H. "Bill" Skinner remedied that problem and the early printings of the song carried their names in addition to Lampert's and Perkins'. "They copyrighted it just to protect Dad," recalled Marcia Lampert. "Dad never bothered with things like that."

Among the things that Lampert did bother with, however, were improvements in the music program. With the band wearing hopelessly out-of-date World War I uniforms previously identified with the university's old ROTC band, Lampert used his own savings to purchase new ones. One of the most vocal opponents to such drastic action was Jeannette Lampert, herself a UK piano instructor. Though the university later reimbursed the Lamperts for the uniforms, Mrs. Lampert remained "quite put out about it," her daughter remembered.

The other half of Lampert's self-assigned mission was to create an alma mater, a formal song to be played at commencements and other fitting occasions at the university. He had completed the melody in 1917 but the words remained unwritten. After the success of the fight song, the Lamperts had dinner one evening with their colleague Dr. William D.

"Delbert" Funkhouser and his wife Josephine. During the conversation that evening Lampert asked Mrs. Funkhouser for help. "Josie," he said, "write some words to this for me, can't you?"

Josephine Funkhouser was as agreeable as Troy Perkins had been, and completed the song soon afterward. The first of the song's four stanzas was not only suitably inspirational for the university's graduates, it also explained the traditional meaning behind the school's colors.

> *Hail Kentucky, Alma Mater*
> *Loyal sons and daughters sing*
> *Sound her praise with voice united*
> *To the breeze her colors fling*
> *To the blue and white be true*
> *Badge triumphant age on age*
> *Blue, the sky that o'er us bends*
> *White, Kentucky's stainless page*

UK's new alma mater debuted on April 2, 1927, at a men's glee club concert. It was another hit, and has been played at commencements ever since.

Lampert spent the remainder of his career conducting orchestras, glee clubs and choral groups. And he pioneered what came to be known as "oratorios," in which orchestras and large choruses would accompany soloists. Upon his retirement in 1944, he recalled his career and said, "I think the happiest moments of my life have been spent at the University of Kentucky."

The retired educator then devoted the next several years to teaching music to Lexington schoolchildren. He died on August 27, 1949, and was buried in Little Rock, Arkansas, his wife's hometown. In a *Lexington Leader* editorial on Aug. 30, 1949, Lampert was hailed as "generous in soul and spirit."

"The memory of Prof. Lampert is indelibly stamped on hundreds of former students and associates whose lives were enriched by his friendship," the newspaper said.

During halftime of the Oct. 15, 1949, Citadel game, the UK Band, which Lampert had founded, formed his nickname, "Prof.," while playing "On, On, U of K" and the alma mater. The tribute plaque placed on the door of the rehearsal room in the Fine Arts Building lists his accomplishments.

The UK band paid tribute to its founder at halftime of UK's Oct. 15, 1949, game against The Citadel, forming his nickname "Prof" while playing "On, On, U of K," and the alma mater.

The music school honored Lampert in 1950 by placing a tablet listing his accomplishments on the door of the rehearsal room in the Fine Arts building.

"He did whatever he did because the need for it was there," said Lampert's daugher Marcia. "Those songs needed to be written, so he wrote them."

* * *

During his college career, Troy Perkins wrote, directed and acted in plays at UK's old Romany Theater, predecessor of the Guignol Theatre. He also operated a local bookstore for a time.

Before arriving at the university, he lived in Oklahoma and worked as a publicist for a Hollywood movie studio. A cousin of U.S. Rep. Carl D. Perkins with a lifelong love of traveling, Perkins became a career diplomat and an expert on China. He served as director of the U.S. State Department's office of Chinese affairs and was a sought-after speaker on the subject at his alma mater.

* * *

The arranger for both the fight song and the alma mater was Elmer G. Sulzer, who joined Lampert's growing music department in 1926. Sulzer was the university's representative in a joint effort with Louisville radio station WHAS to introduce the new medium to eastern Kentucky. The move not only brought education and entertainment to remote areas of the state, it helped establish the early popularity of UK's sports teams. Sulzer also served as UK's first publicity director and founder of the school's efforts to teach radio. He established a radio studio in 1933, began a department of radio arts in 1941 and started WBKY-FM—later WUKY—in 1944.

Somewhat ironically, Sulzer left UK for Indiana University in 1952, becoming director of radio and television communications and professor of radio and television. His lifelong hobby was the history of Kentucky steam railroads and he published numerous articles on the subject.

* * *

Lampert's friend and colleague Dr. William Delbert Funkhouser was one of the nation's leading scientists, having written 327 books and articles on entomology, zoology and archaeology in a 30-year career. He graduated

University of Kentucky Special Collections

Dr. William Delbert Funkhouser, one of the nation's leading scientists, joined UK in 1918 and served as dean of the graduate school from 1925 to 1948. He was chairman of the UK athletic council—and its successor the athletic board—from 1918 to 1945. When he died on June 10, 1948, he was the only secretary the Southeastern Conference had ever had. During his SEC tenure, Funkhouser wrote most of the SEC's regulations and was "chief interpreter of the rules."

from Wabash College in Indiana in 1905 and earned masters and doctoral degrees from Cornell University in 1912 and 1916. Funkhouser joined UK in 1918 as professor of zoology and added anthropology to his duties in 1927. The biological sciences building constructed in 1942 was named in his honor. Funkhouser also served as dean of the graduate school from 1925 to 1948.

At a time when professors and university administrators actively supported athletics, Funkhouser was chairman of the UK athletic council from 1918 to 1945 and chairman of the athletic board beginning in 1945. He was the only secretary the Southeastern Conference had from its 1933 inception until his death on June 10, 1948. In this position, Funkhouser was the writer of most of the SEC's regulations and "chief interpreter of the rules."

Josephine H. Kinney Funkhouser, writer of the words to the alma mater, died in Lexington on Oct. 6, 1972.

9

'Daddy' Boles, Father of UK Athletics

In going from an almost unknown student pastime to a big time collegiate sports program, University of Kentucky athletics has had many guiding hands.

Dr. Arthur McQuiston Miller, professor of geology and paleontology and later first dean of Arts and Sciences, was—despite never having played the game—the school's first real football coach and an unfailing advocate of college sports.

Dr. John J. Tigert, who coached several men's and women's teams at UK before becoming U.S. commissioner of education and later president of the University of Florida, contributed much to the school, as did trustee and board chairman Richard C. Stoll and athletic director Bernie A. Shively.

But none labored so long and hard for the Big Blue as Stanley Atwood "Daddy" Boles.

Described as "one of the most completely easygoing, considerate individuals you'd ever expect to bump into," the redheaded Boles was born in Williamstown, in Grant County, in 1887. As a husky 185-pound, 17-year-old player on the Kentucky Wesleyan College football team, he was walking to practice one day with a rather undersized teammate. "Hey," another team member called to Boles, "you're big enough to be that other boy's daddy!" A nickname was born.

The young man graduated from KWC in 1910 and went on to get a master's degree from Vanderbilt.

Boles entered the coaching ranks at Locust Grove Institute in Georgia, where he directed the football and baseball teams. His next job was as head football coach at a tiny church-affiliated school known as Polytechnic College, Fort Worth, Texas. But the athletics department was a bit shaky and the young man soon left the school.

Arriving at Texas Christian University, he coached the football team to a victory over, among others, SMU. Another year went by and Boles found himself coaching at Trinity University, a small Presbyterian school, when he was invited to apply for an assistant's position coaching football and track at the University of Kentucky

Despite what might have been considered a demotion, the 27-year-old Boles jumped at the chance to become a smaller fish in a bigger pond. He also couldn't resist returning to his native state. He arrived at UK in 1916 as "physical director for men," which meant that he was the gym teacher. His duties also included assisting Tigert, the football and track coach. The football Wildcats posted a 4-1-2 record that season, including an impressive victory over the school that would become Mississippi State.

"Athletics in 1916 were an extra-curricular activity participated in strictly on a volunteer basis," Boles explained. "We had no scholarships, very few spectators for games, and no sports writers."

The following year, 1917, Tigert departed for World War I, and the athletic council named Boles head football and basketball coach. After posting wins over Butler and Maryville, the football team suffered through six consecutive games without scoring on their way to 3-5-1 record that was the school's worst in 15 years. The only saving grace for Boles was that his team finally came together in its season finale, whipping Florida 52-0 on Stoll Field.

> *"Athletics in 1916 were an extra-curricular activity participated in strictly on a volunteer basis. We had no scholarships, very few spectators for games, and no sports writers."*
>
> *—Stanley Atwood "Daddy" Boles*

The new UK coach fared better with the basketball team, which won 9, lost 2 and—incredibly—tied 1. The Wildcats played at Boles' alma mater, Kentucky Wesleyan, on Feb. 9, 1918. The discovery of a scorer's error after the game proved the contest had ended in a 21-21 tie, which may be unique in the history of college basketball. Officials of the two schools intended to resume or replay the tied game, but allowed the season to end without doing so.

The next school year, 1918-19, began with a promotion. Boles was named athletic director, hiring Andrew Gill to coach the football and basketball teams. George Buchheit relieved Gill of his basketball duties the following season.

By 1921, Buchheit had built the hoops team into a contender for the Southern Championship, which it won that year. The season was UK's best ever up to that time and Boles did everything he could to use the momentum to build his program. As excitement—and demand for tickets—grew in anticipation of the Cats' Jan. 29 showdown with Auburn, Boles had University Gymnasium's folding chairs painted and numbered as reserved seats. Tickets were printed and placed on sale at the University Book Store and Lexington Drug Co.

The resulting 40-25 victory—then considered "one of the most thrilling games the Wildcat cage has ever seen"—helped convince school officials and supporters that a larger venue was needed for Kentucky basketball. Three years later, UK had the 2,800-seat Alumni Gym, the finest basketball facility in the South.

As athletic director in those early days, Boles' duties included not only hiring and firing coaches and making scheduling agreements for UK's sports teams, but finding jobs for players who couldn't pay their way to college. The A.D. was also a frequent guest at high school sports banquets, bringing along Wildcat football and basketball coaches. Then as now, such appearances were a recruiting tool.

Boles never stopped learning, often spending time off campus taking courses at Princeton or the universities of Tennessee, Virginia, and Illinois on such subjects as "bayonet drill" and "mass athletics." And when he couldn't find a suitable candidate to fill a coaching position, he took on the task himself. He coached the freshman basketball team to an undefeated season in 1924 and served as coach of the golf team, beginning in 1938.

The A.D. position had grown into a full-time job by 1929, and physical education was dropped from Boles' duties. "Recently the work attached to the office of Director of Athletics has become so strenuous and complicated that it became necessary for the Athletic Council to have his entire time," according to a profile in a football program from that season. "Consequently the new office was created and 'Daddy' became the first full-time Director of Athletics. The new position carries with it great responsibility in that financial management and ticket sales are included under the new office. ...

"Boles is one of the best known and loved persons on the campus of the University of Kentucky," the profile went on. "More than half the Alumni have come in contact with him during their years at the University and to all of them he still is 'Daddy.' During the time that he has been in charge of athletics ... he has brought about many important changes and improvements. The sale of tickets to the different athletic contests has been placed on a new foundation and is now carried on in a most efficient manner. Through his excellent management a good portion of the debt on the stadium and basketball building, which the Athletic Council assumed, has been paid off. Through his efforts the University of Kentucky is recognized throughout the South and contests with our teams are eagerly sought by other universities."

University of Kentucky Special Collections

After spending two years as a gym teacher and coaching football, basketball and track, Boles became athletic director in 1918, a position he held until 1934. During those early days, Boles pioneered ticket sales as a way to finance the program. In addition to founding the boys and girls high school basketball tournaments, he sold reserved seats during UK's 1921 Southern Championship basketball season and helped facilitate the construction and financing of Alumni Gym, the largest in the South at the time, and Stoll Field's McLean Stadium. He added lights and a public address system at McLean Stadium in 1929, allowing for the broadcasting of games. His shining moment, however, took place in 1930, when he hired Adolph Rupp to coach the basketball team.

After leaving the AD position in 1934, Boles became "graduate manager of intercollegiate athletics" and ticket sales manager, in addition to being UK's golf coach. His 1941 team had a 9-0 record. Pictured with him were golfers Lloyd Ramsey, Ermal Allen and Carlisle Myers.

According to the *Kernel* campus newspaper, one of Boles' finest achievements of the 1929 season was the addition of lights and a public address system to McLean Stadium and Stoll Field. The lights—consisting of "twenty powerful flood lights along the rim of the stadium"—allowed UK to schedule night games, which were "gaining in popularity in the larger universities throughout the country.

"Many people, who because of various reasons could not attend a game during the afternoon, are thus enabled to witness the Wildcats' games," read the *Kernel* editorial. "Another feature of the flood lights is the additional practice hours which the Big Blue can use to good advantage."

The public address system brought the "announcement of plays, players, and substitutions" to UK games for the first time, which allowed for the radio broadcast of the Wildcats' 20-6 victory over Washington and Lee on Oct. 12.

"The *Kernel* rejoices with the student body that we have such a man at the helm of Kentucky's athletic department," the editorial went on. "He'll certainly put Kentucky 'on the map'—athletically speaking."

The student journalists' prophesy was fulfilled the following year, when basketball coach John Mauer left the university for a job with Miami of Ohio. Boles decided to act on a recommendation he had received from University of Illinois coach Craig Ruby about a suitable replacement. The recommended man had a 59-22 record in three years at that state's Freeport High School, and Ruby thought he had earned a shot at a college job. The man's name was Adolph Rupp.

After an interview and the favorable report of the search committee, Boles hired Rupp, the single most important and successful decision he ever made. In a 42-year career, the Kansas native and college basketball hall-of-famer won 876 games and four NCAA championships, transforming Kentucky from a respectable regional team into the greatest basketball program in college sports history.

Ending his time as athletic director in 1934, Boles became "graduate manager of intercollegiate athletics" and, from 1939-46, ticket sales manager.

In late 1945, as millions of World War II veterans began streaming back to the United States, universities throughout the nation braced for implementation of the law known as the G.I. Bill. The law, which funded programs allowing veterans free access to higher education, had the effect of deluging colleges and universities with not only veterans, but their spouses and children.

As UK planned for waves of the newcomers—as well as former students whose college careers had been interrupted by the war—it turned to Boles, who was beginning his 30th year at the school. He was appointed manager of Cooperstown, UK's "colony" of more than 400 prefabricated houses built on a portion of the university's agriculture experimental farm and named for agriculture college dean Thomas Poe Cooper.

As UK planned for waves of the newcomers—as well as former students whose college careers had been interrupted by the war—it turned to Boles, who was beginning his 30th year at the school. He was appointed manager of Cooperstown, UK's "colony" of more than 400 prefabricated houses built on a portion of the university's agriculture experimental farm....It was the largest such facility in the United States.

It was the largest such facility in the United States.

"Dean Cooper gave us the worst part of the farm, land on which nothing ever had been grown," Boles said with a grin, building up to his punch line about the Cooperstown birth rate. "And, with all those 500 or so kids and more coming all the time, we claim to have turned it into the most productive 30 acres in Kentucky." By 1949, the place had grown even larger, with the addition of a new complex known as Shawneetown.

Boles' duties included management of house rentals, along with maintenance and repairs and the enforcement of regulations. As he had with his students and players, he soon became simply "Daddy Boles" to the more than 500 families and 1,500 people who lived at the two sites.

"Good, strong men have been driven to a point just this side of complete nervous collapse by jobs much less involved than handling the married-veteran housing situation at a large college," began a 1940 feature article on Boles in the *Louisville Courier-Journal*. "Those who have mulled over the situation say it takes one with the wisdom of a latter-day Solomon, the patience of a prophet and the unflinching firmness of the south slope of the Rocky Mountains to take care of such an assignment."

Boles explained that he handled everything from "leaky roofs and dripping faucets to Junior's croup"—though taking care to avoid "intrafamily spats." The manager took care of everything with "a fine sense of humor," according to another account, "and the happy ability to handle most situations without undue commotion or excitement."

UK offered an opportunity many of the veterans would never have had without the G.I. Bill, and most chose professional fields, a phenomenon not lost on the housing manager. "We have so many law students at Cooperstown," he said, "that we're bound to wind up with someone on the Supreme Court."

Boles' latest assignment was a service to the university and the athletic department, since the returning veterans included Jay Rhodemyre and Phil Cutchin—standouts on Bear Bryant's first two UK football teams—and Cliff Barker, Alex Groza and Kenny Rollins—three starters on the 1947-48 Fabulous Five basketball team, in addition to reserves Johnny Stough, Dale Barnstable and Jim Line.

When veterans' numbers began falling, Boles retired from UK in 1955, ending a 39-year career. He was often called on to recount his experiences at the school as well as his insights about athletics. He invariably told his stories in a humorous way, such as his account of an incident at the 1930 UK-Tennessee football game. "I was standing on the sidelines when a man walked up to me and gave me a live Wildcat," he said. "Not knowing what to do with it I put it under a cheerleader's megaphone." He later gave it to the campus "pep" organization, Suky, which he had helped found.

He said William "Black Doc" Rodes, "who was playing at UK when I came, was the best football player UK has had since I've been here" and "Bob Gain has been the best lineman." Boles also defended coaches whenever he had the opportunity. "An academic professor may teach until his beard reaches his waist without repercussions," he said. "But let an athletic coach lose one or two games and the alumni are yelling for his blood."

Boles died on Dec. 4, 1961, at his Lexington home. That evening, during Kentucky's basketball game with the University of Southern California, a capacity crowd at Memorial Coliseum rose and bowed their heads in prayer and silent tribute to a life lived in service to UK and its athletics program.

It was a job well done.

In 1918, Boles invited all Kentucky high school boys' basketball teams to a tournament on the UK campus.

When he only received seven favorable replies, Boles added the University High team from UK's campus and began the first Boys' High School Basketball Tournament. The field was Covington (now Covington Holmes), Danville, Kavanaugh (now Anderson County High), Lexington (now Henry Clay), Monticello, Paris, and Somerset, in addition to University High.

Games were played in the already antiquated University Gymnasium, with a capacity of only 600. Tickets cost 10 and 15 cents for students, 25 and 50 cents for adults. The admission receipts totaled about $35, which Boles used to pay a single referee to officiate the contests at the rate of $5 per game.

The school that became Lexington's Henry Clay High won the first tournament 16-15 over Somerset.

Teams had to pay all their own traveling expenses. UK fed the 56 players at the campus cafeteria, and they slept in fraternity houses.

Beginning in 1921, Boles held a girls' tournament simultaneously with the boys' until it was discontinued in 1932. He managed the boys' tournament until 1936, when it was taken over by the Kentucky High School Athletic Association.

In 1918, Boles invited all Kentucky high school boys' basketball teams to a tournament on the UK campus....Games were played in the already antiquated University Gymnasium, with a capacity of only 600. Tickets cost 10 and 15 cents for students, 25 and 50 cents for adults. The admission receipts totaled about $35, which Boles used to pay a single referee to officiate the contests at the rate of $5 per game.

Boles said the best tournament game he ever witnessed was the 1928 Carr Creek-Ashland game, which Ashland won 13-11 in four overtimes. The Tomcats, led by Ellis Johnson, also won the national high school championship in Chicago that year.

As with most of Boles' endeavors, the tournament benefited the University of Kentucky in numerous ways. The most important thing was that it placed the best high school basketball talent on campus. Many of these players later chose to play for the Wildcats, including Bill King, who played for Henry Clay in the inaugural tournament and starred on the 1921 team that produced UK's first tournament championship.

Ellis Johnson, a member of the 1928 Ashland Tomcats, earned three letters on the Wildcat football team and became an All-American basketball player. He also served as a student representative on the committee that helped hire Adolph Rupp and starred on the legendary coach's early teams.

10

First Tournament Championship Team
First All-American

As they prepared for the beginning of the 1921 basketball season, members of the University of Kentucky Alumni Association noticed a trend in the school's athletic program. "The demand for winning teams at the University is growing insistent," read an alumni editorial in the *Kentucky Kernel*, the student newspaper.

"Graduates, former students, faculty and undergraduates seem anxious that the Blue and White be represented by champion teams and a spirit of cooperation is beginning to be manifest that may bring a new strength," the editorial continued. "This strength will come with the sending in of better material in the way of new students, in which the University will have to compete with the strongest institutions of the South."

The basketball team seemed poised to make strides in the as-yet-unconquered Southern states at a time when most rooters would have been happy to claim a state championship with a winning record over rivals Kentucky Wesleyan College, Cumberland College, Transylvania University, Georgetown College and Centre College. Second-year coach George Buchheit had 18 players from which to choose a starting five and planned "an intensive practice schedule." One returner sure to be among them was team captain Basil Hayden of Paris, whom the *Kernel* considered the "valiant leader … of the squad" and "one of the best forwards in the South."

Sportswriters looked forward to a schedule that included, in addition to archrival Centre, the University of Cincinnati and—for the first time ever—the school that would become Auburn University, which was such an unknown in Lexington that the *Herald* said it was located in Georgia.

The UK homecourt was "University Gymnasium," a cramped two-story brick room inside Alumni Hall lined with wooden barbells and Indian clubs. The goals were suspended from the second-story steel balcony, from which students would watch games upon seats brought in for the occasion. Long shots were imperiled by the protruding rafters of the vaulted ceiling and a long pipe, from which were suspended strange-looking oblong light bulbs. The metal posts that supported the running track served as exclamation points for the 60- by 40-foot court's out of bounds lines. "We always had to dodge those things," Buchheit recalled.

The gym's varnished hardwood, though normal looking in every respect, was nonetheless a quirky object of amusement to students who had used

UK's home court was University Gymnasium, "capacity 600," a cramped, two-story brick room inside Alumni Hall. Goals were suspended from the second-story steel running track, and protruding rafters and pipes made long shots risky. The track was supported by metal posts that served as exclamation points for out-of-bounds lines. "We always had to dodge those things," recalled coach George Buchheit.

it for everything from compulsory exercises to dancing. A poem, penned by the "Kandid Kid" and titled "Ode to the Armory Floor," advised that:

> If you lose the only girl,
>   Blame the floor;
> If your head begins to whirl,
>   Blame the floor;
> If your dancing seems a sin
> And you break a leg or limb,
> If you paralyze a fin—
>   Blame the floor.

The 1920s was the heyday of flamboyant sports writing, with every aspiring reporter anxious to coin a phrase to rival "Gashouse Gang," the "Four Horsemen," or "Sultan of Swat." Local scribes referred to players as basketeers, sphere-tossers, or—harkening back to the days when crowds were separated from the playing floor by heavy fencing—cagers.

Kentucky's players were at various times dubbed the "Wildcat menagerie," "Buchheit's quintet," "Kentucky warriors," "Bluegrass basket shooters," "blue clad basketeers" or the "feline squad."

Buchheit had yet to pick his starters on the eve of the Jan. 12 opener with Kentucky Wesleyan, but announced that a severely sprained ankle had restricted Hayden's workouts and would keep him from the lineup.

Though Wesleyan had whipped Eastern Kentucky Normal (today's EKU) 37-13 in its opener, it had been trounced by powerful Centre 46-14, going "the way of many another valiant aggregation." UK fans were anxious to "dope out" if a state championship was possible. After all, wrote a *Herald* reporter, "Centre beat Wesleyan by the margin of 32 points. What will State do?"

Sportswriters looked forward to a schedule that included, in addition to archrival Centre, the University of Cincinnati and—for the first time ever—the school that would become Auburn University, which was such an unknown in Lexington that the Herald said it was located in Georgia.

"Every cubic inch of the gallery was taken up" at University Gymnasium to watch the game, which began at 8 p.m. Buchheit's starting five would be "the lengthy" Freddie Fest at center, former Lexington High star Bill King in his collegiate debut at forward, "Poyntz" at forward, Sam Ridgeway at "stationary guard" and football team quarterback Bobby Lavin at "roving guard." After an early 4-0 deficit, the Wildcats "piled up a comfortable lead" in the first half, prompting Buchheit to send in his substitutes, which "increased the margin at a faster rate than had the regulars."

Hayden decided to "don the legless pants" in the second half and scored five points substituting for King as Kentucky ripped an out-manned KWC 38-13.

Next was a Jan. 15 "mix-up" with Cumberland College, which entered University Gym with a five-game winning streak against the Blue and White. "Coach R.P Jones has worked his men into mid-season form, so that the visitors are going to be a tough knot for the university five to go through," wrote a *Herald* reporter. "If the Wildcats are victorious ... the local team will begin to blow some State championship bubbles."

Hayden replaced Poyntz in the starting five, while Adkins—who led all scorers in the opener as a reserve—replaced Fest at center. Adkins was a prolific scorer who befuddled opponents and spectators alike with an unexpected backhanded release to his shot, which was usually on the mark.

Buchheit stressed passing and sticky defense, and his team responded. "Time and again the swift passing combination of ... Ridgeway on one end and Captain Hayden on the other, took the sphere down the floor past the Williamsburgers to hang up two more points for Kentucky," reported the

Herald. "Hayden showed up easily as the best individual player of the night," pouring in 18 points, as the Wildcats went on to win 37-13. Lavin satisfied himself with four points and several assists, while shutting down his opponent.

Like many of his successors, Buchheit managed to keep his talented reserves—dubbed the Wrecking Crew—happy with late-game playing time. It was said Kentucky's players could easily "make a couple of high caliber basketball squads."

The "perennial and unceasing war between the Wildcat of Kentucky and the Tiger of Georgetown" was renewed on Jan. 18. The *Herald* billed the contest as a struggle between the "quick passing" and teamwork of UK against the individual stars of the "yellow-sweatered five."

For the first few minutes it looked as if the Tigers were going to give the "Blues and Whites" the fight of their lives before Buchheit's "chain-lightning system of floor-work"—as the *Herald* reporter called it—took effect. King and Adkins took the scoring honors with 12 apiece in a game filled with "fast and furious" play and "passing stunts," while Hayden had 10 in a 38-23 win.

Three nights later, on Jan. 21, Kentucky entertained the University of Chattanooga before a "record crowd." The Moccasins grabbed the opening tip and took control of the contest early behind center and team captain Bill Redd, whose play was described as "a queer combination of basketball, football, baseball and track, with a little slapstick comedy thrown in." *Herald* writer J.A. Estes reported that Redd "pitched goals like a basketball player, guarded like a football tackle, wound up for his passes like a baseball pitcher, and ran an approximate distance of 10 miles."

Buchheit employed a floor-length 1-3-1 defense that consisted of one player under

University of Kentucky Special Collections

Second-year coach George Buchheit stressed teamwork and passing, in addition to a sticky, floor-length 1-3-1 defense that would today be called a press. Like many of his successors, he kept a talented stable of reserves happy with late-game playing time. After compiling a 44-27 record in three seasons, Buchheit left UK for Trinity College in Durham, N.C., the school that would become Duke University.

each basket and three zoning their five offensive opponents. The strategy was designed to negate outstanding individual play and was usually effective.

Redd's individual antics, which included holding the ball "as much as the rest of his team put together" was no match for UK's teamwork. The Wildcats embarrassed Chattanooga 42-10, with Hayden putting forth "his usual routine of goal shooting, scoring five field goals, and his guarding was of the highest type."

UK's 4-0 start was its best in seven years, but sportswriters were quick to point out that its next four games would be the toughest of the season and the Cats would be playing away from home for the first time.

At about the 17-minute mark of the second half, trailing 20-16, Hayden called a play for King, who "tossed in a neat field goal," pulling the Wildcats to within 2. "It seemed as if the packed galleries had been waiting all night for that moment," read the Herald, "and when the sphere rolled through the iron ring a roar went up that made the old gymnasium shiver." Ten seconds later, Hayden had a stolen ball, which he laid in to tie the score. By the time the onslaught was over, Kentucky had gone on a 14-0 run en route to a 36-20 advantage. "After that every yell was a victory song for the Wildcats, and the Auburn team was soon so far behind it became discouraged and went to pieces."

The away game was against Cincinnati on Jan. 26, a Wednesday evening. Just as it had against Chattanooga, Kentucky's defense clogged the interior, forcing long shots, "with disastrous results." For its part, the UC defense left openings for Kentucky's speedy forward Bill King, who drove for 16 points—including eight free throws—in a 26-19 victory. Hayden contributed four points.

The next challenge would come against the school that somewhat flamboyantly called itself the "Alabama Polytechnic Institute of Auburn, Alabama."

"Auburn comes fresh from a series of victories that would make an enemy less courageous than the Wildcat tremble and fear for his safety," read the *Herald*. The Auburn "net artists" were described as "undoubtedly one of the best basketball outfits of the South." Auburn actually entered the game 3-3, but was riding a two-game winning streak, with an impressive two-point win over Georgia Tech and a 27-7 crushing of Vanderbilt.

Knowing a good opportunity when he saw it, athletic director Stanley A. "Daddy" Boles capitalized on the hype by having the gymnasium's folding chairs painted and numbered and placing a portion on sale at the University Book Store and Lexington Drug Co. as reserved seats.

By the time the regulator clock on the brick wall read 8 o'clock p.m. on

80

Saturday, Jan. 29, the university gym gallery was full and noisy amid the unmistakable atmosphere of a big game. All of the enthusiasm was showered on the Wildcats, with the exception of a "lone rooter" at the end of the visitors' bench.

Adkins got the tip and Kentucky took a 2-0 lead in the opening minute on King's "peach of a basket before anybody had a chance to stop him." But Auburn, with "the advantage of weight and height all the way around" … "launched an aerial attack" that produced a 6-2 advantage.

Kentucky's usual quickness was held in check and Hayden "did little more than give signals during the first half. …" Auburn's dead-eye forwards, team captain H.B. Barks and "Hahn," dominated. "Each time the 'Cats would ring in a goal," wrote the *Herald* reporter, "one of the Auburn forwards would call a halt, and while everybody held their mouths open, would stand in the middle of the court and sail in as pretty (a) field goal as ever was made." The Wildcats could get no closer than four points and the visitors took a 14-10 lead into intermission.

Things got no better in the opening minutes of the second half, as hot-shooting Barks and Hahn—along with the sticky defense of Auburn guard Jimmy Wade—held Kentucky at bay.

But at about the 17-minute mark of the second half, trailing 20-16, Hayden called a play for King, who "tossed in a neat field goal," pulling the Wildcats to within 2. "It seemed as if the packed galleries had been waiting all night for that moment," read the *Herald*, "and when the sphere rolled through the iron ring a roar went up that made the old gymnasium shiver."

Ten seconds later, Hayden had a stolen ball, which he laid in to tie the score. By the time the onslaught was over, Kentucky had gone on a 14-0 run en route to a 36-20 advantage. "After that every yell was a victory song for the Wildcats, and the Auburn team was soon so far behind it became discouraged and went to pieces."

The final score was 40-25, with King leading all scorers with 16 and Hayden adding 12. The game provided a team-concept object lesson in the eyes of the *Herald* reporter. "The thorough coaching and the fighting spirit of the Wildcats … defeated the brawn and high individual ability of the Auburn five." It was, he added, "one of the most thrilling games the Wildcat cage has ever seen."

It seemed that nothing could stop Kentucky, now 5-0 and a "real dark horse" to win the championship of the South—nothing except perennial rival Centre College. The also undefeated Colonels were favored to win because they would be playing at home and Bill King was rumored to be unable to play. Sportswriters also employed their usual who's-played-who reasoning, pointing out that Centre beat Auburn by 18 points, while UK beat the "Plainsmen" by 15.

Despite having the services of King after all, the game started bad for

Kentucky and got worse. "Diminutive running guard" Bobby Lavin had to leave in the first few minutes with torn shoulder ligaments and the Wildcats fell behind, ending the half at the short end of a 17-7 score.

The Cats settled down after halftime, with reserve guard Jimmie Wilhelm replacing Lavin, and staged an exciting comeback. Buchheit's team "got down to work with a near perfect system of passing that was dazzling in its speed and accuracy," outscoring Centre 20-12 in the second half.

UK ended up two points short, however, losing 29-27.

"This game leaves the superiority of the two teams about as much in doubt as ever," admitted a Danville reporter, "as the Kentucky five was completely outplaying the Colonels during the last half and would probably have won with another minute or two to play."

After demolishing Georgetown by a record margin of 56-11 on Feb. 15—including a 26-0 first half lead—the Wildcats turned their attention to the return match with Centre. Predictions were everywhere, which sportswriters based on the usual "dope."

"The Colonels have already stacked up dope against the Wildcat hopefuls," said the *Herald*. "Centre walloped the Georgetown five by a score of 62 to 23, when the best the Kentucky squad could do (in the teams' first meeting) was to beat the Tigers 38 to 23. That gives Centre a dope advantage of 24 points. ... There is a difference in the climate of the U.K. gymnasium and the Centre court, however, and Coach Buchheit and his wards are confident that when the Gold and White squad goes out of the local cage next Friday night, it will be carrying the vivid memory of a stinging defeat."

The blue and white faithful were heartened by the announcement that Bobby Lavin, though still nursing his injured shoulder, was practicing and might be able to play against Centre.

The campuses of both schools were abuzz with talk of the contest, which would decide the state collegiate championship. The *Herald* unabashedly proclaimed it the greatest game ever played on Kentucky's court. "Ordinarily a basketball game gets only a negligible amount of public attention," the reporter wrote, "but the interest in the game of tonight is well attested by the fact that practically all the reserve seats which have been placed on sale have already been gobbled up and fans are clamoring for more."

In testament to the game's importance, two referees would make the calls, instead of the usual one.

The Friday night crowd was in a fever pitch that Feb. 18 as game time approached and "crammed and jammed into every available inch of space, plastered onto the walls, roosting on the rafters, hanging down from the ceiling like flies in winter time, and peeking through the skylights." It was the "largest crowd that ever witnessed a game on the University court," wrote *Kernel* reporter Gerald Griffin. "And as many were turned away as were admitted."

When it was learned that Lavin was unable to play after all, he was replaced by reserve running guard Gilbert Smith of Lexington.

The opening tip produced a "fearful roar" and the crowd continued a "horrible noise" even after a running Centre hit two shots to take a 4-0 lead. But Kentucky overcame the deficit, went ahead, and the contest became a study in suspense. "The game was so full of sensational plays, wonderful feats of goal shooting, and tense seconds when the lead depended on a hairbreadth's turn in the ball that every one of the record audience was kept on its figurative tiptoes during every minute," read the *Kernel* account. "Dignified and undemonstrative elder members of the crowd waxed as enthusiastic as the most vivacious youngsters."

Tempers ran high, with players committing hard fouls, which were met with cries of "football" and "throw 'em out" from the crowd.

The half ended with Kentucky leading 11-7.

Centre surged again when play resumed, however, quickly hitting two shots to tie the score at 11. King was fouled and "the audience was breathless ... as he picked up the ball to try for a foul goal." He made the shot, putting Kentucky ahead for good.

Held to their lowest output of the season by the suffocating defense, Hayden and King nevertheless carried the offensive load, shooting "three or four goals that were nothing short of remarkable." Hayden led all scorers with 8, as the Cats went on to win 20-13.

But Centre was unimpressed. Coach Charles E. McDowell said only a third game on a neutral court could truly decide which was the better team. Kentucky partisans pointed out that the Wildcats had outplayed Centre three out of four halves and in the two games, outscored the Colonels by five points.

The 1921 Southern Intercollegiate Athletic Association tournament, held in Atlanta's "auditorium," was organized by the Atlanta Athletic Club with the assistance of Georgia Tech coach W.A. Alexander and Georgia coach Herman J. Stegeman. It was the first event that brought elite basketball teams to the city. The Atlanta Chamber of Commerce commissioned a "big silver loving cup" to be presented to the winner. The Wildcats quickly became a favorite among the city's sportswriters, and a Feb. 27 issue of the Atlanta Sunday Constitution *featured a multi-column image of the team, along with an individual shot of Hayden in action. The semi-finals attracted 4,000 fans, "with 2,000 more left outside the gates," which was hailed as "the largest turnout of fans ever seen in the South."*

And Hayden held its star forward Bo McMillin scoreless for the first time in his career.

After dispatching Vanderbilt 37-18 on Feb. 22, a game that saw Lavin return to the starting lineup, Buchheit's squad prepared to leave for Atlanta and the Southern Intercollegiate Athletic Association tournament. Still regarded as a dark horse, the Kentucky players had won the respect of their fellow students and the local sportswriters. A *Herald* reporter described the Wildcat attack: "Bill (King) gets the ball anywhere on the floor, dribbles through a five man attack, feeds it to Hayden, and Hayden shoots 'em from all angles and all positions."

The team arrived in Atlanta on Feb. 23 and practiced on the spacious new floor in the "auditorium," where the tournament would take place. Kentucky was "tipped by experts here as the one to furnish the University of Georgia (with its) strongest contention. ... The team seems to be a fast, rangy outfit, capable of playing the big floor to advantage, where a heavy team might find the long distances and passes difficult."

"Captain Hayden, King and (Adkins) grade up with the best forwards ever seen in action on an Atlanta floor. Rangy, fast, clever side steppers, any one of this trio is extremely dangerous on a quick shot. Though Tulane was far from a poor team, and in fact is a first rate aggregation, they appeared slow in company with the Kentuckians.."

—Atlanta Georgian sports editor Ed Danforth

The tournament was organized by the Atlanta Athletic Club with the assistance of Georgia Tech coach W.A. Alexander and Georgia coach Herman J. Stegeman. The Atlanta Chamber of Commerce commissioned a "big silver loving cup" to be presented to the winner.

With Lavin back, the Wildcats reverted to their usual starting lineup of Adkins at center, Hayden and King at forward, Lavin at running guard and Ridgeway at stationary guard. Buchheit had refined his "system" to an offense that involved quickly switching his guards and forwards as they ran toward their basket, often freeing Adkins for lay-ins. An Atlanta sportswriter called it "one of the most peculiar attacks yet uncovered on a basketball court. ... It is a baffling thing."

Facing the Tulane "Greenbacks" in the opening game, Kentucky got off to its usual slow start, this time trying to accustom "their legs to the enormous floor...." But the Cats staged a run and ended the half with a 30-16 lead. "Captain Hayden, King and (Adkins) grade up with the best forwards ever seen in action on an Atlanta floor," wrote *Atlanta Georgian* sports editor Ed Danforth. "Rangy, fast, clever side steppers, any one of this trio is extremely dangerous on a quick shot. Though Tulane was far from a poor team, and in fact is a first rate aggregation, they appeared slow in company with the Kentuckians."

Buchheit repeatedly ran his forward-guard switching play, freeing Adkins for his familiar "freak shots, back-handed and otherwise." Lavin and Ridgeway shut down their opponents on defense. It was a good tournament opener, with Kentucky winning 50-28. Adkins led all scorers with 18, while Hayden accounted for 17 and King 13.

The Wildcats continued their team approach with an impressive 49-25 win over Mercer. "The team from the Blue Grass region simply outclassed their opponents," a reporter wrote. "They were faster, their shooting was superior, and they displayed a defense which was more than baffling to the Macon contingent."

Despite their respective semi-final opponents, everyone anticipated the expected clash between Georgia and Kentucky. Buchheit's innovative running style, along with the Bulldogs' undefeated record, captured the imagination of southern sportswriters, who flocked to cover the event. UK enjoyed unprecedented recognition, with its triumphs splashed in banner headlines and large photos in the Atlanta newspapers. The Feb. 27 issue of the Sunday *Constitution* featured a multi-column image of the team, along with an individual shot of Hayden in action.

Excitement continued to build, attracting more than 4,000 fans—"with 2,000 more left outside the gates"—to the semifinal double-header of Georgia-Georgia Tech and Kentucky-Mississippi A&M, "the largest turnout of fans ever seen in the South" for such an event.

UK cruised to a 12-6 halftime lead over the "farmer five," before emerging "dead on its feet" for the second stanza of its third game in four days. After absorbing a fierce run from the Aggies, however, Kentucky pulled away, winning 28-13. Next up was undefeated Georgia, which narrowly escaped rival Georgia Tech.

The SIAA Tournament championship game, on Tuesday night, March 1, 1921, was, according to the *Herald*, the "most dramatic ever recorded in Southern basketball history." In Lexington, hundreds of "students, alumni and rooters ... jammed every corner of the lobby and mezzanine floor of the Phoenix hotel" awaiting telegrams from Atlanta.

Kentucky ran off two quick baskets as "another great crowd ... rocked the auditorium with cheers for both teams." Not to be outdone, the Bulldogs rattled off a field goal and three free throws to go ahead 5-4.

King hit a shot to make the score 6-5 and, after a defensive struggle, Kentucky headed into halftime with an 8-7 lead. The score, relayed by megaphone to the crowd at the Phoenix Hotel, was "greeted with a roaring welcome."

The teams took up the same struggle in the second half, which featured "magnificent guarding," with Lavin "breaking up Georgia's pass game time after time"—often grabbing opponents' passes in mid-air—and

Ridgeway shutting down the Bulldogs' star forward Billy Anderson, "the best individual goal shooter in the tournament."

"Ridgeway shoots foul; so does Georgia," yelled the megaphone announcer at the Phoenix. "Georgia makes another on foul; score, Kentucky 11, Georgia 10," he added, creating an "uproar (that) drowned out his shouting."

King, Hayden and Adkins worked together "on goal shooting and perfect passing," keeping the Wildcats ahead.

With less than a minute remaining, Hayden tied the score at 19. After a defensive stop, UK regained possession with 20 seconds to play. Adkins received a pass and was fouled under the Kentucky basket.

King went to the free-throw line as Kentucky's designated foul-shooter, according to the rules of the time. He toed the line and was raising the ball toward the basket when a pistol shot sounded—signifying that the continuous-running time had run out. By rule, King was allowed to continue with no time on the clock. His shot swished, making his Wildcats champions of the South, the first Kentucky basketball team to win any championship beyond the state's borders.

"Students cut classes with the most unanimous prodigality Wednesday ever known at the University of Kentucky. The faithful few—and they were more few than faithful."

—Lexington Herald, March 3, 1921

"Hayden ties score; King scores in one point," screamed the announcer to the Phoenix crowd. "Final score, Kentucky 20, Georgia 19. Bring home cup tomorrow."

"Nobody heard the last telegram," wrote the *Herald* reporter, as everyone was screaming "at the top of their voices."

Dawn broke on campus the next morning as usual. But nothing else was the same.

Almost nobody attended classes. Instructors calling roll in nearly empty classrooms were interrupted by "stentorian serenades of the holiday takers, and the latter element was so much in evidence that the professors were forced to chase their classes from the campus in order to free themselves from the torments of the victory-drunk students."

"It was too much," wrote a *Herald* reporter. "Dances were becoming so common that they overlapped and the authorities at the university had to call out the military and lock up the armory and gymnasium to keep down a part of the glad celebration." Transylvania students "pulled down their whistle" and joined the melee. They "gave such evidences of gratification at our triumph as to make Kentucky adherents thrill with pride at (their) sportsmanship."

"The old battling spirit of a decade ago has returned to its own," wrote an impassioned *Kernel* writer of his Transy counterparts, "our former enemies, by now our friends. ... Above the temporary defeats of recent years

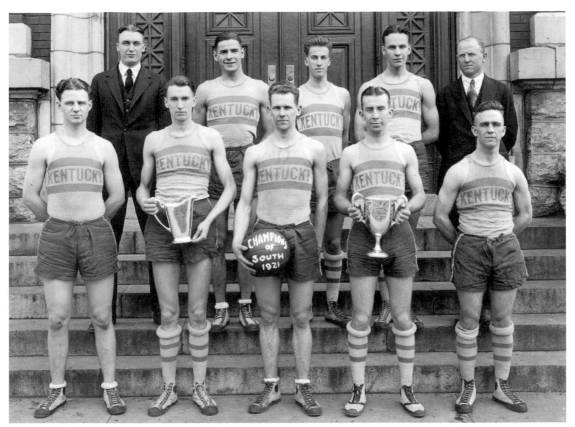

The 1921 Champions of the South. In addition to Hayden (with the ball), the team's starting five included center Paul Adkins (to Hayden's right), stationary guard Sam Ridgeway (to Hayden's left), running guard Bobby Lavin (to Ridgeway's left), and forward Bill King (second row, between Adkins and Hayden). Coach George Buchheit is pictured at top left, with athletic director Stanley A. "Daddy" Boles at top right. For their accomplishment, each team member received a gold basketball watch charm "surmounted with a pearl inlaid K."

shines out the matchless spirit of 'do or die.' Let us arise and march on! Wheep no more my lady—."

The students quit campus and marched downtown to await their heroes at the Southern Depot. They joined fans already filling the train station's waiting rooms to capacity, and the overflow crowd stood all around the outside of the building, jostling in a spring downpour.

The team's 6:30 train arrived on time, prodding the dampened revelers into action once again. Cheers greeted Buchheit and the nine players on the traveling squad as they emerged. The heroes were "hoisted on high and placed in cars of steel, tired with rubber," which had been provided by the "Boosters Club." As the cars made their way downtown, people lined the streets and, according to the *Herald*, "yelled out praises to them through megaphones and hoarse throats."

The Wildcats were sighted as they entered the already packed lobby, and the band struck up "My Old Kentucky Home," as everyone "stood with uncovered heads, solemnly proud of the State's most recent great achievement." Buchheit and his club—dubbed the "Wonder Team"—were escorted to their seats in a banquet hall upstairs and the party really began.

The coach, "the man behind the gun," rose to express his thanks, followed by each member of his team, "their words," wrote a reporter, "though stammered in places and slow to come, were the greatest of eloquence to those who had come to do them honor."

A university delegation including Athletic Council president J.J. Tigert, Dean Paul P. Boyd, Dr. Lyman Chalkley and Professor Enoch Grehan was next to offer congratulations. Tigert presented the team with a silver pitcher from the Lexington Board of Commerce.

Athletic Director Boles directed his comments to Centre College—and its much-discussed challenge. "We have won the championship of the South," he said, "and we believe that includes Kentucky as well."

A man in the crowd named L.L. Harris—a University of Georgia gradu-

Hayden posed with stationary guard Sam Ridgeway, at left, and running guard Bobby Lavin, at right. The *Atlanta Journal* called Lavin "the greatest player that has ever played in a college game," while the *Georgian* called Hayden the "Blond Appollo, who dashes across the floor like a streak of lightning."

Courtesy Stephen M. Vest

Hayden was recruited by UK to take over as basketball coach when Ray Eklund failed to recruit any players for the 1927 season and quit a week before the first game was to be played. The team went 3-13, the worst record in school history. He later moved to Georgia, but often returned to Lexington to appear as UK's first and oldest basketball All-American. He died on Jan. 9, 2003, at age 103.

ate—made it known that he had something positive to say and was invited to speak. I "would rather have Georgia lose to Kentucky than to any other team under the sun," he said, "in accents too passionate to have been insincere…." A cheer for Harris went up, and, according to the *Herald*, he left the podium saying, "I would rather have an ovation like that from a group of college students than be president of these United States."

In the weeks that followed, the South's newspapers made their usual judgments of the 1921 season and its players.

The *Herald*'s "All-Kentucky" team was simply UK's starting five. In an interesting commentary, *Herald* sportswriter J.A. Estes noted that Centre's George Maver was the best individual player in the state. The Long Island, N.Y., native wasn't All-Kentucky, however, because "his work is not team work, and he would not fit into a squad that wished to develop team work to its highest extent."

The *Atlanta American* newspaper chose Hayden, King and Adkins to the All-SIAA team, in addition to players from Georgia and Georgia Tech. The *Atlanta Journal* wrote glowing tributes to Lavin, "the greatest player that has ever played in a college game," while the *Georgian* hailed Hayden as the "Blond Appollo, who dashes across the floor like a streak of lightning."

The *Georgian*'s All-Southern team was Bill King (high scorer of the tournament with 55, in addition to his title-winning free throw) and Billy Anderson of Georgia at forwards, Adkins at center, and Lavin and "Baby" Roane of Georgia Tech at guards.

After the choosing of football and basketball All-America teams became popular in the 1930s, the Helms Athletic Foundation researched previous seasons and retroactively chose All-America basketball teams beginning with the 1920 season. Ten players were chosen for each year, without first or second team distinctions. The Helms All-America team for 1921 was: Arnold Oss, Minnesota; Forrest Di Bernardi, Westminster; Edward Durno, Oregon; R. D. Birkhoff, Chicago; George Williams, Missouri; Everett Dean, Indiana; Dan McNichol, Pennsylvania; Donald White, Purdue; Herbert Bunker, Missouri; and Basil Hayden, Kentucky.

On paper, Hayden seems a worthy, though unlikely All-America choice. He trailed King in scoring in the SIAA tournament 55 to 33 and for the season, with a 9.6 average, to King's 11.4.

But he was the captain of the Southern championship team, the undisputed leader of a good team. He was nearly 22 years old, already a college graduate and an Army veteran, and he brought this maturity to bear by sacrificing his statistics to make the Wildcats better. Hayden often drew the opponents' defensive specialist and was defended almost exclusively by quicker guards in the tournament. The 1921 Wildcats routinely turned back challenges of good opposing players with team play and balanced scoring. They racked up 147 points in the tournament, 23 more than previously undefeated Georgia, which came in second.

King was an outstanding scorer at forward. Adkins had good size for a center, along with an unorthodox shot that made him a constant threat when Kentucky needed points. Lavin was the defensive specialist while playing today's point-guard position. Hayden was the play-caller, an excellent passer and a forward who liked to drive, often getting the clutch basket. The team was lighter and quicker than most of its opponents and Buchheit maximized these advantages.

Basil Hayden was UK's first All-American because he made the Cats better than they would have otherwise been in an era that valued teamwork over individual performance.

* * *

Seven players lettered for the 1921 Wildcats: Hayden, King, Adkins, Lavin, Ridgeway, Smith and Wilhelm. Each received a gold basketball watch charm inlaid with a pearl "K."

* * *

King lived his life in Lexington. In later years, he lost both his legs to "a circulatory ailment."

* * *

By virtue of its showing in the SIAA tournament, Kentucky was one of 15 institutions invited to join the Southern Intercollegiate Conference, which was formed while the teams were in Atlanta. In addition to UK, the charter members were Maryland, Virginia, Washington and Lee, VMI, North Carolina, North Carolina State, Clemson, Georgia, Georgia Tech, Alabama, Alabama Polytechnic (Auburn), Tulane, Mississippi A&M (Mississippi State) and Tennessee. The conference, which officially began on Jan. 1, 1922, included "stringent rules" allowing only certified students to participate in games, in addition to the possibility of an inter-conference schedule with the Western Conference, predecessor of the Big Ten.

* * *

UK organized a "systematic code of extension work," enlisting members of campus clubs to poll their hometowns over the 1920 holiday break. The university announced in January that its traditional name, "State College," had almost completely disappeared as a description, in favor of "Kentucky."

* * *

George Buchheit coached three more basketball seasons at UK, compiling a 44-27 record. He also coached other teams, including the 1923 freshmen football "Kittens." He resigned in 1924 to accept the head basketball coaching job at Trinity College in Durham, N.C., the school that became Duke University, where he remained until 1931. After earning a master's degree from Columbia University, Buchheit moved on to Pennsylvania State Teachers College at Bloomsburg, where he ended his coaching career in 1946. He then moved with his family to Springfield, Ill., where he became an engineer for the state highway department. Accompanied by former athletic director Stanley A. "Daddy" Boles, who had hired him in 1919, Buchheit visited the UK campus in 1953, reminiscing about his early coaching career and marveling at how the place had changed in three decades.

* * *

Hayden's alma mater appealed to him to take over as coach when Ray Eklund quit a week before the 1927 team was to play its first game. Left with a team of novices after Eklund failed to recruit, Hayden compiled a disastrous 3-13 record, worst in UK history. He returned to Paris and became a bank cashier. In later years, Hayden somewhat ironically moved to Georgia, but returned to Lexington periodically to appear at UK events as Kentucky basketball's first and oldest All-American. He died on Jan. 9,

2003, at the age of 103.

* * *

The University of Georgia still plays its games in Herman J. Stegeman arena, named in honor of the Bulldogs 1920-31 coach and organizer of the Southern Intercollegiate Athletic Association's tournament, the first such event that brought elite basketball teams to Atlanta.

* * *

Bo McMillin, who Hayden had held scoreless in the Wildcats' celebrated 20-13 victory on Feb. 18, became a Kentucky legend in his own right. He was born Alvin Nugent McMillin in Texas in 1895 and grew up in Fort Worth as something of a gambling, football-playing ne'er do well. His high school coach, Robert L. "Chief" Meyers, was a Centre College graduate who desperately wanted to bring McMillin to Danville.

Working with a friend living in Somerset, Meyers brought McMillin—along with his teammates James "Red" Weaver and Thad McDonald—to Kentucky and placed them in Somerset High School. Local businessmen paid the boys' expenses.

Moving to Centre in 1917, McMillin almost single-handedly built the football program to national prominence. The resulting publicity placed McMillin and Weaver—along with teammate James M. Roberts—on Walter Camp's All-American team in 1919. Harvard invited the Praying Colonels, as the team was known, to Cambridge in 1920. Though the Crimsons won 31-14, they impressed northeastern sportswriters enough to gain a rematch the following season.

Centre returned to Harvard—which hadn't been defeated in almost five years—on Oct. 29, 1921. Nearly 50,000 fans packed the stands around the muddy field of Harvard Stadium. The Praying Colonels held the Crimsons scoreless in the first half, though they failed to score either.

After a Harvard penalty, quarterback McMillin dashed through the Crimson line in a zig-zag run that put the Colonels ahead 6-0. It proved to be the final score. Then as now, Centre's victory is universally considered college football's upset of the 20th century.

Despite reportedly betting on the game, McMillin became a folk hero in Kentucky and the football world. He later went into coaching, leading tiny Geneva (Penn.) College to another victory over Harvard in 1926. McMillin died in 1952.

11

Voices of the Wildcats

It's hard for many fans to believe, but Cawood Ledford was not the first voice of the Kentucky Wildcats. But Cawood's is the name on the Rupp Arena banner and that's as it should be.

In the years just before and after his 1992 retirement, it was amusing to hear Cawood tell about his life and career, about how lucky he was or that everything he did was just no big deal. Unless he was a very good actor, the man was completely unaware of the magnitude of his talent.

Cawood was, after all, possessor of *The Voice*, a rich, mellow, melodious sound that evoked tradition, achievement, impeccable manners and good humor, all curled around a hint of Harlan County. How could anyone not like that voice? In kind, grandfatherly tones, it introduced untold numbers of small boys—and not a few girls—to the glory of University of Kentucky sports, and took them into droopy eyed-slumber via transistor radio on the nights of late-ending games.

It seems improbable that Kentucky, the nation's greatest college basketball team, could simultaneously have boasted the greatest play-by-play man. But then again, the best team deserved it. And he was indisputably the best, calling the NCAA Finals year after year for national networks whether

UK Sports Information

Cawood Ledford began the UK portion of his career on Dec. 5, 1953, as one of four announcers broadcasting Wildcat games. By the time he retired on March 28, 1992, he was the only "Voice of the Wildcats" many fans had ever known.

the Wildcats were playing or not. He also was routinely the winner of national awards in his 40-year career.

Many writers—and sports announcers—have reminisced about growing up listening to radio sports announcers and seeing the games in their imaginations as they were described.

The Yankees had Red Barber, the Cardinals and later the Cubs had Harry Carey, the Celtics Johnny Most and the Wildcats had Cawood. And we wouldn't have traded him for an NCAA Championship.

Back when a fan's only access to an athletic contest was by listening, the radio announcer was king. Part eyewitness, part actor, the play-by-play man was a guest in the home, bringing the game with him and telling us what it meant. Good announcers connect with their audiences, creating such a bond that fans look on them as friends, people they know personally. In that sense, an announcer isn't a celebrity at all, just a guy with a whole lot of friends. Cawood had millions of friends, and he reciprocated that friendship.

Cawood made everyone understand that Kentucky games were important; that the people involved in them cared about what they were doing and were striving for excellence. He followed the ups and downs of the program in respectful and caring tones, excited about a win and sorry about a loss. He had an almost supernatural way of painting word pictures with nearly imperceptible inflections in his voice. For example, when Cawood said, "G.J. Smith from thurty," the emphasis he chose for the word "thirty" told the listener not only from what distance the player shot the ball, but that it was, in the announcer's opinion, an unwise shot. And when a Wildcat walked, Cawood would hurl the word "walks" into the air like a dagger—just punishment for an unpardonable sin.

Cawood was, after all, possessor of The Voice, a rich, mellow, melodious sound that evoked tradition, achievement, impeccable manners and good humor, all curled around a hint of Harlan County.

He could even communicate things without saying them, merely changing his voice to convey the added excitement of an NCAA Tournament game or the hopelessness of an off-night. Small fans drank these descriptions in and, years later, many would swear they witnessed games they could have only heard on the radio.

As all good announcers do, Cawood had signature phrases he used to quickly describe the action. This was born of necessity, since basketball is a fast sport and he had only a few seconds to describe what he was seeing.

An offensive trip might sound something like: "Woods in a hurry, angles right, looks, over to Farmer; Farmer in to Feldhaus, checks, back out to Farmer, who swings it left to balance the floor. Farmer looks, over to Woods, who had a notion; in to Pelphrey, turns, shoots, no good, tapped up by Hanson, rolling in ... and he's fouled. It took a trip, but stayed. Hanson's really built a fire under there tonight, Ralph." Cawood reduced the complexity of the action into 68 words that left no doubt what had happened.

A player attempting a field goal might fire, launch or shoot the ball, let it fly or miss a "gimme." That miss might roll off, go in and out or fail to "draw iron." A Wildcat was on rare occasions even known to "miss everything." If the player scored, he might "drill" it, or the shot might be good or a beauty—or even a beau-ty! Or, maybe, he would say, "Grevey from 15 ... write it down" with smiling pride in his voice or, in later years, "Reggie Miller for three from downtown ... got 'em."

If UK benefited from a bad call, Cawood's description might be, "Kentucky got a break on that one." If the call was questionable and in the opponent's favor, he would say, "I don't know about that one." If the call was not very good, "They missed it." If the call was really bad, listeners would hear that "They blew that one." Anything worse, and he would give the impression the striped shirts had lost their sanity, "Oh my goodness, they say he traveled." Sometimes it was, "Hord hit the deck, no call."

UK Sports Information

Upon his retirement in 1992, then-Athletics Director C.M. Newton awarded Ledford a permanent "Voice of the Wildcats" banner in Rupp Arena's pantheon of retired jerseys. With Cawood was his wife, Frances.

Of course there were hundreds of other phrases. Dribbling could be walking it up or tom-tomming it, angling it, retreating with it, working it in—and sometimes "losing the handle." Rebounds were "clearing it out" or getting on the boards and sometimes "big-kickers." Defense could be tenacious, sticky or "really getting after them." Opponents could be "all over" a Wildcat. And a good offensive move could leave a defender "nailed to the floor."

The successful player in the center jump circle would get the "tap," as opposed to the tip. Room enough to shoot was daylight, leads could be whittled, and sometimes players just "went to sleep out there." And almost always, Kentucky moved "from right to left on your radio dial," and "the Cats are running." When the game was over, it was time to "head to the barn."

Cawood might give his opinions about officiating or whether this or that player was having an off-night, but he seldom took a stand that might alienate even a portion of his listeners. If such a stand had to be made, he would make it subtly.

After Kentucky's NCAA-record 129 consecutive home victories was ended by Georgia Tech on Jan. 8, 1955, coach Adolph Rupp lowered the boom, scheduling a Sunday practice and taking away some of his players' privileges. Three of them—Linville Puckett, Billy Bibb and Logan Gipe—promptly quit and transferred to Kentucky Wesleyan. Under Rupp,

Puckett said, basketball was not "regarded as a game, but as a matter of life or death, with the resemblance of one going to war." The phrase, "going to war" would enter Cawood's—and Rupp's—repertoire as a description of a player who laid it all on the line when a game was in doubt. It was an eternal repudiation of Puckett and the admission that basketball was indeed life and death in Kentucky.

Cawood called the Fiddlin' Five's unexpected triumph over Seattle to win Rupp's fourth NCAA Championship in Louisville's Freedom Hall on March 22, 1958. He followed the old coach's teams in their ups and downs, from the Rupp's Runts' loss to Texas Western in the 1966 NCAA Finals and the disastrous 13-13 meltdown the following year to Dan Issel and company's rise back to national prominence. He bantered with Rupp in post-game shows and howled with laughter at his colorful language and high-spirited humor.

And when Rupp, after being forced to retire in 1972, was criticized for making a 17-word speech at that year's basketball banquet, the fact was filed away in Cawood's memory.

Dribbling could be walking it up or tom-tomming it, angling it, retreating with it, working it in—and sometimes "losing the handle." Rebounds were "clearing it out" or getting on the boards and sometimes "big-kickers." Defense could be tenacious, sticky or "really getting after them." Opponents could be "all over" a Wildcat. And a good offensive move could leave a defender "nailed to the floor."

As the years passed, Cawood's voice only got better with age. Sometimes radio broadcasting rights would go to a new high bidder, but the new bidder always hired Cawood to call the games. There was the 1978 NCAA Championship, a 94-88 win over Duke, the retirement of Joe B. Hall, the Eddie Sutton era and beyond.

Cawood announced that his last year would be the 1991-92 season, and the farewell ceremonies began. He was presented with all sorts of keepsakes, from a red sweater from Bobby Knight to his own "Voice of the Wildcats" banner in Rupp Arena's pantheon of retired jerseys.

It was quite a season. The overachieving Wildcats went 29-7 to win the SEC East and the conference's tournament championship.

Cawood's last call was March 28, 1992, in Philadelphia, the NCAA East Region championship. UK lost to Christian Laettner and Duke in overtime 104-103 in what has been called the greatest college basketball game ever played. As the final minute or so ticked away, Cawood called on all his powers and his voice switched into some higher, richer plane. His "Woods, to Farmer, in to Pelphrey" took on epic proportions and his entire career seemed to flash before his fans' eyes.

And when it was over, he signed off, choosing, he explained, the words

University of Kentucky Special Collections

UK President Frank LeRond McVey, at left, addressed the WHAS radio audience during the 1929 beginning of a joint venture to bring the news to Kentucky's Appalachian counties. From musical selections and agricultural topics, programming expanded to include the broadcasting of Kentucky football games, beginning on Oct. 12, 1929, a 20-6 win over Washington & Lee. Announcers in the campus studio took their play-by-play from wire reports relayed from Stoll Field.

Adolph Rupp had used: "To those of you that went down the glory road with me, my eternal thanks, good night."

* * *

The Wildcats first found their voice in the 1920s. Radio arrived in Kentucky on July 18, 1922, when station WHAS went on the air in Louisville. WHAS was an experiment of the *Courier-Journal* and *Louisville Times* newspapers and their owner, Robert Worth Bingham. Bingham is said to have looked on the new medium as a public service, an opportunity to bring the arts to Kentuckians "who would never have any

University of Kentucky Special Collections

Contrary to popular myth, the WHAS-UK joint broadcasting effort likely originated with Elmer G. Sulzer, a music professor who started the university's publicity department on Jan. 1, 1929. Once the station earned its clear channel status and the right to broadcast in 50,000 watts, it promptly abandoned its civic high-mindedness and began eliminating UK programming from its schedule. Undeterred, Sulzer switched to Lexington's WLAP-AM and the Mutual and CBS networks, winning a Peabody Award in the process. Sulzer also founded UK's department of radio arts and began WBKY-AM (today's WUKY), the first university-owned and the first public radio station in the United States. He also arranged the music for the school's fight song and alma mater.

access to it otherwise."

One aspect of Bingham's philanthropy began in April 1929, with an innovative joint WHAS-UK effort to bring education to the Commonwealth. Bingham propaganda aside, the idea probably belonged to Elmer G. Sulzer, a UK music professor who had started the school's publicity department that January 1. On broadcasting equipment supplied by the station, university president Frank L. McVey began the first broadcast expressing hope that the new medium would provide the audience with programs that were "interesting, stimulating and helpful." Bingham agreed, saying, "it is for those whose need is greatest who fill my mind as I think what this work of ours may mean to them."

WHAS turned over its programming to UK for 15 minutes each weekday at noon. The time, managed by Sulzer, was filled with musical selections, agricultural topics and various professorial lectures. The broadcasting of football games began on Oct. 12, 1929, a 20-6 win over Washington & Lee. Several games were broadcast in 1930, with announcers doing play-by-play in the studio via wire reports relayed from Stoll Field.

By early the following year, Sulzer was the university's first "radio director" and the rooms housing the equipment were being referred to as its "remote control radio studios." Programming had changed to 45 minutes on Tuesdays and Thursdays and 15 minutes on Mondays, Wednesdays and Fridays, with a 30-minute program every Sunday at 6 p.m. For example, on Wednesday, Aug. 26, 1931, from 12:45 to 1 p.m., WHAS broadcast the "Agriculture period," which featured "Miss Statie Erickson, who speaks as head of the department of home economics on 'Timely Topics of Nutrition.'" This was followed by "Miss Mary L. Didlake, assistant entomologist and botanist, talking on 'Our Insect Friends.'"

Sulzer's next brainchild was a proposal to bring radios—and programming—to remote areas of eastern Kentucky. WHAS cooperated with UK to install radios in "listening centers" throughout the region, allowing the "Kentucky Highlander" access to "the modern slant on almost everything." Soon, there were nearly 40 such centers, from Owsley County's Cow Creek to Vest, in Knott County. Such well-publicized high-mindedness allowed WHAS to win clear-channel status from the Federal Radio Commission—precursor to today's FCC—and to increase its wattage from its original 5,000 to 50,000 by 1933. Upon receiving this plum, WHAS promptly switched to network programming, and, by 1940, had largely cut UK out of its broadcast day.

Sulzer was ready for WHAS's philanthropic amnesia. He began feeding UK's programs to Lexington's WLAP and the Mutual and CBS networks, winning a Peabody Award in the process.

WLAP brought three Wildcat football games to its listeners in 1934 and, by 1935, had expanded its coverage and added a regular play-by-play announcer, Ed Ashford.

Ashford also gave the first "live description" of a UK basketball game, a 46-29 victory over Xavier in that season's finale.

WLAP brought three Wildcat football games to its listeners in 1934 and, by 1935, had expanded its coverage and added a regular play-by-play announcer, Ed Ashford. Ashford also gave the first live description of a UK basketball game, a 46-29 victory over Xavier in that season's finale.

J.B. Faulconer arrived at WLAP in 1940 and put together the University of Kentucky network of stations—the "Ashland Oil-Aetna Sports Network"—which became the largest such enterprise in the South. Faulconer also took over UK's play-by-play duties and conducted coaches' shows and interviews. The station featured a "Football Score Board" show during the season on Saturday nights at 7. Because its coverage was not comprehensive, WLAP would often advertise in local newspapers whenever it was going to broadcast a game. An example, from 1948, read: "Tomorrow; WLAP; 1:45 P.M.; Kentucky vs. Florida; J.B. Faulconer at the mike for the State-Wide Kentucky Football Network."

By the early 1950s, there were three "voices" of UK sports, Faulconer, with WLAP's network, sponsored by Ashland Oil; Claude Sullivan, who broadcasted on WVLK's Standard Oil Network; and WHAS' Phil

Sutterfield. Cawood Ledford became the fourth when he was hired away from Harlan's WHLN in 1953 to call the games for WLEX.

Ledford's debut came on Dec. 5, 1953, as Adolph Rupp's Wildcats downed Temple 86-59 in the home opener. The team went 25-0 that year, and the football Cats posted a 7-2-1 mark in Bear Bryant's final season in Lexington.

As the years passed, Faulconer went on to work in the public relations department of Keeneland Racecourse and Claude Sullivan retired. Ledford moved to WHAS in 1956 and formed his own radio and television production company in 1979, becoming the one and only "Voice of the Wildcats" in the process. He died of cancer in 2001.

* * *

Tom Leach inherited Cawood Ledford's microphone and Voice of the Wildcats moniker in 1997 when he began calling football games and developed his distinctive "Touchdown Kentucky" phrase. Leach now does play by play for the basketball and football teams and is well on his way to becoming "the best" among his peers. A 1983 UK graduate, Leach has said he grew up wanting to be Cawood's successor. And consciously or not, he also says "tap" instead of tip.

* * *

A true renaissance man, Edgar G. Sulzer founded UK's department of radio arts in 1941 and began WBKY-AM, the first university-owned and the first public radio station in the United States. He added WBKY-FM in 1944, in addition to leading the marching band and arranging the music for the school's fight song and alma mater. Sulzer moved on to Indiana University in 1952, becoming director of radio and television communications and professor of radio and television. His lifelong hobby was the history of Kentucky steam railroads and he published numerous articles on the subject. WBKY-AM became WUKY in 1989.

* * *

J.B. Faulconer joined the U.S. Army in World War II, serving as an infantry commander and earning a battlefield commission to lieutenant colonel at age 26. He also won the Legion of Merit and a Bronze Star for valor. He returned to WLAP after the war, but remained in the Army Reserve, eventually rising to the rank of major general and commander of the 100th Division from 1970 to 1973. Faulconer later worked in the Keeneland Race Course public relations department.

No UK sports team has approached the success of the cheerleading squad. The Kentucky cheerleaders have won a record 14 Universal Cheerleading Association Championships and are the only team to ever win back-to-back championships, which it has done three times, not to mention the only one to win three, four, five, six, seven or eight in a row. The first national champion squad was the 1985 cheerleaders, above.

12

Cheerleaders: UK's Champion of Champions

In all the storied years of UK sports, no athletic team has approached the success of the cheerleading squad.

The Wildcat basketball team is the winningest in college history, having won more games than any other school in both numbers and percentage. It boasts more than 40 Southeastern Conference championships, seven NCAA championships and has made more appearances in the NCAA Tournament than any other school.

But that doesn't hold a candle to the success enjoyed by the cheerleading squad. These Cats have won a record 13 Universal Cheerleading Association Championships. The school has won the championship, sanctioned by the Universal Cheerleaders Association, or UCA, in 1985, 1987, 1988, 1992, 1995, 1996, 1997, 1998, 1999, 2000, 2001, 2002, 2004 and

As late as 1941, the cheerleading squad was a co-ed affair. By the end of the decade, however, the team was all-female.

2005. UK's is the only team that can boast of winning back-to-back championships (1987-88 and 1995-2002, 2004-2005) and the only one to win three, four, five, six, seven or eight championships in a row.

In addition to the talent and dedication of its members, the program has benefited mightily by the success and exposure it gains when the basketball Wildcats appear on national television. The squad's other television credits include *The CBS Evening News*, the *CBS Morning Show* and Connie Chung's *Eye to Eye*. It has been the subject of articles in *Southern Living, Gentlemen's Quarterly, ESPN the Magazine* and *Seventeen*.

As dedicated as any UK athletes, the cheerleaders represent the university, in addition to the commonwealth of Kentucky, as goodwill ambassadors wherever they perform. They have entertained during halftime of the NBA's Denver Nuggets—then coached by former UK All-American Dan Issel—and the Miami Heat—then coached by former UK player Pat Riley.

In the early days of the school—when it was known as Kentucky State University—a single, male, "cheer leader" was elected each year to lend enthusiasm whenever a team needed it, during a game or otherwise.

The Wildcat and Scratch mascots—introduced in 1976 and 1996 respectively—are also part of the squad. They are fan favorites and are often called upon to pose for photographs with blue-clad youngsters.

Cheerleading has virtually become a tradition in itself and "Two-Bits," the spelling out of K-E-N-T-U-C-K-Y and the moving pyramid as familiar as the banners in Rupp Arena.

The tradition, however, goes back much farther than many fans know.

In the early days of the school—when it was known as Kentucky State University—a single, male, "cheer leader" was elected each year to lend enthusiasm whenever a team needed it, during a game or otherwise.

On Oct. 7, 1909, for example, when the football team's train left Lexington's Queen and Crescent Depot en route to winning the nickname Wildcats in a game against Illinois, it was the cheer leader who climbed to the depot's roof screaming, "Illinois Rah!; Illinois Ree!; K.S.U.! Ken-tuck-y!"

Cheer leaders presided over many such seeing-offs and welcoming-homes near the Administration Building, where "the entire student body" would assemble to escort the varsity to a nearby train station. The teams would ride in "wagonettes" decorated with blue and white banners, streamers and pennants and pulled by students who had fought for and won the honor.

Hundreds would whoop and scream "all the yells and songs" of their school as they paraded down Limestone Street in class order and led by the Battalion Band,

UK's Wildcat character was introduced in 1976. Recent costume changes include wearing a blue and white bandana with matching pants, a big hit with younger fans.

with "stray Preps, etc." bringing up the rear. Cheers called "S-U-Kentucky" and "The Skyrocket" were among the favorites.

By the early 1920s, "cheer leaders" were elected for each class, with the senior member considered captain of the squad. Those who made the team received letters for their service.

Page one of the Oct. 12, 1923, *Kentucky Kernel* campus newspaper notified students that tryouts for the coming athletic seasons would be held in the "Gym building" before Ryan Ringo, a student member of the athletic council. Each class elected a cheer leader, with the junior class adding a second member so "we are more nearly assured a capable leader for each succeeding year."

The 1940s saw cheerleading go all-female. The eight-member squad sported white knee-high skirts and shirts with blue sweaters and the white "K's" that were awarded all "lettermen." By the 1950s, the squad

Kentucky's "Scratch" character often prowls around Commonwealth Stadium on game days.

had assumed somewhat modern form, with both male and female members, along with pom-pons and recognizable cheers. Cheerleaders wore white sweaters with blue "K's" in 1957, with the women wearing beyond-knee-length white skirts, white socks and saddle-style shoes.

The late 1970s and early 1980s saw the emphasis placed on co-ed squads and athletic performances, which dazzled fans with their daring and precision. The SEC began restricting "large pyramids" in 1979, and the squad became experts at creating smaller ones. They even developed a moving version that would rotate at center court during basketball games. The uniforms were transitioning to their present form as early as the 1980-81 school year, when the female cheerleaders wore an early version of the present "V-stripe" design, while the men wore shirts with "Kentucky" on their chests. There were 15 members that year: seven female, seven male and the Wildcat mascot.

The Kentucky cheerleaders were also competing nationally, placing second in the 1979-80 National Collegiate Cheerleading Championship and finishing in the top 10 every year in the history of the UCA championships.

The first win came in 1985, and the squad has never looked back.

Former cheerleader Jomo Thompson became the team's coach in the 2002-03 school year. The advisor is T. Lynn Williamson. UK squads usually consist of 36 members, 14 of whom represent UK in competition.

13

Kentucky's Wildcats

The Kentucky Wildcats were born on Oct. 11, 1909, two days after the football team's amazing 6-2 victory over powerhouse Illinois. U.S. Army Lt. Phillip W. Corbusier—the school's military commandant—stood up in a Monday morning celebratory chapel session to tell the student body their team had "fought like wild cats."

Corbusier's speech, covered in the local newspapers, created a sensation—and his "wild cat" soon became the subject of student doodles and a long essay on the exemplary qualities of *Lynx Rufus*.

Two years later, the new mascot appeared for the first time in the student annual, and, in January 1921, popular alumnus Richard S. "Dick" Webb arranged to have a real wildcat shipped from San Antonio, Texas. The animal was named "Jim Server," after James "Big Jim" Server, captain of the football team, who took care of it.

"This ferocious animal will be seen on the field at every contest in which the University takes part from now on," said the *Kernel* campus newspaper. "The Wildcat is about three-fourths grown and is ferocious and

Born on Oct. 11, 1909, when the school's military commandant said the football team "fought like wild cats," UK's mascot was confirmed when it became the subject of student doodles.

almost untamable, like the Wildcat teams of the University in their contests."

Webb kept the cat at his "Mammoth Garage" at 319-333 East Main St., which had a fire not long after its arrival. This only served to build the animal's reputation. "At the recent fire," the *Kernel* reported, "which destroyed about ten automobiles, the wildcat slept peacefully through the entire excitement and was uninjured."

The student-fans of the sports teams were overjoyed to have a live wildcat they could show off at games. "When this unusual mascot is seen upon the field, it will create more attention than the teams," one wrote. "When it is taken with the team to play other colleges, the Wildcats of the University of Kentucky will always be remembered by their 'Wild,' mascot."

In a tongue-in-cheek description of the ball game, the student reporter suggested that Whiskers' existence ebbed and flowed according to the team's fortunes. "Perhaps he gave up the ghost when Tech, starting like a whirlwind, ran up a nice lead before his human namesakes got started," the reporter wrote. "Maybe he had heart failure when Jimmie McFarland sent one of his sensation shots sizzling [through] the draperies—or it may be he was tickled to death when State won."

"Jim Server," which apparently had his name changed to "Tom," didn't last long, however, dying, it was said, "from captivity." He was replaced by another wildcat, named TNT.

TNT's companion, Whiskers, died just a few months later, on Feb. 23, 1924, during a UK-Georgia Tech basketball game.

The game, said the *Kernel*, proved too exciting for Whiskers, who was "found dead in its cage under the spectators benches as the crowd was leaving."

Said to be the tamer of the school's two live mascots, Whiskers "was apparently well and happy a few minutes before the game, according to two students who took him from his cage and played with him."

In a tongue-in-cheek description of the ball game, the student reporter suggested that Whiskers' existence ebbed and flowed according to the team's fortunes. "Perhaps he gave up the ghost when Tech, starting like a whirlwind, ran up a nice lead before his human namesakes got started," the reporter wrote. "Maybe he had heart failure when Jimmie McFarland sent one of his sensation shots sizzling [through] the draperies—or it may be he was tickled to death when State won."

By 1928, TNT was also gone and the school was in need of another wildcat. It was in that year that a 15-year-old boy caught one near Williamsburg, which ended up in the hands of a Morehead man who brought it to a football game. This was probably the incident that athletic director Stanley A. "Daddy" Boles remembered as occurring at a UK-

Tennessee football game. "I was standing on the sidelines when a man walked up to me and gave me a live Wildcat," he said. "Not knowing what to do with it I put it under a cheerleader's megaphone." Boles later gave it to the campus "pep" organization, Su-Ky, which he had helped found.

That wildcat may have been "Fuzzy," who lasted until 1930, when it was reported to have "hanged himself by the chain which held him prisoner" in late October of that year, a few days before the home-standing Wildcats were shut out 19-0 by Alabama.

Kentucky lost to Tennessee 8-0 to end its season at 5-3.

"Colonel," who prowled the sidelines of football games from 1947 to 1954, became the victim of a well-intentioned effort to place it in what today is called the Salato Wildlife Center near Frankfort. It died soon afterward of pneumonia.

Salato Wildlife Refuge

Blue, "official mascot" of UK athletics, lives on display at the Salato Wildlife Refuge in Franklin County, the same place where Colonel, a previous live mascot, died in 1954.

Other live cats have included Hot Tamale and later Baby, which appeared briefly in 1969 only to be retired when an elderly woman—perhaps the editorial writer from 1924—complained.

The days of live wild mascots appearing at sporting events long gone, UK adopted a 3-year-old male bobcat in 2000 through the Kentucky Department of Fish and Wildlife. This "official mascot" of UK athletics lives on display at the Salato Wildlife Refuge in Franklin County, the same place where Colonel died in 1954. The athletics department sponsored a name-the-wildcat Internet contest, and the final three choices were Tucky, Blue and Champ, with Blue receiving a plurality of 50,000 votes.

Blue was born in captivity and donated by the "Woods and Wetlands of Cadiz, Ky." His life expectancy is 15 to 25 years.

Adolph Rupp: Architect of the Big Blue

Memorial Coliseum, home to Kentucky men's basketball from 1950 to 1976, is universally known among UK fans as the "House that Rupp Built."

But Adolph Rupp was more than the builder of a field house, he was the architect of the pre-eminent program of college basketball, the man who created the phenomenon that is Kentucky basketball.

Rupp arrived in Lexington in 1930 as a respectable high school coach without college experience. Even so, he was somewhat unimpressed with his step up. UK had only matched the salary he had earned in Freeport, Ill., and its facilities were not as good. Kentucky, for its part, was by no means a team down on its luck. Under departing coach John Mauer—who had left for a job with Miami of Ohio—the Wildcats posted 12-6, 12-5 and 16-3 records en route to three consecutive trips to the Southern Conference Tournament in Atlanta.

Adolph Rupp in the early days of his coaching career. In many ways, his edge was the memory of a virtually impoverished childhood on his parents' Kansas farm. His youthful experiences made him ambitious, driven to succeed and always a bit insecure about the future.

So what special abilities did Rupp have and how did he transform Kentucky basketball?

The primary thing that made the 29-year-old coach tick was the searing memory of a hard-scrabble existence growing up on his parents' 120-acre Kansas farm. Rupp was born on Sept. 2, 1901, in Halstead, 20 miles north of Wichita, the fourth child of Mennonite immigrants. Rupp's father, Heinrich, had come from Austria, while his mother, Anna Lichti, was German.

"Dolph," as his family knew him, spent his childhood doing chores, attending the nearby elementary school and living the life of the average farm-boy of his time. He could be found on Jan. 1, for example, at the neighborhood's annual New Year's Day coyote hunt.

Kansas, known for cyclones, wind storms and droughts, was not the place to prosper in farming, and the young Rupp's school lunch was often a slice of fried potato between two slices of bread.

One of the most exciting events of his youth occurred in 1909, when

The 1923 national championship Kansas Jayhawks, with their coach Forrest C. "Phog" Allen. The journeyman Rupp, top row center, won one letter in four years on the squad. As a senior, the 6-foot-1 Rupp played "left guard" in a reserve role. Coach Allen is said to have used the stocky farm boy as an enforcer when Jayhawks' opponents got too physical.

Halstead High School won the state championship in the still-young game of basketball. Excited school board members quickly provided equipment to allow students in the country schools of Harvey County an opportunity to learn the game.

In many ways, this act was Adolph Rupp's ticket to fame, fortune and immortality.

By the time it was his turn at Halstead High, Rupp was a 6-foot-1 center on a losing team. In his senior year of 1918-19, however, the regular coach departed for World War I and Rupp became the squad's player-coach. He averaged 19 points per game, leading Halstead to the championship of the Little Arkansas Valley League.

The next year, he was what today would be called a walk-on at Kansas University. He got a job to pay his way through school and

The future hall of fame coach had the almost unbelievable opportunity of learning from basketball inventor James A. Naismith, who was a Kansas assistant coach.

earned a spot on the team. His coach was Dr. Forrest C. "Phog" Allen, who was assisted by none other than Dr. James A. Naismith, the inventor of basketball.

The 6-1 Rupp was a member of a group of KU reserves known as the meatpackers, who played the last few minutes of games no longer in doubt. Allen also used him as an enforcer when Jayhawks' opponents got too physical. The young player spent his years at Kansas observing Allen and Naismith and, in his senior season, became a member of the 1923 National Championship team.

Upon graduation, Rupp hoped to go into banking, but times were hard and the Kansas economy was dependent on farming. While doing graduate work back at KU, Rupp periodically traveled to the University of Wisconsin, where he had been welcomed to sit on the Badgers' bench by coach Walter O. Meanwell. As he watched, he drank in Meanwell's basketball philosophy, known as the "fast break." The experience made Rupp a professional coach.

He soon took a job coaching tiny Burr Oak High School in north central Kansas and, by the 1926-27 season, was at Freeport High School in Illinois. Rupp's team went 10-7 that first year and 11-5 the next. Then he really began to make noise, building his reputation on Freeport's rise to 18-6 in 1928-29 and 20-4 for 1929-30.

The speaker at the high school's annual basketball banquet in the early spring of 1930 was University of Illinois basketball coach Craig Ruby. Several of Ruby's former associates at Illinois, including M.E. Potter, football coach Harry Gamage and Gamage assistant Bernie A. Shively, were working in the UK athletic department, and Ruby told Rupp about the open coaching job there.

Armed with Ruby's recommendation, Rupp interviewed in Lexington that May and got the job, telling school officials about his up-tempo style and that if they didn't want excitement they didn't want him.

The three decades of experiences Rupp arrived at UK with made him ambitious, driven to succeed and always a bit insecure about the future. Forty-two years of championship-level coaching and 876 wins would never change that. He knew where he would return if he didn't win basketball games.

By the time November 1930 rolled around—and despite having to help with the football and track teams—UK's young coach was already hard at work changing Kentucky basketball. But he found himself at a huge disadvantage. Seven of his top 10 or so players were still on the football team and he couldn't count on them until after the season-ending Tennessee game on Nov. 27.

As explained at the time, the fast break was designed for "speed and energy." It was dependent on a "team's ability to move, think and act rapidly, in other words to take their opponents by storm and drive through to a goal." It contrasted with the slow-break or "Illinois" style, which involved—in these pre-shot clock days—"slowly and calculatingly" diagnosing and solving a defense.

Courtesy University of Wisconsin-Madison Archives

Rupp learned the fast break system from Walter O. Meanwell, coach of the Wisconsin Badgers. The experience, along with a poor economy, made the young man a professional coach.

But the fast break of 1930 could be only so fast. Jump balls took place after each basket, and players often preferred to stand as far away as mid-court to attempt two-hand set shots that could be surprisingly accurate. The lane was a thin rectangle topped by a circle, which coaches referred to as the "keyhole." From the smooth iron hoops hung nets made of canvas strips held together by brass fittings.

Rupp ran plays out of the jump balls, having one or more players break for the Kentucky basket, as the UK center tried to tip the ball to them to set up a lay-in or "crip" shot.

By the time the football players reported, the 15 others trying out for the team had been practicing for more than a month and Rupp was hopeful. He had instituted his fast-paced practices designed to develop the "inexhaustible energy and speed" required to run his system. His players seemed to respond.

A Dec. 10, scrimmage, however, destroyed any illusions he had about his team's progress. "The fast break system which has been rather dubiously accepted by basketball fans since its advent in Lexington this season is not proving so successful in action," wrote *Kentucky Kernel* sports editor Virginia Dougherty two days later. The new coach worried that he might have to delay complete implementation of his plans.

But Rupp had a good collection of athletes from which to choose a team. Senior captain Carey Spicer, quarterback of the football team, had been an All-American for Mauer as a sophomore. Center George Yates was 6-4 and sophomores Forest "Aggie" Sale and Louis "Little" McGinnis were impressive in practice. Ellis Johnson had been a high school All-American for the Ashland Tomcats that won state and national basketball championships in 1928.

The pleasantly surprised coach said his practices were becoming so competitive that he probably wouldn't decide on a starting lineup until a few minutes before 8 p.m. on Dec. 18, when the Wildcats opened his inaugural season against the Georgetown Tigers. When he finally made up his mind, Rupp's first starting five were Aggie Sale at center and Carey Spicer and Louis McGinnis at forwards, with Bill Trott at shooting guard and Ellis Johnson at "floor guard."

Georgetown traditionally gave Kentucky teams difficult games, but Rupp's new style changed everything, including the minds of the fans. "The Tigers played on even terms with the Wildcats for the first five minutes of the game, but from then on it was nothing more than a practice session for the superior Kentucky team," observed *Kernel* sportswriter Totsy Rose. "This new type of play is a great deal more interesting to watch than the system that was used last year by Coach (Mauer)."

Before it was over, Rupp emptied his bench, playing all 17 members of his squad, who rang up an annihilating 67-19 score. Sale led all scorers with 19—single-handedly matching the Tigers' total—while McGinnis added 16.

After beating Marshall 42-26 and Berea 41-25, the 3-0 Wildcats downed Clemson—their first Southern Conference opponent—33-21 before 2,000 fans in Alumni Gym.

Next up was Tennessee, and UK faced what the campus newspaper called a "real test." The game would not only decide which was the better ball club, it was a contest between Rupp's fast break and the slow break run by UT's Bobby Dodd. "The Volunteer team uses a system similar to that used by Kentucky last year and it will be a good opportunity for Lexington fans to see the faster Rupp system used against one they know so well," reported the *Kernel*. Rupp said his squad had put in a week of hard preparation, "with special emphasis on the shooting department."

But the football players on Rupp's team—which constituted seven of his 17 players and four members of his new starting five—had their own agenda. Dodd's Tennessee football team, which was facing a possible conference suspension for rules violations regarding early practices, had shut out UK 8-0 in the Thanksgiving Day football game, and Spicer—UK's starting quarterback and Southern Conference scoring leader—had revenge on his mind.

His new supporting cast—McGinnis, Yates, Bronston and Johnson—were only too happy to oblige, helping the Cats pummel the Vols, 31-23. Kentucky added the 55-18 destruction of Chattanooga to end its six-game home stand with a perfect 6-0 record. Then came the first away game, against Vanderbilt, a strong conference opponent.

The Southern Conference had 23 members in 1930. Eventually filling the majority of places in the modern SEC, ACC and Big East, they were Georgia, Alabama, Maryland, Kentucky, Auburn, Vanderbilt, Duke, Georgia Tech, Mississippi, North Carolina, Virginia, N.C. State, Washington and Lee, Sewanee (or University of the South), VPI (today's Virginia Tech), Clemson, LSU, Florida, Tennessee, Tulane, VMI, South Carolina and Mississippi A&M (today's Mississippi State).

Rupp would have to beat Georgia, Alabama and Maryland to have a chance to win the conference championship.

With Spicer pouring in 27 points, UK dispatched Vandy 42-37, before turning its attention to the return match against the hated Volunteers in Knoxville.

Now with five former football players starting—Spicer, McGinnis, Yates, Johnson and Bronston—the Wildcats pounded Tennessee and ended the first half with a 24-9 lead. But the Vols fought back behind their high-scoring center Leclair Greenblott, tying the game at the end of regulation. Kentucky pulled away in the overtime, however, winning 36-32. Bronston fouled out; and Johnson left the game "painfully injured" and was expected to miss at least the next contest.

Rupp's first team stood at 8-0 for only the second time in school history and the first since Edwin R. Sweetland's undefeated 1912 squad went 12-0 in winning the championship of the South. "The victory ... proves conclusively that Rupp has whipped a green team into shape," said the Kernel, "and when the conference tournament rolls around in three weeks, Kentucky will be a favored team to win the title."

Rupp's first team stood at 8-0 for only the second time in school history and the first since Edwin R. Sweetland's undefeated 1912 squad went 12-0 in winning the championship of the South. "The victory ... proves conclusively that Rupp has whipped a green team into shape," said the *Kernel*, "and when the conference tournament rolls around in three weeks, Kentucky will be a favored team to win the title."

Returning home, the Cats dispatched Washington and Lee 23-18 before

In addition to being the quarterback and captain of the football team Carey Spicer was Adolph Rupp's first All-American.

meeting the Georgia Tech "Golden Tornado" on Feb. 9. They would do so without Johnson, whose injury turned out to be a chipped anklebone that would sideline him for several weeks.

Tech, which also ran the fast break, was the defending regular season conference champion and had a 6-2 record heading into the game. It was a fast-paced, see-saw affair from the start, with both teams running but often missing easy shots. The score was knotted at 21 at the intermission. Kentucky ended the half only 9 of 44 from the floor, while the Yellowjackets were 6 of 21.

The Wildcats took the initiative in the second half and led 26-23, before Tech surged back to take the lead 27-26. With 10 minutes to go, the score was 32-30 in favor of the Georgians. Bronston made a long set shot to tie the score and Spicer hit two free throws to put UK up for good. When time expired, the Wildcats had a 38-32 victory and a 10-0 record.

But there was a three-game road trip at hand. The "Ruppmen," as sportswriters were beginning to call them, would play three games in four days. Trott was set to replace Johnson in the lineup and junior center Ercel Little was elevated to a spot on the traveling squad.

Kentucky went to Athens, Ga., by train and met the Bulldogs on the worst of all possible nights for the superstitious Rupp, Friday, Feb. 13. With their football coach standing in for the absent Herman J. Stegeman, Georgia's defenders turned physical, shutting down Spicer and holding the visitors to a season low total of 16. The Bulldogs' 25 points won the game and propelled them into sole possession of first place in the conference.

The following day, Kentucky was entertained by Clemson, whose members had just been cleared to play after being quarantined for meningitis. But it was the Wildcats that made Rupp sick, losing their second consecutive game, 29-26.

Next up was a revenge-minded team in Atlanta. "Georgia Tech still feels that they have the best ball club and intends proving it at the 'Cat's expense Monday night," wrote a *Kernel* reporter. But the Kentucky coach was at his best when cornered, driving his team to a defense-minded 35-16 victory that saw McGinnis and Yates both score 12.

On Feb. 20, with Spicer scoring 27 points, UK added an impressive 43-23 trouncing of Vanderbilt to run its regular season record to 12-2.

Five days later, more than 300 fans assembled at the train station to see Rupp and his Wildcats board the "Big Blue limited" for the Southern Conference Tournament in Atlanta. Intermingled with the sounds of "On,

On, U of K" and the "defying screeches of the engine," Rupp told the crowd a few "good breaks" would help the team bring home a championship. "Although it is practically impossible to predict the outcome of a tournament," he said, "we are going to Atlanta with a lot of confidence and determination. ..." Traveling overnight, they arrived in Atlanta at 8 a.m. on Thursday, Feb. 26, and settled into their rooms in the Georgian Terrace Hotel.

The team worked out in the Georgia Tech gym "for the purpose of limbering up their traveling kinks." Rupp said his players were in good condition and, according to *Kernel* reporter Edgar Turley, "they were displaying their old time zip and drive," which had been "sadly lacking on their last southern trip."

To satisfy fans' thirst for information about the game, the Kentucky Theatre hired local sportswriter James Kerr to wire the play by play from courtside in Atlanta to the throngs waiting inside the theater. Fans, who enjoyed free admission to the theater that night, could presumably be counted on to buy enough sodas and popcorn to make the arrangement worthwhile.

At 4 p.m. on Feb. 27, the telegraph wire began buzzing between Atlanta and Lexington. Rupp's starters for the tournament were Yates, Spicer, McGinnis, Worthington and Bronston.

The Cats got past N.C. State 33-28 and beat Duke 35-30 the next afternoon. On Monday, March 2, they would play the upstart "Florida University Alligators," which had surprised Georgia Tech and Tennessee to earn their spot in the semifinals.

Kentucky jumped out to a 10-4 lead after a lay-in by Spicer and a Worthington assist to a breaking Yates. Rupp's players were already playing the quick-passing, chance-taking style that would make him famous. Florida had the ball in the middle of the first half when Bronston "speared a pass and whipped one to McGinnis who shot in full stride. ...The ball sailed high in the air and came straight through the basket for another goal."

Kentucky jumped out to a 10-4 lead after a lay-in by Spicer and a Worthington assist to a breaking Yates. Rupp's players were already playing the quick-passing, chance-taking style that would make him famous. Florida had the ball in the middle of the first half when Bronston "speared a pass and whipped one to McGinnis who shot in full stride," Kerr reported. "The ball sailed high in the air and came straight through the basket for another goal." The Wildcats ended the half leading 25-18.

UK went on a 9-2 run when the contest resumed, taking a 41-20 lead on a three-point play by Carey Spicer. With an 18-point advantage as the second half dwindled, Rupp emptied his bench, sending Sale, Darby, Little, Kleiser and Trott in for Spicer, Yates, McGinnis, Bronston and

Worthington. "Spicer was given a tremendous hand as he walked off the floor," said the *Kernel*, and "McGinnis was given a cheer that shook the auditorium." After the second-team mop-up duty, the Wildcats entered the tournament finals with a 56-36 victory.

Rupp's final hurdle proved to be Maryland, which had beaten Georgia 26-25. "Kentucky and Maryland have powerful teams," wrote Totsy Rose. "The Wildcats ... have been capable of rising to great heights in coming from behind to win a large majority of their games. Maryland has displayed wonderful basketball against strong opposition. ..."

The attention of many Lexingtonians, however, was turned to a flu epidemic that had taken hold at UK's campus, disrupting so many classes and forcing the postponement of so many tests that university officials briefly considered closing the school.

> *"Kentucky lost to a great team by two points after putting up a basketball fight that would have brought tears of joy to the United States Devil-Dog Marines."*
>
> *—Frank Phipps, Kentucky Kernel, March 6, 1931*

By the time the championship game was held before 7,000 screaming fans on Tuesday night, March 3, it had become apparent that starting center George Yates had brought the flu with him to Atlanta. Suffering from a high fever, Yates remained in bed "when not actually on the playing floor."

Hampered by Yates' illness and a stifling Maryland defense, Kentucky started slowly, falling behind the "Old Liners" 5-0 at the game's start and further and further as the first half ticked by. Two late-half baskets by Yates and Bronston left UK down 18-7 at the intermission.

"Staging one of the greatest comebacks ever witnessed" in the tournament—and undoubtedly prodded by an excoriating Rupp halftime speech—the Cats clawed back in the second half to 25-19 with five minutes remaining.

Rupp's fast-break offense continued to erode the Maryland lead, until Louis McGinnis put the Cats ahead 27-25 on a long shot with less than a minute to play. Maryland's Bozzy Berger, however, took the inbounds pass at a run and hit a driving lay-in to tie the score. After Spicer missed a heavily contested shot, Berger took the rebound and stopped at mid-court with 15 seconds to go. He let go a two-hand set shot that swished though the basket to give Maryland the championship, 29-27.

Though the Wildcats lost the game, they made a considerable splash in Southern basketball. Four of Rupp's players—Spicer, McGinnis, Yates and Bronston—were named to the Associated Press All-Southern team and Spicer became an All-American for the second time.

Four hundred fans awaited the team when it arrived home at the Southern railway station the following evening. The crowd reconvened inside Alumni Gym to hear tributes by UK President Frank McVey and

Rupp's first team, 1930-31 (bottom row, from left): Ercel Little, George Yates, Carey Spicer, Forest "Aggie" Sale, and ____ ____; (middle row) George Skinner, Bill Trott, John "Frenchy" DeMoisey, Gordon George, Louis "Little" McGinnis, Cecil Bell and manager Maurice Levine; (back row) Rupp, Jake Bronston, Bill Kleiser, Ellis Johnson, Charles Worthington, and Darrell Darby.

other school officials and students. Rupp, reported the *Kernel*, "paid tribute to the fighting spirit of his team, which overcame an almost hopeless lead only to lose in the final 40 seconds of play by a shot that was almost marvelous." The new coach also praised the courage of center George Yates, who—in spite of losing 20 pounds during the tournament while suffering from the flu—"played a brilliant brand of basketball which won him a place on the all-Southern team."

Though it fell short, everyone marveled at the Wildcats' comeback. "Kentucky lost to a great team by two points after putting up a basketball fight that would have brought tears of joy to the United States Devil-Dog Marines," wrote Frank Phipps in the *Kernel*.

Sportswriters also gave high praise to Rupp. "The will to win, the most important thing in basketball, which he instills in the team pulled the 'Cats through many a tight place," wrote Lawrence Crump. "The skeptics who watched the entire Wildcat squad work out against Georgetown College in the season's opener returned in increasing numbers to pack the gymnasium during the remainder of the season."

Rupp's first year at Kentucky didn't result in a championship, but it was a perfect reflection of his style, his ambition and his emphasis on creating an exciting product to attract fans to his program. It was a strong beginning to a legendary career.

* * *

Armed with a somewhat cutting-edge style and a soaring drive to succeed, Adolph Rupp quickly guided his teams to near-domination of the new Southeastern Conference, which was founded in 1932 with Alabama, Auburn, Florida, Georgia, Georgia Tech, Kentucky, LSU, Mississippi, Mississippi State, Sewanee, Tennessee, Tulane and Vanderbilt. At least one player from Rupp's first five teams became an All-American. Aggie Sale was chosen for both 1932 and 1933, sharing the honor with Ellis Johnson in the latter season.

After going 15-2 in 1931-32, Kentucky went 21-3 the following year, winning the first SEC Tournament championship over Mississippi State by the score of 46-27. Having established the Wildcats in the South, the young coach looked to break onto the national stage, adding New York University and Michigan State to the schedule in 1934-35. More than 16,000 fans crowded into Madison Square Garden to watch the Kentucky-NYU game that year.

In 1935-36, Rupp began his long rivalry with powerful Notre Dame, which served as a microcosm of his rise in the basketball world. UK lost that first contest 41-20. By the time three years had elapsed, Rupp had trimmed the Irish advantage to only five. In game eight of the series— which took place on Jan. 23, 1943—the Wildcats won, 60-55. After that 1-7 start, Rupp ended his career with a 19-14 advantage over the South Bend, Ind., school.

UK won the National Invitational Tournament—more prestigious than the NCAA Tournament at the time—in 1946.

Then, as hundreds of returning World War II veterans arrived on campus, Rupp armed himself with the best talent in the nation and went on a tear no coach has ever matched. It was the beginning of the Fabulous Five. With two All-Americans, four all-SEC players and three former starters, Rupp delicately juggled his players' egos to win 159 games in five years, while losing only 15, picking up three NCAA championships and an Olympic championship along the way.

The Wildcats won 129 consecutive home games in 12 years from Jan. 4, 1943, to Jan. 8, 1955, which included 32 victories in a row beginning with an 86-59 win over Temple on Dec. 5, 1953.

Rupp added a fourth NCAA championship in 1958 and was poised to win a fifth in 1966 when Texas Western upset the ailing Wildcats 72-65 on March 19 of that year. The game, often called the "Brown vs. Board of Education of college basketball," became a symbol of the civil rights era because the Miners were an all-black team and Kentucky was all white.

In spite of the fact that Rupp helped integrate Southeastern Conference basketball, sportswriters have spent years portraying Rupp as a symbol of racism. In truth, Rupp was one of the most forward-thinking coaches of his time in the SEC. As coach of the conference runner-up, he accepted NCAA Tournament bids in 1959, 1961 and 1962 when SEC champion Mississippi refused to play against African Americans.

Rupp routinely coached African American players in all-star games and conducted an annual basketball clinic at Kentucky State University, the state's historically black university. His protégé, C.M. Newton, integrated basketball at Alabama.

When recruiting blacks, the coach accurately explained what a pioneering player would face on road games in a segregationist South. As Tom Payne, Kentucky's first African American player, explained after a 1971 game against Tennessee, "The players, the coaches on the bench, everybody, was trying to provoke us into a fight."

Forced to honor the university's rule requiring retirement at age 70, Rupp ended his 42-year career at Kentucky with an 876-190 record. Other coaches have broken some of his records—especially as the number of games per season has increased—but his 82.2 winning percentage over four decades has never been approached.

In spite of the fact that Rupp helped integrate Southeastern Conference basketball, sportswriters have spent years portraying Rupp as a symbol of racism. In truth, Rupp was one of the most forward-thinking coaches of his time in the SEC. As coach of the conference runner-up, he accepted NCAA Tournament bids in 1959, 1961 and 1962 when SEC champion Mississippi refused to play against African Americans.

* * *

After enduring a youth in a cloud of racism that prevented him from playing basketball in high school and in the NBA, Don Barksdale became the only African American player on the 1948 U.S. Olympic Basketball Team.

Barksdale was selected on the strength of his career at UCLA and on AAU teams in the early 1940s. The Olympic team also included the Phillips Oilers AAU team, along with Rupp's Fabulous Five, reigning champions of the NCAA Tournament.

According to a 1984 article in the *Philadelphia Inquirer*, as the team traveled the country playing exhibition games, segregationists forced Barksdale to stay with local black families instead of with his teammates in top-notch hotels. One of the people offended by the situation was the Olympians' assistant coach, Adolph Rupp. "Son, I wish things weren't like that," Rupp said. "But there's nothing you or I can do about it."

Rupp's son, Adolph Rupp Jr., better known as "Herky," recalled that his father personally chose Barksdale for the Olympic team. "My father was the sole reason he was on the team and I think his only friend," said Rupp.

* * *

Because of his unprecedented winning percentage, Rupp's teams often faced near-ambushes on the road. From Starkville to South Bend, the Wildcats suffered almost every imaginable indignity, from having coins thrown at them to having the hairs on their legs pulled out during out-of-bounds plays.

One of the most notorious games took place on Dec. 18, 1953, against St. Louis University. The Kiel Arena crowd was loud and belligerent, and several fights broke out between Billiken fans and those of the Wildcats, many of whom had traveled the relatively short distance from western Kentucky to see their team play.

As the final seconds of the third quarter elapsed—immediately following an altercation on the court—Pat Hickey again fired the pistol at Lancaster. At this point a melee ensued, which involved Lancaster, the younger Hickey, several fans and at least two clergymen from Owensboro.

Among his friends it was well known that Rupp despised Billiken coach Ed Hickey, referring to him only by an unprintable nickname of his own invention. It is likely that the UK coach was not very popular in the Hickey household either.

College games were divided into quarters at the time and it wasn't unusual for periods to end with the sound of a blank pistol instead of a whistle or air horn. Unknown by the UK coaching staff was that the person in charge of shooting the pistol that night was the official scorer, who was none other than Pat Hickey, the coach's son. The young Hickey was seated at the end of the scorer's table closest to the coaches' end of the Kentucky bench.

Tensions ran high from the opening tip, and the opposing fans continued to insult each other as the game progressed. As the first period ended, Pat Hickey pointed the blank pistol directly at Wildcat assistant coach Harry Lancaster and fired, sending a smoldering chunk of wadding bouncing off Lancaster's leg.

Rupp's burly assistant jumped up screaming at Hickey—whose identity he did not know—and told him not to let the incident happen again. "Go to Hell," Hickey replied.

As the final seconds of the third quarter elapsed—immediately following an altercation on the court—Pat Hickey again fired the pistol at Lancaster. At this point a melee ensued, which involved Lancaster, the younger Hickey, several fans and at least two clergymen from Owensboro.

After several arrests were made, order was restored and the Wildcats

120

prevailed, 71-59.

* * *

Kentucky's all-time largest margin of victory took place on Feb. 27, 1956, at the old Armory in Louisville, when it destroyed Georgia by 77 points, 143-66. Assistant coach Harry Lancaster said Rupp—who owned a 19-2 record against the Bulldogs—was unimpressed. Beating Georgia, the head coach said, was like "kissing your sister."

* * *

"Coach Rupp was the most successful superstitious person I've ever known," recalled Dan Issel, UK All-American and all-time leading scorer.

Rupp admitted to carrying buckeyes in his pocket and was known to follow cat tracks and pick up loose bobby pins, which were often strewn wherever he might walk by his players in the aftermath of a loss.

Many of his superstitions, including the brown suit, had come about when he departed from his usual routines. One example was the Noll Hotel, where the Wildcats stayed whenever they were in Knoxville. As times changed, the hotel had become somewhat seedy, and Rupp was pressured to pick a new place to stay.

"My sophomore year, coach Rupp moved us out of the Noll and into a new Sheraton," Issel recalled. "Well, it was just unfortunate, but we were beaten by 28 points that night. It was the worst defeat Rupp had ever suffered in the SEC."

The next year, Issel said, "we were back at the Noll Hotel."

* * *

After Rupp's UK retirement, he took several basketball-related jobs. One of them was serving as a board member for the Kentucky Colonels franchise of the old American Basketball Association.

His new position gave Rupp the opportunity to see three of his former players—Dan Issel, Louie Dampier and Mike Pratt—who were then playing for the Colonels.

In his 1985 book *Parting Shots*, Issel recalled one night after a game, when the old coach accompanied him to his home for a visit. Knowing Rupp's favorite drink was bourbon, Issel brought him a glassful but was refused. "The doctor told me to lay off the hard stuff," Rupp explained. "You got any vodka?"

15

Clyde Johnson, First Football All-American

For the first 50 years of UK athletics, football was king.

The Wildcats boasted good teams during many of those years, posting a string of 14 winning records in one stretch and winning the mythical Championship of the South several times.

There were the Immortals of 1898, still the only team in UK history unbeaten and untied. Edwin R. Sweetland's 1909 squad went 9-1 and beat powerful Illinois to earn the school's Wildcats nickname. There were great players too, from John "Shipwreck" Kelly and Ralph Kercheval to Bob "Twenty Grand" Davis and Bert "Man O' War" Johnson.

But in all those football-crazy years, no Kentucky player had ever been named an All-American. The first was a mountain of a man, 6-foot-6, 235-pound Clyde Elmer Johnson of Ashland.

Described as a "mild-mannered, brown-eyed giant," Johnson began his football career as a left tackle for Ashland High School and played on the 1934 Tomcats team that went 10-1 en route to a 365-2 point total. He learned line play

At 6-foot-6 and 235 pounds at a time when the average collegiate lineman played at about 195 pounds, Clyde Elmer Johnson of Ashland became the SEC's dominant tackle in 1941 and 1942. "Big John" or "Big Stoop," as he was known, almost single-handedly forced a 7-7 tie with Georgia during his sophomore debut in 1940 and narrowly missed upsetting the top-rated Bulldogs during his 1942 senior season. Johnson was unable to sleep on the nights before big games, usually reading or pacing until morning. Most offenses ran away from him.

under Ashland coach Fayne Grone and was also a two-year member of the basketball team.

Highly recommended by Grone, Johnson arrived at UK in 1939 and continued his football education under line coach and athletics director Bernie Shively—a former All-American guard at Illinois—whose philosophy was "get across the line low and hard."

"Big John," as his fellow players called him, made his Wildcat debut against Georgia in Athens on Oct. 26, 1940. "Fighting and determined," he "clawed his way through the Georgia line to stop the Bulldogs cold," forcing a 7-7 tie.

By his senior season of 1942, Johnson was a three-year starter and the dominant tackle in the Southeastern Conference. Most opponents confined their offenses to the right side of the Kentucky line and several had their hopes of victory dashed when Big John broke through to make a key play.

Imaginative sportswriters referred to Johnson as a "raw-boned giant," or "durable chunk of Kentucky manhood," but their most common description was "huge." He "stood straight up on defense to fight off blockers with his huge hands and reach for the ball-lugger," said one, explaining his playing style. Some SEC players tested Johnson, doubting that

Athletics Director Bernie Shively—who had been an All-American guard at Illinois—also served as the football team's line coach. Shively's advice to Johnson was to "get across the line low and hard."

someone so big could be fast, but big number 8 proved them wrong, moving "his big body around with unsuspected speed and agility."

"Johnson is gifted with the two attributes that make a great tackle," Shively observed, "size and the determination to go when the game is the hardest. He plays better against a good team than he does against an easy club."

It was a war year, with the United States fighting for its life, gearing up to take on Germany in Europe while holding Japan at bay in the Pacific. World War II affected virtually everyone and everything. The government controlled much of American life, from the supply of food, tires and gasoline to a nationwide 35-mile per hour speed limit and 5,000 annual mileage limit for cars.

The war also affected college football, as it vied with the armed forces for the same 18- to 22-year-old male population to fill rosters. Ole Miss' 1942 team, for example, had only eight returning lettermen, having lost 25 of its returning players and all of its assistant coaches to the war.

But, as it had every year since 1892, autumn brought football to the University of Kentucky. The head coach was Louisvillian Albert Dennis "Ab" Kirwan, a kindly, scholarly man, attorney and former UK player (an All-SEC halfback and 1925 team captain), who had come to his alma mater in 1938, after coaching at Male and duPont Manual high schools in Louisville. His was a cerebral approach to the game, along with strict

Described even in football literature as "scholarly," head coach Albert Dennis "Ab" Kirwan had mellowed since his days as an All-SEC halfback and captain of the 1925 Wildcats. He taught a cerebral approach to the game and didn't even bother to sign as many players as he could under the rules. "I am one of those unfortunate people with a tender conscience," he said. When UK didn't field a team in 1943, Kirwan earned a master's degree in history, resigned from coaching with a 24-28-4 record and became a history professor. He later wrote the standard biography of U.S. Senator John J. Crittenden and served as university president from 1968 to 1970. The Kirwan Tower and complex was named in his honor.

adherence to the rules. He had an 18-16-3 record heading into the 1942 season.

The 1942 Wildcats were truly a team of Kentuckians, with most of the players hailing from Lexington, Cynthiana, Mayfield, Somerset, Paris, Fort Thomas, Corbin, Catlettsburg, Tompkinsville, Louisville, Harrodsburg and Glasgow and most of the others from such nearby locales as Cincinnati, Evansville or Huntington, W.Va.

Kentucky suffered a setback, however, before the season even began when projected starting halfback Gene Meeks "accidentally rammed his right arm through a window pane in the K Club room of the Student Union building," severing two tendons. He was expected to miss at least six weeks as the wound healed.

There were only 40 varsity players on that war-year team, which was captained by 200-pound junior center Charley Bill Walker of Corbin. Rumors were flying that, following the lead of many other conferences, the SEC would drop its freshman eligibility ban "for the duration (of the war)" to help teams fill out depleted varsity rosters.

Throwing out his normally gradual shift into "heavy work," Kirwan scheduled double session practices and hitting for both the varsity and freshmen.

Practice began at 9:30 on the morning of Sept. 2 with a 1 1/2-hour session full of "blocking and tackling, passing, charging" and "the thud of leather against leather and grunt against grunt." The team went for another two hours that afternoon and reported for "skull work" in the evening. Gene Meeks spent his time catching passes with his good arm, prompting onlookers to dub him "Ambidextrous Meeks."

The Wildcats had 16 days to prepare for Orange Bowl champion Georgia and its All-American back Frank Sinkwich, "the Youngstown, Ohio, flash" scheduled to join the Marines as soon as the season was over.

Coach Kirwan was impressed with his returning starters, including 190-pound senior fullback "Roarin' Bob" Herbert of Fairmont, W.Va., and punter Phil Cutchin and his ability to place the ball in the "coffin corners." Still present, however, was the "same bugaboo" of limited reserves.

As the days went by, reporters noted an unusual enthusiasm and sense of urgency among the Wildcat players as they whispered to each other, "Only 15 days to Georgia ... 14 days to Georgia. ..."

Kirwan scrimmaged his team before a "sizable crowd" on Saturday, Sept. 5, pitting his projected starters and second-teamers against two squads of freshmen running known Georgia plays for 60 minutes. The coach said the Wildcats were in the best shape he'd seen since he arrived in 1938, probably because of the season's early start.

The coach was forced to take a break from practice to attend the funeral of his mother, Margaret, who died of a heart attack in Louisville on Sept. 6.

A series of scrimmages punctuated days of double-session practices, as the Wildcats hit hard to prepare for the opener. The veterans defeated the reserves and freshmen 72-6 on Sept. 8, 60-0 on Sept. 10 and—after a "secret" practice in the morning—79-0 on Sept. 12. Team members had bruised themselves for 10 days before the coaches began to back off in favor of "polishing."

"I've worked this squad harder than any I've ever coached," Kirwan said. "But it hasn't complained yet, and they're still going strong."

"He was tremendously effective on defense, standing straight up to his full six feet, six inches, batting would-be blockers out of the way with wide-swinging swipes of his huge paws and then lunging in to tackle the ball carrier."

—Herb Barker, Associated Press sportswriter

Hundreds of "railbirds" showed up to see practices and scrimmages, forcing the athletic department to erect grandstands on the west side of Stoll Field, the portion used for practices.

But traveling was not encouraged. On Sept. 12, Joseph B. Eastman, director of the U.S. Office of Defense Transportation, ordered a "drastic curtailment in travel to football games and other sport events ... to conserve transportation facilities." Colleges and universities were asked to transfer games to larger cities "where as many people as possible will have an opportunity to attend the games without traveling."

The Vandy-Ole Miss game scheduled for Nov. 7 was moved from Oxford to Memphis. Kentucky's game with Georgia would be held at Louisville's Manual (High School) Stadium.

National sportswriters gave UK little chance against the Orange Bowl champs. The contest was generally billed as a contest between "Fireball Frankie Sinkwich and Company' versus whatever Coach Ab Kirwan has handy around Kentucky's campus." It was conceded, however, that Kentucky's "pair of bear-like tackles"—Johnson and Clark Wood—might

The captain of the 1942 Cats was 200-pound center Charley Bill Walker of Corbin, pictured at right with his brother George.

slow down the Bulldog running game.

Kentucky suffered another setback when starting guard Rich Colvin left practice on Sept. 14 with a bruised kidney and spent the night at Good Samaritan Hospital.

Because the game was a week earlier than most teams' openers, it was the nation's pre-eminent contest of Saturday, Sept. 19, 1942, making Louisville briefly the "epicenter of the pigskin world" in a game of "mid-season stature." The Wildcats, it was said, had "nothing much to lose and a bucketful of prestige and confidence to gain."

"If they hold the Bulldogs to a two-touchdown margin or less," wrote a *Leader* sportswriter, "they'll ruin half the bookmakers in the country and gain a lift that should enable them to proceed through the remainder of their 10-game schedule with something approaching assurance."

Georgia arrived in Louisville on Thursday night after a "17-hour ride in day coaches." The Wildcats left Lexington on Friday afternoon after a blocking practice and lunch and settled into their rooms at the Seelbach Hotel. Even sumptuous quarters couldn't calm Johnson, however. A pre-game insomniac, the big tackle spent the night reading and pacing in his room until sunrise, when he walked around downtown Louisville awaiting breakfast.

As game time approached, sportswriters pointed out that the contest would be only the third between Kentucky and Georgia. The Wildcats defeated the Bulldogs 13-6 in 1939 and played them to a 7-7 tie the following year in a game that produced two stars, Sinkwich for Georgia and Johnson for UK.

Sinkwich, of Croatian descent—"the runningest, passingest, kickingest man in college football"—became an All-American tailback in 1941 in spite of playing almost the entire season with a broken jaw. Doctors wired the jaw nearly shut and Sinkwich lived on a liquid diet until it healed. He was the reigning ground gainer in college football and Red Grange's pick for player of the year in the Southeastern Conference. Georgia, in turn, was the projected conference champion.

Bulldog coach Wally Butts, who had coached against Kirwan's Manual High School teams when he was at its archrival Louisville Male, was nevertheless wary about the early season scrap. "It will be the earliest conference game in history, and probably the weather will be the hottest. This means both teams will have to substitute often," Butts said. "Any football coach can tell you how inexperienced men can be expected to perform with only 16 days of fall practice. Yes sir, it certainly looks like a wild and woolly game to me.

"If the game is close—and don't worry, it will be close—then we can't afford to take chances with our second line, which includes four men without game experience.

Kirwan, for his part, was confident in his team's strength if not its prospects for victory. "I am very well pleased with the boys," he said. "They have been working hard for this game, and I believe that they will give the Georgians something to think about before they leave the field tomorrow."

"Roarin' Bob" Herbert, the Wildcats' 195-pound fullback, got many of the tough yards in Kentucky's 7-6 near-miss against top-rated Georgia. The game, which was played at Manual (High School) Stadium in Louisville, briefly made the place the "epicenter of the pigskin world."

That afternoon, the SEC announced, by a vote of 9-3, that it had granted eligibility to freshmen. Committee member C.M. Surratt of Vanderbilt described the move as "the last rites for big time football."

"Next year, if we have eleven men and you have eleven men, we may get together and play," Surratt said. "That is about how it'll be." Voting yes were Auburn, Florida, Georgia, Georgia Tech, Louisiana State, Mississippi State, Mississippi, Tennessee and Vanderbilt. Kentucky, Alabama and Tulane voted no.

The game began at 3 p.m. before 10,000 fans at Manual Stadium. They included thousands of Kentucky's celebrated "railbirds" cheering for the blue-clad Wildcats, along with a sizable contingent of fans from Ohio, anxious to see their fellow Youngstown resident Fireball Frankie Sinkwich in live action.

Sinkwich met UK captain Charley Bill Walker and the officials at midfield, called the toss correctly and elected to defend the south goal. Kentucky would receive.

Grabbing the kick off at their own 35, the Cats could do little with it. They punted to "Race Hoss" Lamar Davis at the Bulldog 17, who streaked 49 yards to the Kentucky 37 before he was finally tackled.

After a failed Georgia field goal attempt and another Wildcat punt, the Bulldogs were in business at their own 28. Sinkwich tried a reverse, handing off to Davis.

Johnson crashed through the line, forced Davis to fumble, and fell on the ball. Big John, it was said, spent "most of the afternoon folding up the Georgia interference like it was a busted accordion."

The teams battled to a scoreless tie until the third quarter. With four minutes remaining, a Phil Cutchin punt and touchback gave the ball to the Bulldogs at their own 20. Sinkwich sent his team into a spread formation and, after faking a run, dropped back to pass. The Wildcat defense swarmed "over the All-American halfback like he was just another guy in a white sweater." UK tackle Bill Griffin "knifed into the protective cordon," knocked the ball from Sinkwich's arm and recovered his prize at the seven-yard-line.

Halfback Charlie Kuhn of Louisville got four yards for UK on first down. It was second and goal at the three. The Wildcats' 195-pound fullback Roarin' Bob Herbert received the ball and "pounded" it to the one.

On third and goal—"with Georgia's seven-man defensive line drawn in tighter than a dollar derby"—Tommy Ewing handed off to Kuhn, who raced around left end untouched for the score. The moment was sweet for Kuhn, who had played for Butts at Male.

Kuhn trotted over to the spot from which he would place-kick the point after attempt. Walker's hike sailed to the holder, who placed the ball in the turf; and Kuhn kicked into a stiff Georgia defense. The ball was blocked, the score Kentucky 6, Georgia 0. The fourth quarter had begun.

Georgia received the Kentucky kick off and had first down at its own 37. Sinkwich ran twice, then hit Van Davis for a 31-yard pass play that put the ball deep in UK territory. In five straight "smashing" runs, Fireball Frankie got the ball to the two. On fourth and goal, Sinkwich finally hit pay dirt, to tie the score at 6.

Georgia called on Leo Costa, "a burly fellow kept around just to boot ... extra points." Costa had hit 26 consecutive attempts and 62 in three years as a Bulldog. The senior "trotted into the game and automatically toed the ball between the uprights." The score was Georgia 7, Kentucky 6.

The Bulldogs had their victory.

"We're very proud of the way our boys fought," Kirwan said after the game. "They battled all the way and gave everything they had."

But it was a game of might-have-beens. Kentucky recovered all three Georgia fumbles in the struggle and narrowly missed blocking several punts. But it also had three passes intercepted and produced only 115 total yards to the Bulldogs' 266.

The Wildcats, however, had come close to beating one of the nation's best teams and in the process had won the respect of the football world. "The Kentucky boys went into the game as hybrids—a combination of dark horse and underpooch," wrote sportswriter Alex Bower. "They came out as heroes. Not even their best friends would have told them beforehand they could march through Georgia as they did here today. But march they did and part of the time on double."

Butts also was impressed with Kentucky, calling Herbert the best defender he'd seen in two seasons and saying the Bulldogs were lucky to have won the game.

Kentucky played its first night game of the season the following Friday, Sept. 26, against the Xavier Musketeers at Corcoran Field in Cincinnati. Xavier had revenge on its mind, nursing the memory of its 21-6 defeat at the hands of the Wildcats in 1941 that marred an otherwise perfect season.

Johnson recovered a first-quarter fumble in a game that had Kirwan "substituting freely" en route to a 35-19 victory and a 1-1 record.

On Tuesday evening, Sept. 29, at the invitation of athletics director Bernie Shively, Kentucky football season ticket holders packed into Alumni Gym to watch movies of the UK-Georgia game.

The team's home debut took place on Oct. 3, with the Wildcats demolishing the Washington and Lee Generals 53-0 in the 20th meeting between the schools.

After a 7-6 home loss to Vanderbilt, UK played Virginia Tech to a 21-21 tie in Roanoke. Its record was 2-2-1 heading into its Oct. 24 homecoming game against Alabama in Lexington. Hopeful fans, however, pointed out that the Cats were two points away from being 4-0-1 and that sophomore halfback Gene Meeks' arm was sufficiently healed for him to make his first start of the year.

Kentucky kicked off to Alabama and pinned the Tide on its 16. The Wildcats fielded the punt and quickly moved to the visitors, 15-yard line. Cutchin was tackled for a one-yard loss on first down. Receiving the snap on second down, he connected on a seven-yard pass to end George Sengel, which brought the ball to the Alabama nine. As Cutchin dropped back to pass again, Sengel was virtually tackled by Tide defender Al Sabo "without so much as a reprimand from the field judge."

The 35 "Red Elephants" on coach Frank Thomas' traveling squad, fresh from an 8-0 shutout of powerful Tennessee, were 4-0 and wary of a letdown. A homecoming crowd of 12,000 packed into Stoll Field stadium for the 2 p.m. start.

Kentucky kicked off to Alabama and pinned the Tide at its 16. The Wildcats fielded the punt and quickly moved to the visitors' 15-yard line. Cutchin was tackled for a one-yard loss on first down. Receiving the snap on second down, he connected on a seven-yard pass to end George Sengel, which brought the ball to the Alabama nine. As Cutchin dropped back to pass again, Sengel was virtually tackled by Tide defender Al Sabo "without so much as a reprimand from the field judge."

Kentucky piled up the statistics against 'Bama throughout the first half, routinely gaining healthy yardage on running plays and passing well, only to be thrown back by the referees on everything from holding to intentional grounding. The half ended with the 'Cats leading the visitors 6-1 in first downs, 57-21 in rushing yards and 31-0 in passing yards.

A Wildcat fumble on their own 22 in the third quarter led to Alabama's first score and an interception on the UK 44 doomed the Cats 14-0 in the fourth. The Kentucky line, it was said, played well but was worn down by the talented 'Bama reserves. Second stringers Jay Rhodemyre at center and Bill Griffin at tackle impressed everyone with their solid play. They met Tide quarterback Russ Mosley simultaneously for a double sack that ended a drive and Rhodemyre got an interception after Griffin pressured Mosley into a bad pass.

Johnson and Griffin, were reported to have "battled as far as they could go." Big John spent the game "moving his tremendous 235-pound bulk with surprising agility and speed," wrote Associated Press sports editor Herb Barker. "Johnson was an impressive figure in the Wildcat line, and what is more, an immovable one," he continued. "Alabama finally quit running plays at his side of the line because it cost them an average of three yards every time they did it. He was tremendously effective on defense, standing straight up to his full six feet, six inches, batting would-be blockers out of the way with wide-swinging swipes of his huge paws and then lunging in to tackle the ball carrier."

Kentucky rebounded to beat George Washington 27-6 in the nation's capital, before being demolished by Georgia Tech 47-7 in Atlanta on Nov. 7.

Johnson was injured for the first time in his college career on Nov. 14 at home against West Virginia. He left the game at the close of the third quarter with a knee injury that ended his season.

The Wildcats had battled the Mountaineers to a scoreless tie. As the final minute ticked away, West Virginia quarterback Richard Leonard flung two incomplete hail marys from the Kentucky 39. Receiving the third down snap, Leonard faded back to avoid a fierce Wildcat pass rush and sailed a wobbling pass into a waiting crowd at the five-yard line.

Mountaineer William Bell outjumped Kentucky's Charlie Kuhn for the ball, but it bounced off him before ricocheting off Kuhn's hands and into the air. The errant pass dropped into the waiting arms of West Virginia reserve end Fred Morecraft, who walked into the end zone. The visitors kicked the extra point and successfully defended against three Wildcat hail marys for a 7-0 win.

"Kentucky is a real hard luck team," said WVU coach Bill Kern. "(It) stopped our offense better than any team we've played this season." Kirwan agreed, praising Johnson's effort as "one of the finest games I ever saw a tackle play." Leonard's pass was long remembered in West Virginia as the "Cigarette Play," because it was such a "lucky strike."

Johnson's injury forced him to watch the Wildcats' final game of the season, a 26-0 loss to Tennessee in Knoxville on Nov. 21.

UK's final record was a disappointing 3-6-1, having only beaten Xavier, Washington & Lee and George Washington and tying Virginia Tech. Fans, however, were hopeful for

Big number 8 in action against Vanderbilt, 1942.

the future because its losses were to SEC and Rose Bowl champion Georgia, Orange Bowl champion Alabama, Sugar Bowl champion Tennessee, and Georgia Tech, which posted an undefeated regular season before losing to Texas in the Cotton Bowl. After all, they reasoned, Kentucky lost to Georgia by only one point and the Bulldogs' 35-13 win over Cincinnati was on par with Kentucky's 35-19 victory against the Bearcats. Georgia coach Wally Butts was named SEC coach of the year, while Georgia Tech's Bill Alexander took national coach of the year honors.

Johnson had played in 23 games as a Wildcat, averaging "between 50 and 55 minutes" per contest, which *Herald* reporter Roy Steinfort termed "almost the feat of a superhuman."

On Nov. 30, the Alabama football team announced its annual all-opponent squad. Unanimous picks were Frankie Sinkwich, Vanderbilt quarterback Jack Jenkins and Johnson. Number 8 was also on the all-opponent teams of West Virginia and Vanderbilt.

On Dec. 4, "Big Stoop" was named to the 10th annual Associated Press All-SEC team, a group chosen by "20 Southern sports writers." Johnson also made the team chosen by the International News Service, which polled coaches, sportswriters and radio announcers. He was Kentucky's first All-SEC player since Bert Johnson made the team in 1934.

His knee sufficiently healing, Johnson was preparing—along with fellow UK tackle and roommate Clark Wood—to play in the annual Blue-Gray game in Montgomery, Ala., on Dec. 26.

The big news broke on Dec. 11 in New York, when the Associated Press announced Clyde Johnson's name as a member of its All-America team.

Both the *Lexington Herald* and the *Louisville Courier-Journal* proclaimed it in banner headlines. The player was described as "awed but overjoyed." In an editorial, the *Maysville Independent* called the big man's achievement even more remarkable because UK had won only one SEC game—a 26-7 victory over Georgia Tech in 1940—during his career. Big John, it was said. "'worked his way through college', so to speak, without benefit of a Rose Bowl team to help him."

The SEC and Big Ten dominated the All-America squad, placing three players each on the first team. Johnson shared the SEC spotlight with Alabama senior center Joseph J. Domnanovich along with Sinkwich, who was chosen "captain" of the squad. It was noted that the first team All America linemen averaged 204 pounds, far lighter than Johnson's 235.

"It's just a dream—just something that you think about that never happens," he said, grinning. "I still can't believe it."

With the announcement came instant recognition and notoriety, which "the big boy from Boyd County" handled with his usual humility. "He played football in a big way, his ability has been recognized in a big way, but his ego is small, and that makes him a bigger man than ever," read a Leader editorial. "It takes a huge mantle of glory to cover him, because he wants it large enough to take in some of his sidekicks.

With the announcement came instant recognition and notoriety, which "the big boy from Boyd County" handled with his usual humility. "He played football in a big way, his ability has been recognized in a big way, but his ego is small, and that makes him a bigger man than ever," read a *Leader* editorial. "It takes a huge mantle of glory to cover him, because he wants it large enough to take in some of his sidekicks. As he was being photographed and admired and quizzed and calipered and congratulated when the good news became known, he stipulated quite seriously: 'Don't forget to mention George Sengel ... and Arch Colvin and Hut Jones ... and Bob Herbert and Charlie Walker ... They made the job a lot easier.'"

UK officials immediately scheduled a testimonial dinner for Tuesday, Dec. 15, at the Lafayette Hotel. It was attended by Gov. Keen Johnson, former Wildcat star and local businessman William "Doc" Rodes, Barckley Storey, president of the Lexington Board of Commerce and Russell Scofield, president of the Lexington Lions Club.

Johnson was presented a gold watch and chain with a matching penknife, $300 in war bonds and the Lion's Club's annual award for "outstanding athlete at the University of Kentucky."

"Coach Shively had a speech all prepared for me, but it just won't come out," the guest of honor said. "I am very proud to have attended Kentucky. I will be even more proud to be an alumni of Kentucky."

Kirwan was next behind the podium. "In my opinion, an All-America honor has never been bestowed on a more worthy boy," the coach told the crowd. "Stoop has character, intelligence, and personality in keeping with the size of his body. He's a regular fellow on and off the field. That's the reason that his teammates are very devoted to him, and are proud to have played on the same team that he did."

The coach gave the credit for the player's achievement to Johnson himself, along with Shively, who "got the full ability out of him."

"Now that we have had Johnson as All-America," Kirwan added, "it should be easier to persuade prep school boys to come to the University of Kentucky to play football. Now they will know that it's just as easy to become a great ball player at Kentucky as it is at any other school."

The following night, Johnson was at Ashland High School to receive that city's congratulations during a halftime ceremony of a basketball game between Morehead Teachers College and Salem College of West Virginia. The home folks presented him, along with Vincent "Moose" Zachem—who had been named to the Associated Press "Little All America" team—with plaques as Ashland's All Americans.

As a military science major, Johnson was scheduled to enter the Army upon graduation as a second lieutenant. But his long-range plans involved his sport. "If I am still able physically when I get out of the Army, I would like to play a couple of seasons of pro ball and then get a crack at college coaching," he told a reporter. "There's something about football that gets in your blood."

After signing with the Green Bay Packers and leaving the team in a contract dispute, Johnson finished his football career with the Los Angeles Dons of the West Coast League and later taught and coached football at East Los Angeles Junior College.

* * *

With its numbers further depleted UK canceled football for the 1943 war year.

* * *

After his military career ended, Johnson signed a two-year contract in 1948 to play for the Green Bay Packers. The contract, signed by Packer coach E.L. "Curly" Lambeau, included a written notation by the coach agreeing to pay Johnson $7,000 per year for two years. After being released after playing in only two exhibition games, Johnson sued and—eight years later—was awarded $8,918 by the Wisconsin Supreme Court.

He finished his football career with the Los Angeles Dons of the West

Coast League), before becoming a teacher and football coach at East Los Angeles Junior College.

* * *

Punter and halfback Phil Cutchin played in 1941 and 1942 before joining the armed forces during World War II. He returned to finish his collegiate career in 1946 as captain of Bear Bryant's first UK team.

Jay Rhodemyre returned to UK after the war as an All-SEC center and linebacker for Bryant, helping the Wildcats earn their first bowl bid in 1947—a 24-14 win over Villanova in the only Great Lakes Bowl ever played—and being named most valuable player in the 1948 college all-star game. He played four years of professional football for the Green Bay Packers.

* * *

Ab Kirwan spent the 1943 football season—when UK didn't field a team—teaching history to soldiers housed on campus while simultaneously earning a master's degree. He returned to coach the 1944 team to a 2-8 record, before resigning to become a history professor. His record as coach of the Wildcats was 24-28-4.

Kirwan later served UK as dean of men, dean of the graduate school, and finally as university president from 1968 to 1970. His biography of Senator John J. Crittenden—the Kentuckian who unsuccessfully sought to avert the Civil War—remains the standard work on the subject. One historian called him the "most distinguished scholar who had ever occupied the president's office."

"We broke no rules while I was coaching at Kentucky," Kirwan recalled later in life. "We had only sixty scholarships in football at that time, forty varsity and twenty freshmen. We not only broke no rules in awarding grants-in-aid, we did not even grant the full scholarships permitted. We gave only board, room, books and institutional fees at Kentucky at that time. We gave not a cent to any athlete for laundry or for any other purpose. And yet I had many opportunities to do so. Frequently sports fans came to me with offers of money to make illegitimate inducements to promising athletes to enroll at Kentucky, but I spurned all such overtures. I claim no particular credit for having done so. I am one of those unfortunate people with a tender conscience. ..."

16

The Original Mr. Wildcat: Richard C. Stoll

Bill Keightly is universally known among Kentucky fans as Mr. Wildcat for his loyalty and dedication in a 40-year career as the team's equipment manager.

But there was another Mr. Wildcat, another man who served the athletic program in many ways over many years. His name was Richard Charles Stoll.

Stoll, a member of a prominent Lexington family, was a student in 1891 when Kentucky State College—as it was then known—began playing football again after a 10-year lapse.

Following a victory over Georgetown College 8-2 in April and an aborted meeting with Transylvania on Dec. 12, the KSC students and football players were planning for their big game against Centre College. On Dec. 18, the night before the contest, "an enthusiastic crowd" met in the chapel. The group elected Civil Engineering professor James P. Nelson its chairman and W.S. Page, secretary.

Professor J.W. Newman announced that the purpose of the meeting was to end the longstanding disagreement between the all-male Patterson Literary Society and the all-female Philosophian Society over school colors. The Patterson group's colors were "old gold" and purple, while the Philosophians, who held a reception and dance in honor of the football team each November, had chosen red and black. The faculty, Newman said, "had decided to settle that question."

The KSC students and football players were planning for their big game against Centre College. On December 18, the night before the contest, "an enthusiastic crowd" met in the chapel [to decide the school's colors]. Stoll recalled that blue was suggested, and "someone on the other side of the chapel said, 'What color blue will it be?' I happened to have on a blue necktie and took it off and held it up," he said. "That was the color blue which was adopted." The Lexington Transcript reported the next day that state college's colors were "dark blue and light yellow. A motion was made that the colors selected be adopted, which was carried by a big majority." By the following year, light yellow was replaced by white.

Stoll recalled that blue was suggested, and "someone on the other side of the chapel said, 'What color blue will it be?' I happened to have on a blue necktie and took it off and held it up," he said. "That was the color blue which was adopted. The blue at the University is a peculiar color of blue,

Richard Charles Stoll (front row, seated, third from right) was a standout junior fullback on the 1893 team, in addition to track team captain and manager of the baseball team his senior year. At a meeting two years before, he helped choose the school colors. The "dark blue" adopted for the Centre game that year was the shade of the necktie he had worn to the meeting. An interesting sidelight is that the colors were chosen to end a controversy between the Patterson Literary Society, whose colors were "old gold" and purple and the Philosophian Society, whose colors were red and black.

but it so happened that was the color in my necktie." The *Lexington Transcript* reported the next day that state college's colors were "dark blue and light yellow. A motion was made that the colors selected be adopted, which was carried by a big majority." By the following year, light yellow was replaced by white.

The young man played four years for KSC, lettering as a fullback in 1893 and 1894. During his senior year, he was captain of the track team and manager of the baseball team.

After graduating from Yale Law School, Stoll was appointed to KSC's board of trustees in 1898 at the almost unprecedented age of 22 and was the subject of glowing tributes in the annuals of several succeeding graduating classes.

His hero status on campus was not only founded in his successful law career and university boosterism, but in his ability to get things done. When the 1898 football team was bankrupt and its appeal to the board of trustees fell upon deaf ears, money to hire a coach was miraculously found just after Stoll had served as a referee in one of its games. "College athletics is of value when it hardens the muscles, puts courage in the heart, builds up esprit de corps, moulds character and insistently demands fair play," he said. "It is from the friction of contact with manly characters that the sparks of truth are struck out."

By 1902, Stoll was a promising attorney with a law office in the McClelland Building in downtown Lexington and the home on West Third Street he would live in the rest of his life. He was a lecturer during night-time classes at UK's College of Law in 1913 and donated a needed set of law books for its benefit.

According to one of his law partners, historian William H. Townsend, Stoll had "an uncanny ability to find pertinent and important court decisions in obscure places." In one case from about 1900, "the very existence of a large public service corporation" was in question. Though the company had many seasoned attorneys on its staff, Townsend said, "it was Stoll, then only a few years out of law school, who found the court decision that had won the case and saved the company's life."

Stoll was a tireless proponent of athletics and its staunchest ally on the board of trustees. He had already done so much for the school's athletics program by 1916 that the football field was dedicated to him. The bronze plaque placed at the stadium read "Alumnus, trustee, and benefactor."

The young lawyer served as general counsel to numerous Lexington businesses, including Kentucky Utilities, the *Lexington Herald-Leader* and Lexington Water Co. Over the years, he also served as president of the Fayette County and Kentucky bar associations and the Kentucky Trotting Horse Breeders Association and as director of the Keeneland Association.

Described as a "large, imposing man" and an "inveterate smoker," Stoll also possessed an ability to "prevent ill feeling and the bitterness which makes so difficult the reaching of decisions in public matters." He used these considerable skills to assist his school in overcoming numerous obstacles as it grew from a small college to a modern university. He helped ease school president James Kennedy Patterson—who had been in his position for 31 years—into retirement and helped hire the next three university presidents. He assisted UK president Frank L. McVey in securing state funding for a much-needed building improvement program and personally dispelled Depression-era rumors that the university might close.

Stoll was a tireless proponent of athletics and its staunchest ally on the board of trustees. He had already done so much for the school's athletics program by 1916 that the football field was dedicated to him. The bronze plaque placed at the stadium read "Alumnus, trustee, and benefactor."

University of Kentucky Special Collections

Stoll's portrait, the only one of a non-UK president ever displayed in the Board of Trustees Room. With the exception of the years 1905-08, Stoll served continuously on the UK Board of Trustees from 1898 until his death on June 26, 1949, and as chairman of the board's executive committee from 1918 to 1948. During that period, enrollment grew from 376 to more than 7,800. "No man," said UK President Herman L. Donovan, "was ever more devoted to any institution than was Judge Stoll to the University."

During World War I, he directed the Public Safety Committee of Kentucky Council of Defense and was head of the state branch of the American Protective League.

Stoll served as Fayette Circuit Court judge from 1921 to 1931, before founding the Lexington law firm that became Stoll, Kenon and Park.

With the exception of the years 1905-08, Stoll served continuously on the UK Board of Trustees from 1898 until his death on June 26, 1949, and as chairman of the board's executive committee from 1918 to 1948. During that period, enrollment grew from 376 to more than 7,800. At his death, his was the only portrait of a non-UK president displayed in the board's meeting room.

"In listing those men and women who have been the builders of the University, Judge Stoll ranks with those who are at the top," said UK president Herman L. Donovan. "He has long given the University the benefit of his best judgment and wisdom."

"Towering above all his other interests," read a eulogy in the June 28, 1949, *Lexington Leader*, was the University of Kentucky, which he served through the years both as a friend and as an official. No man was ever more devoted to any institution than was Judge Stoll to the University."

Stoll set up his $225,000 estate into two trust funds, one for his wife Angelene, the other for his son, Richard P. Stoll. It was directed that if the younger Stoll had no heirs at the time of his death, the fund would go to "the University of Kentucky to be used by the board of trustees for the school."

* * *

On Nov. 13, 1948, Stoll received UK's first Alma Magna Mater award for service to the school. A citation that accompanied the award read: "Serving without recompense and at the sacrifice of his own personal interests, Judge Stoll's contribution to the advancement of his alma mater has been without precedent in the history of American education."

* * *

After Commonwealth Stadium became home to the football Wildcats in 1973, McLean Stadium was demolished and replaced by an addition to the Student Center on one side and the Singletary Center for the Arts on the other. The middle portion, which is used by the UK marching band for practice space, retains the name Stoll Field.

The marching band's practice area, site of the old football field, retains the name Stoll Field.

17

Integrating the SEC

They can arguably be called five of the most important football players in the history of the Southeastern Conference—and they all played for the University of Kentucky.

Greg Page, Nat Northington, Wilbur Hackett, Houston Hogg and Albert Johnson didn't win any championships or set any on-the-field records.

UK Sports Information

Nat Northington signed to play for UK in December 1965, becoming the first African American to sign with an SEC athletic program. On Sept. 30, 1967, Northington became the first black athlete to play in a game between SEC football teams when he took the field in Lexington against Ole Miss.

But, as the first African Americans to play in the SEC, they were pioneers in the struggle for racial equality.

But being a Jackie Robinson in the South of the late 1960s wasn't for the faint of heart. It required courage, discipline and a profound willingness to turn the other cheek in the face of almost indescribable hatred. These men—teenagers in 1967-68—had all of those qualities and more.

Integrating football at Kentucky wasn't easy. For many years, in fact, it was illegal for a state-supported college or university to admit African Americans. As the northernmost school in the Southeastern Conference, UK was in a leadership position when it came to changing attitudes. The law was changed and coaches were given the green light to recruit.

What were needed were pioneers, black high school athletes willing to help desegregate the SEC in the face of unreconstructed, tradition-bound football fans in the Old South.

Kentucky coach Charlie Bradshaw found two recruits willing to cross the color line: Greg Page, an all-state defensive end from Middlesboro High School—who became the first African American to sign to play for an SEC school—and Nat Northington, a running back from Louisville's Thomas Jefferson High.

Wilbur Hackett and Houston Hogg, members of UK's second African American recruiting class, recalled Page as an "exceptionally special person" with an awe-inspiring physique. "He came close to where I was from," Hogg said. "He was really a nice guy. He had come from a real nice family too."

Hackett said his friend's body looked like it was "carved from granite." Hogg agreed. "He was an exceptional football player. He was a picture of what a football player should look like. He looked like a rock."

Hogg grew up in Hazard in an atmosphere, he said, of equality. "Most of my friends were white. It was like everybody was the same. I didn't understand any form of prejudice." After playing for Hazard High School as a quarterback through his junior year, Hogg's family moved to the Owensboro area, where he played running back for the county high school. "I was the only black on the Daviess County football team," he said.

Hackett, a two-time all-state player for Louisville Manual High School at fullback and linebacker, was recruited personally by Bradshaw. "He strongly wanted me to go to UK. He pretty much told me he would take care of me if I went to UK. He looked me in the eye and told me it would be successful, a positive experience. Not that he would protect me or anything, but that I would be treated right."

UK Sports Information

Wilbur Hackett Jr., a member of UK's second African American recruiting class, became the first black captain of an SEC football team in his junior year of 1969. He is today an SEC referee and a successful building contractor.

Page and Northington also helped convince Hackett to become a Wildcat. "Nat and Greg really sold me on UK because they told me they needed help," he remembered. "They said we needed to get more African Americans in school to help turn this around."

Hackett also fondly recalled the social aspects of his recruitment by the older players. "They went all out. There was no limit on the number of trips at the time. I'd visit, then we'd all drive back to Louisville and go to the clubs. We really enjoyed it. I felt good about coming here."

Being treated right was an important point during the Civil Rights era. Hackett said his UK experience was mainly positive on the field and off. "It was a normal college campus," he said. "It was a good life. I don't think we were hated or disliked. People basically treated us OK." Hogg agreed. "The players and everybody, they accepted us. They treated us pretty good."

"I believe the University of Kentucky was trying to reach out and modernize the program by being the first team in the SEC with black play-

Greg Page was paralyzed during a scrimmage on Aug. 22, 1967, the third day of preseason practice. He died on Sept. 29, as the Wildcats prepared to play Ole Miss. Teammates remembered him as "an exceptionally special person" and "a picture of what a football player should look like."

"Most of my friends were white. It was like everybody was the same. I didn't understand any form of prejudice."

—Houston Hogg, on his childhood in Hazard

ers," said Roger Greer, a member of the 1967 freshman class, who roomed with Albert Johnson.

"The social movement was a reality," explained Hackett. "People were starting to accept the fact that integration was a thing they were going to have to deal with."

The one exception occurred in the aftermath of a campus speech by white separatist and Alabama governor George Wallace, who was running for president. "After the George Wallace speech we had problems," Hackett said. "We had incidents. On occasion you'd have to deal with a situation. I fought more than once and I mean that."

Hogg said a group of white students surrounded him at a gathering one night, and began threatening him. "Hackett, he jumped in and kind of helped me out," Hogg remembered. "It was all because of George Wallace I guess."

The tragedy of those years, however, happened on the field. On Aug. 22, 1967—the third day of preseason practice—Page was paralyzed from the neck down during a drill. "We were getting ready to play Indiana," Hogg said. "It was a rushing drill. We were in shorts and shoulder pads."

"I was standing right next to him when it happened," Hackett remembered. "It was a freak thing, a spinal injury."

Not long afterward, defensive end Cecil New was paralyzed while tackling running back Dick Beard during a scrimmage. "That happened shortly after the accident with Greg Page," said Greer, New's running mate at defensive end.

Page, who had been breathing with the aid of an "iron lung," died on Sept. 29, as the Wildcats were preparing to play Ole Miss. "The boys were crushed at the news," said Bradshaw of his team. "They felt very deeply for Greg."

History was made at 2 o'clock the next afternoon, when Northington took the field as the first African American to play in an SEC football game. Hackett, who witnessed the event sitting in the stands with the other members of the freshman team, recalled that the milestone went almost unnoticed in both local and national media. "It was almost like you don't talk about it and it will go away," Hackett explained, "but it was a big deal to Nat."

For Wildcat football fans, however, it was a familiar story. Northington, playing safety, went down early in the game with a shoulder injury and—in spite of the heroic efforts of quarterback, punter and kick returner Dicky Lyons—the vaunted Rebels ran away with a 26-13 victory.

Afterward, the players walked to the west end zone, where a memorial service was held for Page in front of the remainder of the 34,000 fans in attendance. Speakers included UK president John W. Oswald, Bradshaw and Page teammate Don Britton, president of the local Fellowship of Christian Athletes. "He broke some pretty strong barriers," Hackett said of his friend. "He broke some ground."

So had Northington—and the experience was more than he could handle. After suffering another shoulder separation in an away game against Auburn on Oct. 8, he quit the team. "He made history and he left," Hackett recalled. "His injury was the straw that broke the camel's back. He just couldn't take it anymore."

"He didn't want to stick around no more," Hogg said. "It was pretty rough times." But Northington told the younger players he didn't want them to leave. "We've got it going now," Hogg recalled him saying.

UK Sports Information

Houston Hogg Jr., who grew up in Hazard and later played in Daviess County, said none of his experiences in Kentucky prepared him for the racism he experienced during SEC road games.

History was made at 2 o'clock the next afternoon, when Northington took the field as the first African American to play in an SEC football game. Hackett, who witnessed the event sitting in the stands with other members of the freshman team, recalled that the milestone went almost unnoticed in both local and national media. "It was almost like you don't talk about it and it will go away," he explained, "but it was a big deal to Nat."

143

Much of what Nothington couldn't take was playing on the road in the SEC of the late 1960s.

Left to carry on by themselves, Hackett, Hogg and Johnson routinely left the relative calm of Lexington and traveled the South never knowing what they would face. Much of it was pure, hate-filled racism. "When we played down South we were scared to death," said Hogg. "Some games we were harassed and heckled and called names … you heard it all," added Hackett. "At Ole Miss people said, "Hang the n_____.""

After losing to LSU in Baton Rouge on Oct. 19, 1968, the team returned to its hotel and Bradshaw sent each off with $5 to eat dinner wherever he chose. "We lost the game and I just don't think the coaches wanted to look at us anymore," said Greer.

Hackett, Hogg, Greer and Hugh Bland decided to walk a short distance down the road to a nearby restaurant.

"They had a big George Wallace picture up in there," Hackett remembered. "We just went on in there anyway."

When they arrived back in Lexington, Hackett and Hogg received a letter signed by the governor of Louisiana. "He was apologizing to us for the way we were treated," Hogg said. "A lot of good that did. They beat us to death on the field and then they wouldn't even let us eat."

After sitting quite a while without service, a waitress finally emerged and began taking the orders of the white players. Then she whispered something to Bland. "We asked Hugh what the waitress whispered to him and Hugh said she couldn't wait on us," said Hackett. Hackett and Hogg were told that if they wanted to be served, they would have to leave the restaurant, walk to the back door and stand outside and wait for their food.

Nobody budged.

"I remember Wilbur said 'Oh, no,'" Greer recalled. "That's all he said."

"I was sitting there looking," Hogg remembered. "Nothing like that had happened to me before. One guy got really upset. He threw a saltshaker or something."

"This was years after the Civil Rights Act and I thought all that was over, but it wasn't," said Greer. "It was very disgusting to think that that was still going on. That was 1968."

When informed the police were being called, the Kentucky players jumped up and began running for the door, knocking over at least one table in the process. "We ran out of there," Hogg remembered. "Somebody slammed the door before I could get out and I was running down the street with that screen. I had all of it. I couldn't get rid of it."

"A few things got broken on the way out," said Greer.

By the time the athletes ran the short distance back to the team hotel, they were met in the parking lot by the Louisiana State Police.

"They were typical southern policemen," Hogg said, recalling several holding German Shepherds on leashes and several others with jaws filled with chewing tobacco. "You know it was funny, when the white players walked by those dogs, they didn't do anything, but when they saw me and Hack, those dogs went off. I think they were trained that way."

As things outside began to escalate, a concerned Bradshaw sent his black players to their hotel rooms and told Hackett: "You keep an eye on Houston and make sure he don't get out of that room." "He knew I would fight anybody anytime," said Hogg. "That's just the way I was brought up."

Kentucky was able to leave Baton Rouge without further incident. When they arrived back in Lexington, Hackett and Hogg received a letter signed by the governor of Louisiana. "He was apologizing to us for the way we were treated," Hogg said. "A lot of good that did," he added with a wry laugh. "They beat us to death on the field and then they wouldn't even let us eat."

When Hogg, then a 230-pound junior running back, trotted onto the field at Georgia on Oct. 25, 1969, it was in a hail of epithets that shocked both him and his Wildcat teammates. "They were coached by Vince Dooley. I remember Standish, a tackle. It was their whole team," he said. "They said 'there he is, get that nigger. We gonna kill that nigger.'"

In the huddle, when he looked at the Wildcat offensive linemen, he saw tears streaming down their faces. "They said 'listen to what those guys are saying about you.' And then they called my number and I said 'I'm in trouble.'

"I bet all of them hit me.

"Them kids. I don't know how they could have that much hate in their heart."

In the huddle, when he looked at the Wildcat offensive linemen, he saw tears streaming down their faces. "They said 'listen to what those guys are saying about you.' And then they called my number and I said 'I'm in trouble' ... I bet all of them hit me....Them kids. I don't know how they could have that much hate in their heart."

When it was over the scoreboard read Bulldogs 30, Wildcats 0.

"There was a lot of verbal abuse," said Greer. "There's a lot of verbal things in a football game anyway. I know we had a lot of racial slurs slung at us."

Hogg said three years of varsity football took a tremendous toll on his body. "I got beat up in college. I was as big as some of the linemen that was trying to block for me. I took a beating."

Hackett, an outside linebacker his final two seasons, was elected team captain his junior year, which made him the first black captain of an SEC football team. He made All-SEC honorable mention that year on a team

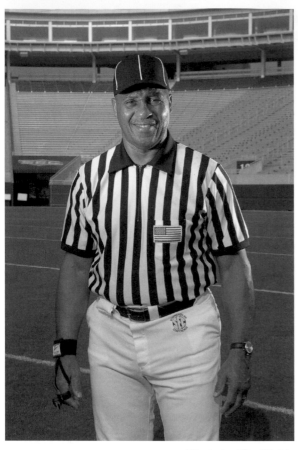

Photo by Tim Webb

After having helped integrate the SEC in the 1960s, Wilbur Hackett is today a referee in the conference. He said his playing days are an advantage in his current job. "I can read a play and know where they're going as soon as the ball is snapped," he said.

that went 3-8.

"Wilbur and Houston were just tremendous athletes," said Greer. "For Wilbur to play linebacker in the SEC at his size is phenomenal."

Returning home to Louisville, Hackett began his own construction business while commuting to a job at Toyota Motor Manufacturing in Georgetown. He also founded a little league for African American children and began working his way into refereeing. After serving in the high school and lower level collegiate ranks, Hackett's career has come full circle. He is today a referee in the Southeastern Conference.

Sometimes, he said, he still gets flashbacks of playing. "I'm glad I played then and not now," he said. "Athletes have really developed in 35 years. Look at the difference in the average weight of a lineman. It's unbelievable. And the speed: Today you see linebackers running down backs in the open field."

The playing experience has paid big dividends.

"I might not be the best official, but I feel like my football experience has allowed me to see things that I wouldn't be able to if I hadn't played," Hackett explained. "I can read a play and know where they're going as soon as the ball is snapped. The ability to anticipate things has really helped me as an official."

One of his career highlights, he said, was working the first victory of Mississippi State's Sylvester Croom—the SEC's first African American coach—a 38-31 win over Florida on Oct. 23, 2004.

Hackett said there are still vestiges of racism in the SEC, but also opportunity. "Too many people make that a crutch. There are still issues, but not so many we can't get through." The answer to many of the problems, he said, is perseverance. "I won't let you tell me no. I'm going to work a little harder, so next time they won't be able to skip over me."

Hackett said the nature of the SEC tends to restrict change, even if that change might be for the better. It took 40 years after the conference was integrated for it to hire Croom. The reason, he said, is that in many southern states a football coach is much more than a coach. "Football in the SEC started as a sport, became a religion and now it's big business," Hackett said. "In the SEC, the football coach has more power than anybody in the state. That's just how strong the feeling is about their football."

Greer said he thinks Page would have made his mark at UK. "I believe Greg would have been a starter. He was just a great player. He never got that opportunity.

"Every year I get very disgusted when I look down there at Commonwealth Stadium and see 'C.M. Newton Field,'" Greer added. "Not that I dislike C.M. Newton, but if they ever wanted to name that field for someone they should have named it for Greg Page...."

Hogg said he looks much more at the present than the past. "Now I look at all the black players playing at those SEC schools. We've come a long way. "We kind of opened the door for the rest of them," he said. "We helped make the world a better place."

"Every year I get very disgusted when I look down there at Commonwealth Stadium and see 'C.M. Newton Field.' Not that I dislike C.M. Newton, but if they ever wanted to name that field for someone they should have named it for Greg Page...."

—Roger Greer

The university memorialized Greg Page by placing a plaque at a housing complex named in his honor.

18

Derek Abney: All-Time Kick Returner, Receiver

In all the history of college football, there has never been a better all-purpose back than Derek Allen Abney.

Abney was the first player in NCAA history to gain 2,000 receiving yards, 2,000 kickoff return yards and 1,000 punt return yards in his career. He holds five NCAA records for special teams play: most punt return touchdowns in a game (two), most punt return touchdowns in a season (four), most total kick return scores in a game (two), most total kick return touchdowns in a season (six) and most total kick return yardage in a season (1,348). His SEC records include 2,315 kickoff return yards and 3,357 total return yards. Abney was also the first player to lead the conference in kickoff and punt returns in the same season.

The young man arrived in Lexington in the summer of 1999

UK Sports Information

Derek Abney was the first player in NCAA history to gain 2,000 receiving yards, 2,000 kickoff return yards and 1,000 punt return yards in his career. He holds five NCAA records for special teams play and set numerous other school and SEC records.

as a recruit for Hal Mumme's pass-happy Air Raid offense. Though a high school All-American wide receiver at D.C. Everest High School in Scholfield, Wis., and that state's player of the year, Abney was considered undersized for the SEC at 5-10 and 175 pounds and was largely overlooked. "There were three main reasons I came to Kentucky," he explained. "I wanted to play in the SEC. Speed was what I hung my hat on. I wanted to come to a league known for speed and the best league in the country in my opinion. And coach Mumme offered me the opportunity to catch a lot of footballs. If you're a receiver, that's what you're looking for."

But the newcomer would have to wait a year before he could prove himself. He was redshirted after suffering a pulled hamstring during fall drills. He had to endure rehab and watch from the bench as the Wildcats went 6-5 en route to the Music City Bowl.

As the 2000 season neared, Abney was just another unknown player trying to establish himself among a platoon of receivers led by Dougie Allen and Jimmy Robinson. But in the second game, against South Florida, Number 12 sent fans and announcers scrambling for their programs, as he caught five passes for 72 yards and two touchdowns. Ending the year with three receiving TDs and 40 receptions for 413 yards, Abney was named to the freshman All-SEC team. He ironically received one punt in 2000, which he returned one yard.

As a sophomore, Abney was introduced to new special teams coach Mark Nelson, a veteran of the Canadian Football League, brought to Lexington by new head coach Guy Morris. Mark Nelson was a theory man and innovator, who believed in elevating special teams to equal status with offense and defense. The new coach took the almost unheard of steps of scouting opponents' special teams units, breaking down film and tracking tendencies. If an opposing player often leaned to the left, for example, Nelson would craft a blocking scheme to take advantage of the tendency. He issued scouting reports to his players and had them ready with schemes that placed special emphasis on scoring.

Abney, second on the punt returning depth chart, suddenly found himself elevated when Kendrick Shanklin left the team. "I was just left over when he transferred," Abney recalled. "The coaches saw the stats that I had 17 TDs on special teams in high school. They pretty much said, 'We've got to give this guy a shot.' It wasn't said, but was sort of understood that I'd get my chance." The chance came against Louisville, when Abney returned a Cardinal punt 47 yards for a touchdown.

"There were three main reasons I came to Kentucky. I wanted to play in the SEC. Speed was what I hung my hat on. I wanted to come to a league known for speed and the best league in the country in my opinion. And coach Mumme offered me the opportunity to catch a lot of footballs. If you're a receiver, that's what you're looking for."

—Derek Abney

Locking down the punt returning duties, Abney continued his ascendancy among the receivers, becoming the starter at the "X" wide receiver spot. He started all 11 games, leading the team in receptions (66), receiving yards (741), touchdowns (six) and scoring (42).

Abney also began rewriting the UK record book, piling up statistics in ways that didn't fit established categories. After catching 12 passes for 123 yards against Mississippi State, he had seven receptions for 113 yards and two touchdowns against Vanderbilt, amassing 244 all-purpose yards. The following week, he had 10 catches for 118 yards and a touchdown against Tennessee. It was the first time in school history that a player had 100 yards receiving in three consecutive games.

Coach Mark Nelson's belief in elevating special teams to equality with offense and defense, in addition to tracking opponents' tendencies, led to Abney's breakout sophomore year in 2001. A starter in all 11 games that year, he lead the Wildcats in receptions, receiving yards, touchdowns and scoring. In addition to a number 2 ranking in SEC all-purpose yards, he made academic all-SEC.

"Coach Nelson had the experience and he knew what to look for. But he went above and beyond. He was always watching film. He told me where the guys would be. The first year, we had an all-right season. But that second year, the combination really became successful. He knew who to put in those positions. He knew who was good at what: who could rush the punt, who could hold a block. That first year, he had no idea. There was an increase in knowledge."

—Derek Abney

The performances ran Abney's all-purpose yards per game to 153.8, ranking him second in the SEC and 11th in the nation. On top of everything else, he was named to the conference's Academic Honor Roll.

But that was just the beginning. With a year of experience behind them, Nelson and his special teams unit were poised to launch Derek Abney onto the national stage.

After consecutive 2-9 years, not much was expected of the 2002 Wildcats, and the so-called experts issued their annual predictions of further catastrophe. Guy Morris was considered to be a good assistant coach who still hadn't earned his stripes as a headman.

The Cats were riding a 4-0 record by the time they set their sights on Florida, which would be their first game of the season outside the state. Having outscored their opponents 170-75, Kentucky was in a refuse-to-lose mood as the players boarded the plane for Gainesville. This was their chance to upset the Gators, they said, and they were going to make the most of it.

But the national television audience saw the expected 19-0 Gator advantage in the third quarter, as the orange and blue-clad fans of the Swamp screamed wildly for the home team to continue the rout. At the 11:03 mark, Kentucky quarterback Jared Lorenzen sent Abney on a fade pattern. Getting past the fleet Gator cornerback and safety, number 12 brought in the pass at the corner of the end zone to get the Wildcats on the board.

Florida answered with another

touchdown and—confident in its special teams—sent a kickoff straight into Abney's hands. Two steps and a head fake later, he broke free, outrunning the Gator coverage for a second score and narrowing the Gator lead to 26-14.

Forced to punt, Florida again sailed a ball to Abney, who faked left, broke a tackle and sped down the sideline for his third touchdown of the day. Usually quiet on the field, the sky-high Abney stuck the ball into the Gator turf with an exclamation point that—after the extra point—made the score 26-21.

Though the Wildcats lost 41-34 that day, Abney had almost single-handedly put a scare in the Gators for the first time that season and won the undying affection of Kentucky fans everywhere.

"All the situations were right. It was in the Swamp, it was on TV and we were playing horrible," Abney said. "We needed a momentum swing and I had been just so motivated to turn our team around and everyone else was also on the special teams, so it just worked out. It was, he said, "my favorite moment at Kentucky."

Derek Abney was making a big splash. Everyone from fans to network play-by-play men considered him to be a scoring threat whenever he touched a football. But the SEC is loaded with speedy talent and many players and coaches are hard to impress. Whether lined up as "X" receiver or running to his return spot before a kick, Abney was often taunted by opposing players who didn't think he was

UK Sports Information

Abney's signature point to the sky became a familiar sight in the SEC. Coaches who chose to kick to him were burned time after time. By his junior year, television sportscasters considered him to be a scoring threat whenever he touched a ball.

Forced to punt, Florida again sailed a ball to Abney, who faked left, broke a tackle and sped down the sideline for his third touchdown of the day. Usually quiet on the field, the sky-high Abney stuck the ball into the Gator turf with an exclamation point. "All the situations were right," he said. "It was in the Swamp, it was on TV and we were playing horrible. ...We needed a momentum swing and I had been just so motivated to turn our team around and everyone else was also on the special teams, so it just worked out. (It was) "my favorite moment at Kentucky."

Abney attributed much of his kick return success at UK to quick players with good blocking skills like Adetayo Agboke, above, and Tommy Cook, below. "Agboke was a big part of it," he said. "Nelson always counted on Tommy Cook," he added. "He was the middle guy on the front line as a receiver. He's taking on the biggest guys every time and taking them out of the play every time. Tommy Cook is a different breed. Coach Morris and coach Nelson really respected him as a player and a person."

quicker than they were or that his statistics were over-hyped. For their part, special teams coaches often ordered balls kicked straight to him, anxious to show the world that this Kentucky upstart could be neutralized.

Time after time, Abney burned them, leading the Wildcats to a 7-5 record, their best since the Outback Bowl year of 1998. Many pundits even give him sole credit for the team's success, saying his kick return touchdowns meant the difference in several games.

The player attributed the success of his junior year to Nelson and his special teams supporting cast. "Having a coach there for a second season was really a novelty during my career at Kentucky," he said. "Coach Nelson had the experience and he knew what to look for. But he went above and beyond," Abney explained. "He was always watching film. He told me where the guys would be. The first year, we had an all-right season. But that second year, the combination really became successful. He knew who to put in those positions. He knew who was good at what: who could rush the punt, who could hold a block. That first year, he had no idea. There was an increase in knowledge."

But a return man must have blockers. Abney said the best were not the biggest hitters on offense and defense, but fast receiver types and often-unsung special teams veterans. Three of them were Adetayo Agboke, Aaron Boone and Tommy Cook. "Nelson always counted on Tommy Cook," he said. "He was the middle guy on the front line as a receiver. He's taking on the biggest guys every time and taking them out of the play every time. Tommy Cook is a different breed." Abney said Cook never got the recognition he deserved, "but coach Morris and coach Nelson really respected him as a player and a person."

"Agboke was a big part of it," Abney added. "And Aaron Boone, he really knew how to sustain blocks. He's a special player."

Abney said returning kicks is as much mental as physical. "If you don't believe in yourself, no one else will. You've got to know in your heart that you're going to get things done. When you have that, you can produce some wonderful things. And you can flip it and say that instead of 'I'm going to score every time,' 'what if I drop it?' Then you're in trouble."

He described a typical TD run: "I'll see the first couple of steps and then it's all instinct. I really don't remember anything. Every once in a while I'll remember a great block or something, but I don't remember choosing a direction or setting up a block. Really what goes through my head is nothing."

Abney's efforts in 2002 earned him a trophy case full of awards. He was named a first team All-American as an all-purpose back by the Associated Press, the Football Writers Association of American, the Walter Camp Football Foundation, The Sporting News, CollegeFootballNews.com, ESPN.com, CBSSportsline.com, CNNSI.com and The Sports Xchange. He was first team All-SEC, as chosen by conference coaches, the *Associated Press*, *The Sporting News*, the *Birmingham News*, the *Mobile Register* and CollegeFootballNews.com. His kick off return average of 26.8 yards broke the SEC season record.

When Rich Brooks replaced Morris for the 2003 season, Abney was introduced to Steve Ortmayer, his third special teams coach in four years. On paper at least, it seemed that the kicking game wouldn't skip a beat. Ortmayer arrived at Kentucky with 25 years of experience as an NFL assistant, including serving as special teams coach for the 1981 and 1984 Super Bowl champion Oakland Raiders. In testament to Brooks' priorities, however, Ortmayer was also the team's assistant coach and tight ends coach.

"If you don't believe in yourself, no one else will. You've got to know in your heart that you're going to get things done. When you have that, you can produce some wonderful things. And you can flip it and say that instead of 'I'm going to score every time,' 'what if I drop it?' Then you're in trouble."

—UK All-American Derek Abney

Abney was well on his way to becoming a folk hero by the time the Brooks era began. He was in big media demand and was the central figure in Commonwealth Stadium's pre-game video, which had him in the center of a group of players in the locker room screaming the *On, On, U of K* fight song while wildly swinging his right arm to the beat.

As a wide receiver, Abney was better than ever in 2003, leading the team with 51 catches for 616 yards and five touchdowns. Though he still gained big return yardage—compiling a 24.1 average on kickoff returns—Abney only managed one special teams score in 2003.

There are several theories on why his TD production dropped during his senior year. The primary reason is thought to have been the abolishment

Abney Records

NCAA

Most punt return touchdowns in a game (two)

Most punt return touchdowns in a season (four)

Most total kick return scores in a game (two)

Most total kick return touchdowns in a season (six)

Most total kick return yardage in a season (1,348)

SEC

2,315 kickoff return yards

3,357 total return yards

26.8 kick off return average

First and only player to lead conference in kickoff and punt returns in the same season

of the "halo" rule, which allowed a punt receiver a two-yard buffer to catch the ball. The rule was changed to read that a returner "must be given an unimpeded opportunity to catch the kick," making it much more of a judgment call. Another theory is that SEC opponents—having been burned so many times in the past—finally began kicking away from the All-American. Abney himself thought it was a combination of the two, along with the coaching change. "Obviously that was part of it," he said of the loss of Mark Nelson. "It's hard to reproduce what coach Nelson did, but my first year with him wasn't as good as my second."

After the disappointing 2003 campaign, Abney was still named a first team All-American by the *The NFL Draft Report* and earned a spot on the second team by the Associated Press. He was first team All-SEC for the third consecutive year and was UK's MVP and special teams player of the year. Abney also received the Jerry Claiborne Award as the senior exemplifying the ideals of academic success and team attitude championed by the former player and head coach.

Abney graduated from UK with a degree in civil engineering and was chosen by the Baltimore Ravens in the seventh round of the 2004 NFL Draft.

Looking back on his college career, Abney points to being a first team All-American as his finest honor. "I look at it like no one can deny that you were the best. It's a justification that I really was the best. I can't believe it that I was the best in college football at least for that year. That is very gratifying. It's something that I can keep with me forever."

19

The Fan Phenomenon

Football Fan Day 1998 was a day like many others in the athletic history of the University of Kentucky.

It was billed as an afternoon of planned activities for children and an autograph session for everyone. I, along with my father and our fellow UK fan and friend Tom Appleton, arrived at Commonwealth Stadium early despite a threat of rain in the air and waited an hour or so before the gates were opened.

When we fans—perhaps 400 strong—were finally allowed onto the field, we were expected to assemble around the football throwing station or the field goal-kicking station, but we didn't. Everyone in the place formed a line in front of a table labeled "Tim Couch."

The guy running the event for the athletics association couldn't believe it—and he was angry. He grabbed a microphone and told us in instructive tones that we had an hour and a half before any players would appear and we might as well get a free soft drink, try out the football-throwing station or buy a football guide.

Nobody budged.

The fans didn't care that they had to wait for the Hero of Hyden to

Courtesy Tom Appleton

Fans lined up to get Tim Couch's autograph during UK football's Fan Day 1998.

appear. They came for the autograph and the autograph they were going to get.

Finally, Mr. Event Manager was going to teach us a lesson. He grabbed the sign from the table and walked toward the locker-room entrance at the opposite end of the field. Everyone in line followed him. He began running—and we ran after him. At his wit's end, he finally disappeared into the tunnel.

We luckily struck up a conversation with an athletics association employee who told us Couch would appear in the stands, which were behind a locked gate. The man told us where to stand and, when the end zone gate was finally opened and the players arrived with pens in their hands, we were the first three fans to collect the autographs of Couch, Craig Yeast and Jeff Snedegar.

Finally, Mr. Event Manager was going to teach us a lesson. He grabbed the sign from the table and walked toward the locker-room entrance at the opposite end of the field. Everyone in line followed him. He began running—and we ran after him. At his wit's end, he finally disappeared into the tunnel.... I sometimes still see the event manager in my mind, running with the Tim Couch sign, and being chased by 400 ravenous Wildcat fans with permanent markers in their hands.

I sometimes still see the event manager in my mind, running with the Tim Couch sign, and being chased by 400 ravenous Wildcat fans with permanent markers in their hands.

The University of Kentucky athletic program is a fan-driven phenomenon. Few people—including its own coaches, administrators or an event manager—understand just how big the Big Blue really is.

According to 2003 figures, Kentucky is one of only five NCAA Division I schools boasting top 25 attendance figures in the three "major" sports of men's and women's basketball and football.

Every gymnasium, arena or stadium UK has ever built was labeled a folly or boondoggle in the planning stage and too small after construction. Rupp Arena was ridiculed before it opened by critics who said there weren't enough fans to fill it. It was full for the first game and winner of the annual college attendance record season after season. My father always says they should have built a Cat Dome and he's right.

No other football program in the country of similar stature could have built—much less expanded—a stadium the size of Commonwealth, which is routinely filled with more fans than 2002 champion Miami and many other so-called football powerhouses. Kentucky often goes to bowl games with a 6-5 record because bowl committees know tens of thousands of fans will follow the Cats wherever they go, spending millions of dollars on anything printed, painted or dyed blue and white.

Newspapers in southern cities hosting the annual SEC basketball tournament—most notably the *Atlanta Journal-Constitution*—have been known to print "Go Kentucky" signs to boost sales.

The UK program is larger than any player, coach or university president. It can't be diminished by rivalry, scandal, betrayal or even mismanagement. It is so big that an endless stream of sportswriters try to build their careers on tearing it down, to no avail.

There are more Kentucky fans in the state's largest city, for example, than for any other school, as illustrated by a fan-store owner who recently jump started sales by turning half his place over to UK merchandise.

I heard somebody say once that the Kentucky Wildcats are the New York Yankees of college athletics. That is

Kentucky fans might wear almost anything to a Wildcats game, as long as it's blue and white.

wrong. The New York Yankees are the Kentucky Wildcats of professional baseball.

And yet there are critics who would criticize Big Blue loyalty as proof that fans have nothing else to live for. But fans are everywhere. There are those blindly loyal to the Chicago Cubs, which haven't won a championship in more than 80 years; or the New York Yankees, the best champions money can buy; or those like the Fighting Irish fan who drives around with a vanity license plate that, in code, professes that God roots for Notre Dame.

But the fans keep coming, to every fan day and practice and game. And they always will—whether they are understood or not.

* * *

The first followers of UK sports teams were the students and a few faculty members who attended its early games. The football team first played in 1881, the men's and women's basketball teams in 1903. There was no shortage of curious onlookers at any of those games, with respectable numbers of Lexingtonians appearing—and sometimes even closing down their businesses—to see what the fuss was about.

By 1892, when football became a permanent fixture at the university, students had a growing interest in the outcome of games. They held a

C.C. Clarke, a member of the Immortals of 1898, also served as a member of the athletics association during his collegiate career.

meeting that year to choose the school colors and showed up by the hundreds to cheer on their "Cadets"—as they were then known—in the Thanksgiving game against archrival Centre.

When coach J. White Guyn allowed students to compete for spots on his 0-1 football team in October 1906, he attracted crowds that must have resembled those at modern practices. "The interest upon the part of the student body is alert," reported the *Lexington Leader*. "In addition to the large number of fans who are on the ground every afternoon several of the girls grace the stands with their presence."

In 1909 students able to afford the $15 cost of a round-trip ticket traveled to Urbana, Ill., in a special railroad car covered with blue and white streamers and stickers to watch the football team become Wildcats in its celebrated 6-0 victory over the Illini.

"Encouragement is what the team needs," a student wrote in the *Idea* campus newspaper beforehand. "This only can come from a loyal bunch of rooters. A game has been won by cheering the team hard when things looked against us. ... Let us then keep up our good reputation for noise."

"The entire student body" assembled at the Administration Building that Thursday, Oct. 7, to escort the varsity to the depot. Team members boarded a "wagonette" festooned with blue and white banners, streamers and pennants. By virtue of their victory over the sophomores in the annual "flag rush" the day before, the freshman class won the privilege of pulling the wagon, and each member in attendance grabbed his portion of a long rope tied to its tongue.

Hundreds whooped and cheered as the parade, led by the Battalion Band, began on Limestone Street, with upperclassmen following the wagon in senior-junior-sophomore order and "stray Preps, etc." bringing up the rear. This sight "created considerable sensation" as it made its way along Main Street, with students reciting "all the yells and songs" of their school, including "S-U-Kentucky" and "The Skyrocket."

Reaching the Queen & Crescent depot, the crowd filled its platform, while the "cheer leader" climbed to its roof, to calls of "Illinois Rah!; Illinois Ree!; K.S.U.! Ken-tuck-y!" The 15 players making up the traveling squad—on whose shoulders rested the honor of Kentucky—jumped from the wagon and boarded the special coach, hanging out of its windows to answer the cheers.

As the train pulled away at 6:10 p.m., students formed a line on either side of the track, shaking hands with team members as they passed by and covering the KSU car with stickers and pennants.

Kentucky's first away game in 1914 took place against Cincinnati. So many fans traveled by train to watch their Wildcats that they left their opponents feeling somewhat threatened. Witnessing blue sweaters filling up the stands, Pat Lyons, the UC "cheer leader," exhorted the home team's supporters to get loud or they "would be outrooted on their own home grounds."

The 1921 basketball team—which became UK's first tournament champion and produced its first All-American—helped accelerate interest in the Wildcats. As an important game against archrival Centre on Feb. 18 of that year neared, fans were in a near-frenzy, as reported in local newspapers. "Interest in the game of tonight is well attested by the fact that practically all the reserve seats which have been placed on sale have already been gobbled up and fans are clamoring for more," wrote one reporter.

Kentucky's first away game in 1914 took place against Cincinnati. So many fans traveled by train to watch their Wildcats that they left their opponents feeling somewhat threatened. Witnessing blue sweaters filling up the stands, Pat Lyons, the UC "cheer leader," exhorted the home team's supporters to get loud of they "would be outrooted on their own home grounds."

At game time, fans were "crammed and jammed into every available inch of space, plastered onto the walls, roosting on the rafters, hanging down from the ceiling like flies in winter time, and peeking through the skylights." It was the "largest crowd that ever witnessed a game on the University court," wrote *Kernel* reporter Gerald Griffin. "And as many were turned away as were admitted."

As Kentucky was winning the Southern Intercollegiate Athletic Association Tournament championship game, in Atlanta on March 1, 1921—the "most dramatic ever recorded in Southern basketball history"—hundreds of "students, alumni and rooters … jammed every corner of the lobby and mezzanine floor of the Phoenix hotel" awaiting telegrams about the game's progress.

Every few minutes a man with a megaphone would appear at a second-floor balcony and yell the latest score and situation. "Ridgeway shoots foul; so does Georgia," he screamed at one point. "Georgia makes another on foul; score, Kentucky 11, Georgia 10," he added, creating an "uproar (that) drowned out his shouting."

When the megaphone man announced that UK's Bill King swished a free throw to give the Wildcats the 20-19 win after time had expired,

"Nobody heard the last telegram," wrote the *Herald* reporter. Everyone was screaming "at the top of their voices."

Dawn broke on campus the next morning as usual. But nothing else was the same.

Almost nobody attended classes. Instructors calling roll in nearly empty classrooms were interrupted by "stentorian serenades of the holiday takers, and the latter element was so much in evidence that the professors were forced to chase their classes from the campus in order to free themselves from the torments of the victory-drunk students."

"It was too much," wrote a *Herald* reporter. "Dances were becoming so common that they overlapped and the authorities at the university had to call out the military and lock up the armory and gymnasium to keep down a part of the glad celebration." Becoming Kentucky fans themselves, students at traditional cross-town rival Transylvania "pulled down their whistle" and joined the melee. They "gave such evidences of gratification at our triumph as to make Kentucky adherents thrill with pride at (their) sportsmanship."

> *Becoming Kentucky fans themselves, students at traditional cross-town rival Transylvania "pulled down their whistle" and joined the melee. They "gave such evidences of gratification at our triumph as to make Kentucky adherents thrill with pride at (their) sportsmanship."*

In the early 1920s, UK was seeking to upgrade its athletic facilities with a new basketball facility at Limestone and Euclid and the addition of a modern stadium around Stoll Field half a block away.

Students spread all over campus collecting money for the effort, which came to be known as the Greater Kentucky Campaign Committee. Those wanting to give could also do so on an installment plan managed through the Alumni office by alumni treasurer George B. Carey.

In a bid to have the basketball arena named for the class of 1927, "Forty Freshmen Leaders" raised $4,000 toward construction of the stadium and basketball building.

Alumni received postcards printed with the slogan "To Gain a Friend is Profitable" soliciting money for alumni dues, the following year's subscription to the *Kernel* and the Greater Kentucky fund.

The *Kernel* devoted page two of every issue to a feature called "Alumni Notes," written and edited by the "Alumni Secretary," whose moniker became "Al." The feature allowed former students space to provide updates about the progress of their lives and careers, in addition to a forum to put pressure on them to pony up funds for Greater Kentucky.

It worked.

"Dear 'Al,'" began a letter from 1898 alumnus and Memphis bank attorney Thomas Luther Campbell that appeared in the Oct. 12, 1923, issue.

"Put me down for ten bucks per year for five years to that GLORIOUS enterprise for 'GREATER KENTUCKY,' and especially for POSTERITY. I have been dilatory in this matter but my heart is with the University all the time."

New York commercial banker Howard P. Ingels, class of 1905, raised money on his own, securing $1,000 subscriptions from several of his customers or friends, including oilman Harry F. Sinclair—owner of 1923's Kentucky Derby winner, Zev.

"Your communication received today made me realize that the small sum that I could give to the Greater Kentucky campaign fund would be accepted in the same spirit as if it were a hundred times as much," wrote Carrollton teacher Marie C. Becker, class of 1917. "A long illness and serious operation last year, 'knocked' me out, not only physically, but financially, in an overwhelming manner," she continued. "That explains my silence during the campaign. I am now trying to get 'square' with the world. I wish I could send Old State a real contribution because I love her so dearly."

As of Thanksgiving Day 1923, the fund had pledges from 5,215 people, including almost 40 percent of the 2,601 alumni then living. The campaign raised more than $200,000 for construction of the two facilities. When it opened in 1924, the basketball portion of the building was named Alumni Gymnasium to honor the former students whose contributions had made the effort a success.

"Your communication received today made me realize that the small sum that I could give to the Greater Kentucky campaign fund would be accepted in the same spirit as if it were a hundred times as much. A long illness and serious operation last year, 'knocked' me out, not only physically, but financially, in an overwhelming manner. That explains my silence during the campaign. I am now trying to get 'square' with the world. I wish I could send Old State a real contribution because I love her so dearly."

—Marie C. Becker, class of 1917, in response to a fund-raising letter for the construction of Alumni Gym

By order of the state legislature, the university was officially known as "State University, Lexington, Kentucky" from March 16, 1908, until March 15, 1916. In a sincere attempt to make the best of a bad situation, students devised a cheer in which they would yell "S.U.—Kentucky." The athletic "pep" organization that subsequently formed became "Su-Ky" and later the Su-Ky Circle. In the 1920s, Su-Ky members borrowed cars to entertain school officials and members of visiting football teams at a time when a "visiting team" still required hospitality.

The group raised money for its efforts in many ways, including the sale

The "Su-Ky Circle," the school's pep organization, encouraged students to decorate their "machines" with blue and white streamers for football games. Early fans also wore "Kentucky buttons" with ribbons on their lapels for train rides to away games.

of blue and white streamers. In 1923, for example, the group sold the streamers "for people to wear to the State-Centre game and also for decorative purposes for automobiles. The proceeds will be used to buy a satin K banner. Show your loyalty by buying your streamers from the Su-Ky Circle."

As they prepared to send the team off to Danville, the *Kernel* told students to "Be sure that you have the blue and white on before you enter the stadium. Decorate your machines for the pep meeting tonight."

Speaking at the "pep meeting" was football coach Jack Winn, who contended that the upcoming contest was not simply one between football teams but one between the two schools. "In the opinion of the writer Coach Winn hit the nail on the head," wrote a *Kernel* reporter. "The team is no stronger than its backers. Without the pulling and fighting of the students Kentucky will not come out of the fray with a whole skin. It is not eleven trained athletes pitted against eleven others; it is The University of Kentucky against Centre College. If the student body fails in doing its part in this, the crucial game of the season, the team cannot be expected to win a victory and bring it to us on a silver platter."

Wildcat rooters traveled to Danville trailing the streamers from their "machines" and from the windows of the special trains and wore "Kentucky buttons" and blue and white ribbons to the game.

Sometimes, however, celebrating got out of hand. "There are students of the University of Kentucky, reputedly freshmen, who painstakingly celebrate, in a manner peculiarly their own, the numerous victories of our athletic teams. Now victory, we think, should by all odds be celebrated; one should ring the proverbial welkin, clash the loud timbrel, perform mid-air calisthenics, and in general disport one's self without much regard for decorum. But when a celebration includes weekly theatre rushing, annoyance to the townspeople and a general rough-neck program, that celebration is doing the University a grievous injury. To see why the University suffers from such tactics requires only a minimum of intelligence, and we earnestly believe that college freshmen are not totally deficient in this commodity."

The *Kernel* reported that the "one hundred and fifty 'State' rooters" at the Nov. 27, 1923, game against Georgia Tech in Atlanta, "led by our doughty little freshman cheer leader, made more noise than the entire student body at Georgia Tech."

By the late 1920s—as the athletic program grew in prominence—the phrase Big Blue began appearing in the *Kernel*. It wasn't long before Alumni Gym and Stoll Field resounded with the chant "Go Big Blue!"

Frances Wells Evans of Owensboro, a freshman in 1935, recalled attending games at Stoll Field and Alumni Gym. Each student paid for books of basketball and football season tickets as part of the "athletic fee," which was due at registration. She recalled leaving Patterson Hall with a group of fellow co-eds, walking across Euclid Avenue and filing into Alumni Gym.

"One hundred and fifty 'State' rooters" ... "led by our doughty little freshman cheer leader, made more noise than the entire student body at Georgia Tech."

—Kentucky Kernel, November 1923

"That was when Happy Chandler was governor," Evans explained. "Happy Chandler had the highway put down from Frankfort to Lexington so he could breeze in to watch the games." Pre-games, she said, were much like those of today, with players warming up and students milling around, talking and finding their way to their seats. When the governor arrived at the gym, however, the place fell absolutely silent. "We all stood," Evans recalled, "And when he took his seat, we sat down."

The stellar success of Adolph Rupp, along with the strong football program built in the 1940s and 1950s by Bear Bryant and Blanton Collier, contributed much to the development of a fan base that went beyond students, alumni and Lexingtonians. Coverage of these teams by Louisville radio station WHAS, whose broadcasts at times could reach virtually the entire eastern half of the United States, also helped develop a following for Wildcat sports teams.

In 1942—despite severe limits on wartime travel—hundreds of "railbirds" showed up to see football practices and scrimmages, forcing the athletic department to erect grandstands on the west side of Stoll Field, the portion used for practices. The railbirds also showed up by the hundreds at away games that year and their numbers only increased after the war, as Rupp's squads took the NCAA Tournament by storm and Bryant's teams went to four bowls in five years, winning a mythical national championship in 1950.

Stoll Field and McLean Stadium looked more like a modern football facility by this time, with low-rise bleachers at the end zones and white-painted metal "H" type field goal uprights. Fans of this era—just as they had in Memorial Coliseum—quickly became accustomed to a high level of success and games during these golden years were quieter, more formal affairs than they would become later. In the late summer heat of early season games, men left their sport coats at home in favor of white shirts, dark ties and hats. Hats were also worn by female fans, who wore cotton dresses and, often, gloves.

By the late 1920s—as the athletic program grew in prominence— the phrase Big Blue began appearing in the Kentucky Kernel, the campus newspaper. It wasn't long before Alumni Gym and Stoll Field resounded with the chant "Go Big Blue!"

Fans saw great wins and great teams during UK football's second era of glory. Such scores as 25-0 over Georgia, 14-0 over LSU, 40-6 against Florida and 27-0 over Mississippi State became commonplace.

They also continued traveling in great numbers. In 1951, more than 13,000 fans traveled to New Orleans to watch the Bear's Wildcats defeat Oklahoma 13-7 to win the Sugar Bowl and crown an 11-1 season.

The Kentucky mystique was also developed in the days before TV coverage by the almost impossibility of the average person to watch a basketball game. Neither Alumni Gym's 2,800 seats nor Memorial Coliseum's 11,500 could begin to supply the tremendous demand for tickets.

After UK won the 1958 NCAA Tournament in Louisville's brand-new Freedom Hall—receiving tremendous support from Wildcat fans in that city—UK began playing a game there each December. Kentucky won its first two Louisville games over Illinois and Temple in 1958 and 1959, and the wily Rupp negotiated a contract with Notre Dame to play annually on Freedom Hall's "neutral court."

The result was another fan phenomenon that could only happen for the Kentucky Wildcats. On the morning of the evening game, fans flocked to UK's hour-long "open shoot-around" during which thousands of blue-starved Louisvillians could gaze upon their heroes in person. It wasn't unusual for the event's crowd to be second only to that night's game in Freedom Hall's yearly basketball attendance figures.

In Rupp's time, fans watched the "practice" in respectful silence, applauding good plays or well-run drills. Sometimes the baron addressed the crowd, sometimes he didn't. Mimeographed, blue-toned team photos—complete with autographs in facsimile—were passed around, and fans could purchase the latest Wildcats souvenirs, including a pennant or a bronze-toned coin featuring the UK logo and a schedule for the upcoming season.

By the time Joe Hall had taken over the program in the early 1970s, UK's morning appearance at Freedom Hall had developed into part-practice, part-pep rally, with screaming fans cheering for their favorite players and autograph seekers crowding onto the edges of the playing floor, reaching out with hands and pens and paper at players as they ran up and down the court. After shooting practice and some drills—including Rupp's old favorite, the three-man-weave—Hall would fire up the crowd for the upcoming game and open the floor to everyone for a 30-minute autograph session.

Staring back at the fans in respectful silence and trying to sign anything they might produce—from basketballs to arm casts—Kentucky's players were reported to be so moved by the adoration that they were determined to pay them back with top-notch performances.

For many fans, the open practice was all they would see of their beloved team until the next year. For those lucky enough to have received tickets in the lottery distribution, however, the fun was just beginning.

Freedom Hall was a fine place to watch a basketball game. It had theater-style seats

It was a spine-tingling, adrenaline-producing experience that was known to send small boys back into their seats ashen-faced and on the brink of unconsciousness. Afterward, fans headed for the doors sweating and exhausted, as if they had participated in the game, which indeed they had.

like Memorial Coliseum, but more of them and in a lower tilt that brought strange acoustics into play. Combined with often-inspired play and the heightened decibels of game-deprived local fans, the place usually became a perfect storm for the Fighting Irish of Notre Dame.

Simply put, the Wildcats' advantage at Freedom Hall was noise.

From the opening tip to the final horn, nearly everyone in attendance stayed on their feet, anxiously awaiting any spark that could set them to screaming. It would usually begin with a Kentucky steal and a basket, which would be met with general sounds of approval. If Notre Dame missed a shot and the Wildcats got the rebound, the noise would grow into a low rumble of clapping and yells of encouragement. But if a string of such plays was put together, Freedom Hall would explode into a roaring inferno of sound that energized the Wildcats and demoralized their opponents, removing any instinct they might have had to resist.

It was a spine-tingling, adrenaline-producing experience that was known to send small boys back into their seats ashen-faced and on the brink of unconciousness. Afterward, fans headed for the doors sweating and exhausted, as if they had participated in the game, which indeed they had.

There is no question that the Kentucky fans of Louisville won more than a few games in the Freedom Hall of the 1960s and '70s.

A perfect example is the Dec. 30, 1978, game. Notre Dame was the best team in the nation; Kentucky was unranked. Since top-ranked UCLA had lost earlier in the day, the number-two Irish were poised to take over the top spot in the polls the next week. All Digger Phelps' team had to do was beat a graduation-depleted team of Kentucky Wildcats.

As the crowd-noise began to grow, Macy and Claytor fed the ball to Anderson, whose quickness was more than Notre Dame could handle. The remainder of the first half was an ear-splitting whirl of Kentucky steals and scores, topped of by a floor-length Anderson drive and soaring dunk that produced a roof-trembling roar from the crowd that wouldn't die. It was just before halftime. Unranked Kentucky had a 34-point lead.

A capacity crowd packed into the arena—for the morning practice. The Louisville crowd had come to see the youthful successor to the '77-'78 national champs. Everyone seemed shocked by the turnout, and Hall apologized to his players before making them available to the Big Blue hordes.

It's true that UK was the defending national champions, but the squad had lost three members of its starting five in Mike Phillips, Jack Givens and Rick Robey, and the majority of its scoring production. The Cats brought a 4-2 record into the game.

Replacing the big frontcourt in the starting lineup were sophomores Chuck Aleksinas and Freddie Cowan, along with junior forward Lavon Williams.

Floor general Kyle Macy and senior Truman Claytor lent stability at the guard positions.

The game began slowly, with the veteran Notre Dame team asserting itself and the Wildcats—"Outgunned in size and experience at each position"—testing their sophomores to see if they could produce.

Dissatisfied, Hall did the unthinkable, replacing Aleksinas, a 6-foot-10-inch center, with 6-3, 180-pound Dwight Anderson. The flashy freshman guard immediately inserted a volatility into the game that brought the crowd to a frenzy and left the Irish completely unstrung.

As the crowd-noise began to grow, Macy and Claytor fed the ball to Anderson, whose quickness was more than Notre Dame could handle. The remainder of the first half was an ear-splitting whirl of Kentucky steals and scores, topped off by a floor-length Anderson drive and soaring dunk

One of the biggest wins in UK history was the 40-34 victory over Alabama on Oct. 4, 1997. The Couch-to-Yeast final touchdown marked a huge step forward for the Wildcats, in just the fifth game of the Hal Mumme era. Both field goals—original to Commonwealth Stadium—fell to reveling fans and members of the student body.

that produced a roof-trembling roar from the crowd that wouldn't die. It was just before halftime. Unranked Kentucky had a 34-point lead.

The Wildcats hung on for an 81-76 win.

The following year, Hall was forced to suspend Anderson and Bowie for the Notre Dame game, giving an obviously overjoyed Phelps his best chance in years to beat the Cats. Kentucky won anyway, 86-80. In the last year of the Louisville series, the Irish resorted to a slow-down strategy and lost 34-28 in overtime.

In the 22-year history of UK-Notre Dame games in Freedom Hall, Kentucky won 18 and lost four. UK continues playing a December contest there every year and has won 75 percent of the time.

Another fan phenomenon revolves around the football program. On the verge of becoming a dynasty under Bear Bryant in the 1940s, the team was mismanaged and mishandled over the next several decades.

After hampering Blanton Collier with a rule limiting the number of out-of-state players he could recruit, UK lost the coach to the NFL, where he won a championship his first year en route to a hall-of-fame career. UK next hired ex-Marine Charlie Bradshaw, whose toughening-up experiments left him with small, defection-riddled teams of over-achieving, NFL-bound players that posted one winning record in seven seasons. Former Notre Dame assistant John Ray arrived on the scene in 1969 arguing for better facilities while going 10-33 in four years.

And yet, Kentucky built the $12-million, 58,000-seat Commonwealth Stadium in 1973 and filled it on opening day and virtually every year since. The average attendance for a UK home football game is more than 55,000, which is higher than many recent national championship teams, including the 2002 Miami Hurricanes. And UK is one of only five NCAA Division I schools averaging Top 25 attendance in the three "major" sports of football and men's and women's basketball.

More than 40,000 Kentucky fans traveled to Tampa, Fla., for the 1999 Outback Bowl against Penn State, the Wildcats' first New Year's Day appearance in 47 years. It was the first sell-out in Outback Bowl history, with Kentuckians almost doubling followers of the storied Nittany Lions.

When Fran Curci's 8-3 team went to the Peach Bowl in 1976, more than 37,000 fans traveled to Atlanta to watch them. Filling the 54,000-seat stadium to capacity, the blue and white faithful cheered the Wildcats to a 21-0 victory.

Undoubtedly the greatest game in Commonwealth Stadium history took place in the electric atmosphere of October 4, 1997. Led by All-American quarterback Tim Couch, Hall Mumme's Wildcats passed their way to a 40-34 victory over Alabama in overtime. It was Kentucky's first win over the Crimson Tide since 1922 and fans roared their approval after the Couch to Craig Yeast game-winning pass. Fans stormed the field, tearing down both goal posts and parading them around the field.

More than 40,000 Kentucky fans traveled to Tampa, Fla., for the 1999 Outback Bowl against Penn State, the Wildcats' first New Year's Day appearance in 47 years. It was the first sell-out in Outback Bowl history, with Kentuckians almost doubling followers of the storied Nittany Lions.

If Memorial Coliseum could gain the moniker the "House that Rupp Built," Commonwealth Stadium can truly be called the House that Tim Expanded. Upon completion of the 7-5 Outback Bowl season of 1998 that saw Tim Couch set UK, SEC and NCAA offensive records on a weekly basis, the lower level-portion of the stadium was enclosed and topped in the corners by 40 luxury suites. Seating capacity was brought up to 67,530, which was surpassed on November 20, 1999, when 71,022 fans saw Couch's Cats play host to the Tennessee Volunteers.

University of Kentucky athletics is truly a fan-driven phenomenon—and the best is yet to come.

* * *

Over the course of the 1920s and 1930s, articles about freshman football games would appear in the *Kentucky Kernel* campus newspaper topped with headlines like "Kittens to host greenies." The idea was to convey junior status to freshman teams, with the Vanderbilt Commodores becoming Midshipmen, the Centre Colonels becoming Lieutenants and so on. Near the end of season after season during those years, and for a reason now lost, it was announced that the Kittens would play the Tennessee "Rats."

* * *

UK graduate and fan Wayne Breeding was traveling on a commuter bus from Tokyo to Kobe, Japan, in the late 1990s when he gazed out his window for a glimpse of the Japanese countryside. As the bus passed a small building, Breeding noticed that painted on one outside wall were the words "Wildcat Grill" in English, complete with the UK logo and an image of a Wildcat. "I just cracked up," Breeding said. "I think they just wanted to be as American as they could, so they set up a 'Wildcat Grill.'"

* * *

Calvin Colson of Middlesboro used to send notes to friends and family members on stationery that included the words: "We believe: Jesus Christ—the American Way—Big Blue of Kentucky."

Calvin Colson of Middlesboro used to send notes to friends and family members on stationery that included the words: "We believe: Jesus Christ—the American Way—Big Blue of Kentucky."

* * *

Big Blue Madness—the first day of practice allowed under NCAA rules—began on Oct. 31, 1982, at midnight. Proclaiming "the Cats will run at 12:01," coach Joe B. Hall began that year's first practice before 8,500 fans in Memorial Coliseum, after a women's volleyball game and numerous contests and other activities.

Today's versions of Madness are held in Rupp Arena, and routinely draw capacity crowds, with fans competing with one another to be first in line. Robert Vallandingham and his son Ronald of New Albany, Ind., were first in line for many years, arriving, for example, in 1994 on Oct. 10 and remaining there to become the first fans admitted three weeks later. In 1996, Wally Clark of Lexington decided it was his turn to be first in line. He showed up with a sleeping bag that year—on September 10.

* * *

Kentucky fans can't resist posing with Wildcats, whether they are real or statuary.

Linda Redmon of Frankfort has been a UK fan since childhood. One of her fondest memories was watching her parents get ready for their annual tradition of attending the University of Kentucky Invitational Tournament, which was held from 1953 to 1989. In the days of Memorial Coliseum, she said, "They would dress up. I mean they would really dress up. ... I will never forget when I got to go to the UKIT." Redmon tries to attend most SEC Tournaments in Atlanta, which is often called "Catlanta" when Kentucky is in town. In response to the tens of thousands of fans who follow the Wildcats, local businesses compete with one another for Big Blue dollars. The *Atlanta Journal-Constitution*, for example, prints UK-themed special editions and mini-posters. One year, Redmon had a corner room at the Atlanta Omni Hotel, the team's headquarters. She thought it would be a good idea to tape her UK newspaper poster onto the window glass, which came together at the room's corner. Later, when returning to the hotel, she looked for her poster, only to find a poster in the window of every corner room on that side of the hotel.

* * *

A photo arrived at the UK Athletics Association office in 2004 that would seem commonplace anywhere in Kentucky. It was of a group of 30 or so blue-clad fans holding "Go Cats" signs, toasting each other with UK cups or giving the Number 1 sign. The photo, however, wasn't taken in Lexington or Paducah or Hyden, but in Baghdad, Iraq. It was sent by Senior Master Sergeant Steve Peters in appreciation for tapes of basketball games his unit had received. The group had assembled to cheer on the Wildcats before a 2003-04 basketball game. "When we were asked to come here to help in the fight against terrorism, none of us hesitated," Peters wrote. "We also had no problem with missing the past holiday season away from our family and friends. Our biggest disappointment was the fact that

Since the War on Terror began in 2001, UK fans in the military have been sending images via the Internet from around the world.

we would miss our beloved Wildcats' entire basketball season."

Every Kentucky fan's dream: Getting the autograph.

CATS Program

According to a story from the 1930s, one of coach Adolph Rupp's early teams showed up at the local train station raggedly dressed for a road trip. The coach sent his players home to retrieve suits, on the grounds that college men should look like college men.

The commitment to represent the university and the state well is a long tradition at Kentucky. UK was one of the first universities in its region to take a stand against "ringers" in athletic contests, instituting an enlightened 1906 rule that only those who had completed a full academic year could participate in athletics. Though the rule placed the school in a competitive disadvantage in athletics, it stressed to everyone that athletes were students first.

The commitment to represent the university and the state well is a long tradition at Kentucky. UK was one of the first universities in its region to take a stand against "ringers" in athletic contests, instituting an enlightened 1906 rule that only those who had completed a full academic year could participate in athletics. Though the rule placed the school in a competitive disadvantage in athletics, it stressed to everyone that athletes were students first.

In the 1970s, when Joe B. Hall coached the basketball team, UK's commitment to academics became part of the institution itself.

Under Hall, four graduate assistants oversaw the academic progress of the players in the program. They were supervised by Bob Bradley, whose title was assistant athletics director for academic affairs. Under the system, players met with their academic advisers over breakfast each morning and attended a mandatory study hall each evening. Tutors were available to any player needing help.

The coach received weekly reports on academic progress from professors and academic advisers and daily reports on class attendance.

"The idea of our program is to provide the day-to-day guidance toward the degree," Bradley explained. "We believe in preventative counseling and advising as opposed to crisis. You know, Kentucky has such a proud faculty, you can't go to a professor and 'patch after crash.'"

"We talk to the parents," Hall explained. "We sell them on our program here at Kentucky....I graduated here at the University and I had prodding to stay in line, I had people who cared about me and my future."

Hall often took the "tough love" approach with his players, even suspending starters for failing to attend class or letting grades slip. "You know you are doing what's right for them and they are going to know it sooner or later," he said. "Very seldom does one fail to come back and thank us."

The coach said his approach was simply a concern for the welfare of his players. "If our program is built on a foundation of caring about our athletes, caring about the way they live, the medical attention they get, the food they get, the discipline that they receive and the encouragement academically they get, then you have a sound program. We can build on that."

UK did indeed build on that, launching—in 1981—the first academic center in the United States dedicated exclusively to student-athletes. Known as the Center for Academic and Tutorial Services, or CATS, the program is part of the Athletics Association and helps players manage the almost overwhelming demands on their time.

(UK launched)—in 1981—the first academic center in the United States dedicated exclusively to student-athletes. Known as the Center for Academic and Tutorial Services, or CATS, the program is part of the Athletics Association and helps players manage the almost overwhelming demands on their time.

Bradley said the man who deserves the credit for CATS is former athletic director Cliff Hagan. When presented with the groundbreaking idea of a student-athlete academic center, Hagan facilitated the funding. "Cliff is the one," Bradley said. "He set it up with (then-UK President Otis) Singletary. The board approved it in about 10 minutes. I didn't even have to stand up."

The CATS director attributed Hagan's interest to a hardscrabble childhood in Daviess County. "He grew up in difficult circumstances," Bradley said. "Cliff did really care about the student athletes. He had a soft spot for kids that need help. He told me: 'Make it good for the kids.'"

The program has served UK and its student athletes well over more than two decades. Kentucky won the College Football Association Academic Achievement Award in 1989 for the highest Division I-A graduation rate in the nation and routinely leads the SEC in numerous academic categories. "We lead the conference in academic All-SEC and we lead in football," Bradley explained. "And that's been going on for 15 years, since Jerry Claiborne was here."

CATS has been managed over all those years by Bradley, whose title has evolved to become associate athletics director for student services.

Expanded in 1998 at a cost of $2.4 million, CATS is now located in Memorial Coliseum and features a computer room, a study area that can accommodate 100 students, 24 tutoring rooms and a career development and life skills resource center. With an annual budget of $1 million, CATS

Expanded in 1998 at a cost of $2.4 million, CATS features a computer room, a study area that can accommodate 100 students, 24 tutoring rooms and a career development and life skills resource center. With an annual budget of $1 million, CATS employs a full-time staff of 10 academic counselors, managers and assistants to operate the program, along with part-time graduate assistants and tutors.

employs a full-time staff of 10 academic counselors, managers and assistants to operate the program, along with part-time graduate assistants and tutors.

"Our center provides our student-athletes with a definite advantage over student-athletes at many other institutions," Bradley said. *"Our goal is to show that we care about the student as well as the athlete."*

—Bob Bradley, CATS founding administrator

"We are extremely proud of what we have accomplished in the academic arena," said Bradley, who was named National Academic Advisor of the Year in 1989 and 1992. "The CATS program is focused on winning in the classroom. We look at each student-athlete's individual needs, set goals and develop strategies to attain those goals."

And players are appreciative, either during their time at UK or later in their lives. "One thing that really stands out about my time at Kentucky is CATS," said UK Board of Trustees member Dermontti Dawson, who lettered at Kentucky from 1984 to 1987 and went on to an All-Pro career in the NFL with the Pittsburgh Steelers. "We had access to computers, tutors, study halls.... It was very nice to have those resources available. Academically, it was great."

Part of the CATS mission is to prepare student-athletes—most of whom won't have professional careers—for life after college. Internship opportunities are explored, along with career counseling and assistance with resume writing and establishing a career plan.

For these efforts, UK was named a "Program of Excellence" in 1999 as part of an effort to recognize NCAA Division I-A athletics programs that have established student-athlete welfare as the basis of their operating principles. The recognition, called the CHAMPS/Life Skills Award, is based on student-athletics commitments to academics, athletics, community service, career development and personal success.

"Our center provides our student-athletes with a definite advantage over student-athletes at many other institutions," Bradley said. "Our goal is to show that we care about the student as well as the athlete."

Since its founding, CATS has been a profound success. From 1984 to 2002, 256 UK players had been placed on the Southeastern Conference Academic Honor Roll, the best such record of a conference member. In 1996, a league-record 20 Wildcats were on the SEC Honor Roll. UK's continuously rising standards placed 53 athletes on the list for the fall semester of 2003.

Since its founding, CATS has been a profound success. From 1984 to 2002, 256 UK players had been placed on the Southeastern Conference Academic Honor Roll, the best such record of a conference member. In 1996, a league-record 20 Wildcats were on the SEC Honor Roll. UK's continuously rising standards placed 53 athletes on the list for the fall semester of 2003.

"One of the most attractive aspects of UK basketball is the academic support," said Tubby Smith. "When we bring a young man into our program, we expect him to perform in the classroom first and on the hardwood second. CATS provides the resources and personnel to help us reach that goal from day one of their freshman year."

"There is nothing more important in athletics than this," Bradley said. "We change history. We take kids that grew up in families where no one has graduated from high school in generations. We ask them to do what we say for four years and they have opportunities they never dreamed of. "We change the mindset of how important education is. We elevate people from circumstances. That's everyone's dream."

* * *

"One of the most attractive aspects of UK basketball is the academic support," said Tubby Smith. *"When we bring a young man into our program, we expect him to perform in the classroom first and on the hardwood second. CATS provides the resources and personnel to help us reach that goal from day one of their freshman year."*

—UK coach Tubby Smith

A 2003 series in the *Louisville Courier-Journal* made much of statistics appearing to show that UK's student athletes had a comparatively low five-year graduation rate. The series failed to mention that the statistics were skewed because the school had produced many athletes that signed professional contracts in the years studied or left the school for reasons unrelated to academics. When actual academic performance is compared, Kentucky stands atop achievement lists among the state's NCAA Division I schools and its graduation rate for athletes who had exhausted their eligibility by the end of the 2004-05 academic year stood at 86 percent, best in the SEC.

At Kentucky, Bradley explained, students can't major in "general studies," "leisure," "parks management" and other fields that have become dumping grounds for athletes with questionable academic credentials. The School of Social Work, for example—another place often found for athletes—has a selective admission policy and requires a minimum 2.5 grade point average. Another, "Arts and Sciences," requires four semesters of foreign languages.

UK academic All-Americans

Louie Dampier (1966, 1967)
Larry Conley (1969)
Dan Issel (1970)
Mike Pratt (1970)
Mike Casey (1971)
Tom Ranieri (1974)
Jimmy Dan Conner (1975)
Bob Guyette (1975)
Mark Keene (1978)
Jim Kovach (1978)
Chuck Verderber (1979)
Kyle Macy (1979)
Ken Petrowiak (1985)

Greg Lahr (1989, 1991)
Doug Pelfrey (1992)
Dean Wells (1992)
Mike Schellenberger (1995)
Jef Zurcher (1998)

More First Cats

The first UK basketball player to score 2,000 points in a career was Dan Issel, who reached the mark during his 1969-70 senior season. Issel, who only played three varsity seasons under the rules of the time, finished with 2,138 points, still first on the all-time scoring list. Issel holds numerous other records. His career scoring average of 25.8 points per game is the highest among UK players. He set the single game scoring record of 53 points against Ole Miss in Oxford on Feb. 7, 1970, and his 948 points (1968-69) and 33.9 percent scoring average (1969-70) remain the best in school history. Kenny Walker (2,080) and Jack Givens (2,038) are the only other 2,000-point scorers in men's basketball history.

Kentucky's all-time basketball scoring leader is All-American Valerie Still, who scored 2,763 points from 1979 to 1983. Still is also the career leader in rebounds, with 1,525.

Valerie Still posed with a young fan in 2005.

The champion single-game punter in UK history was Bert Johnson, who set Washington & Lee back a phenomenal 1,155 yards on Sept. 29, 1934. The closest player in the modern era to Johnson's achievement was Jimmy Carter, who punted for 539 yards against Florida on Sept. 28, 1996. Paul Calhoun (1981-84) is UK's career punting leader with 8,432 yards on 198 punts for a 42.58 average. Calhoun's 80-yard punt against Indiana on Sept. 17, 1983—which rolled for as many as 30 yards—is the longest in school history.

Of all the NCAA, SEC and UK records owned by passing king Tim Couch, perhaps the most impressive is the fact that no other UK quarterback has ever thrown 40 completions in a game. Couch accomplished this feat five times in three seasons. His best game was against Arkansas on Oct. 3, 1998, when he completed 47 passes on 67 attempts. Couch's 74 career pass completions broke All-American Babe Parilli's 1949-51 record by 24.

The first UK basketball player drafted into the NBA was Jack Tingle, who was taken by Washington in the 1st round in 1947.

UK's first Wildcat mascot was Gary Tanner, who began the tradition in the 1976-77 season.

The first UK basketball team to score 50 points in a game was the 1912 squad, which demolished Central University (today's Centre College) 52-10 on Feb. 1 of that year. The 1912 team, which finished 12-0 and won the so-called Championship of the South, was also Kentucky's first undefeated team and the only one until Adolph Rupp's 1953-54 Cats went 25-0 en route to that season's Number 1 national ranking by the Associated Press.

The basketball Wildcats first scored 100 points in a game on Jan. 29, 1951, when they shellacked Tulane 104-68. The most points ever scored by a Kentucky team is 143, which the Cats put up against Georgia's 66 on Feb. 27, 1956, setting an SEC record that still stands.

The first Wildcat football player to break 180 yards rushing in a game was Moe Williams, who gained 199 yards on 40 carries in a 35-30 victory over South Carolina on Sept. 23, 1995. Until then, no UK player had ever topped John "Shipwreck" Kelly's 180-yard performance against Maryville on Oct. 11, 1930. Williams had the best game ever by a UK running back that day, also piling up 57 receiving yards and 73 kick off return yards for an all-purpose grand total of 429.

One of the most universal sayings among a football team's defensive ends is "Meet you at the quarterback." UK's best end tandem jelled in 1986-87. Taking maximum advantage of coach Jerry Claiborne's wide-tackle-six defense, Oliver Barnett and Jerry Reese squeezed opposing defenses relentlessly, piling up quarterback sacks at a record-setting clip. Barnett is the UK sack champion with 26 from 1986-89—the first to reach 20 in a career—while Reese had 16 from 1984-87. Barnett went on to play six seasons in the NFL, and Reese played for the Pittsburgh Steelers in 1988.

The first and only UK football player to record 20 tackles for loss in a season was Art Still, who set the mark in 1977. Still was a first round draft choice by the Kansas City Chiefs in 1978 and played 12 NFL seasons for Kansas City and Buffalo.

One of the most exciting plays in football is an interception return for a touchdown. The first and only player to have three such plays was Dallas

Owens, who played from 1974-77. Two of Owens, scoring interceptions took place in the 1977 season. Owens was drafted by the Baltimore Colts in 1978. Kentucky's longest interception-TD was David Hunter's 100-yard return on Nov. 2, 1968, against West Virginia.

James Whalen was the first and only walk-on football player at Kentucky to be named a first team All-American. The tight end gained a spot on the team after his father sent a tape of his high school highlights to coach Hal Mumme. Whalen began his NFL career with the Dallas Cowboys in 2000.

Kentucky's champion tackler is Jim Kovach, who racked up 298 solo tackles and 223 assisted tackles in his career (1975-76, 1978). Kovach is also the first and only Wildcat to be credited with more than 500 total tackles, having ended his career with 521. The Wildcat with the most tackles in a game is Randy Holleran, who had 29 against LSU on Oct. 20, 1990.

The first and only Wildcat to kick a 53-yard field goal was Doug Pelfrey, who had one against Indiana on Sept. 21, 1991. Pelfrey kicked another 53-yarder later that season against Cincinnati. Pelfrey was chosen by the Cincinnati Bengals in the 1993 NFL draft and played seven years for the team.

The first and only UK player to kick 50 field goals in a career was Joey Worley, who kicked 57 from 1984-87. Worley, who also kicked 75 point after attempts, is the all time school scoring leader with 246 total points.

Kentucky's first bowl game was a 24-14 victory over Villanova in the Great Lakes Bowl on Dec. 6, 1947. It was the only time the Great Lakes Bowl was ever played.

Adolph Rupp's Wildcats won the first Southeastern Conference tournament championship on Feb. 28, 1933, in a 46-27 game against Mississippi State. UK also won the regular season crown with an 8-0 conference record and finished the season 20-3 overall. Rupp's teams won 27 conference championships in 40 seasons, including nine consecutive from 1944 to 1952.

It is doubtful that any college basketball team has dominated a conference more than Kentucky has owned the SEC. In 71 years from the conference's founding in 1933 until 2004, the Wildcats have won 40 conference championships. Kentucky has also won 22 SEC tournament titles in the 43 years the event has been played.

The basketball Wildcats first played in a televised game on March 23, 1951, against St. John's in the NCAA Tournament. Kentucky won that game 59-43 and would win 10 games in a row on television before suffering its first loss.

Kentucky's first appearance in the NCAA Tournament was a 46-44 victory over Illinois in New Orleans on March 20, 1942.

The Wildcats placed three players on the inaugural All-SEC team, center Forrest "Aggie" Sale, forward John "Frenchy" Demoisey and guard Ellis Johnson.

Coach Rupp was the first UK representative in the Basketball Hall of Fame, inducted in 1969.

In addition to helping start the UK radio network, J.B. Faulconer earned a letter as a manager of the basketball team in 1939.

Kentucky became the first team in college basketball history to win 1,000 games on Jan. 13, 1969, with an 88-68 whipping of Georgia in Memorial Coliseum.

The Fabulous Five—Alex Groza, Wallace "Wah Wah" Jones, Cliff Barker, Ralph Beard and Kenny Rollins—won the Wildcats, first NCAA Championship on March 23, 1948. The final score was UK 58, Baylor 42.

In 1989, Kentucky became the first football team in the history of the SEC to win the College Football Association Academic Achievement Award for the nation's highest graduation rate.

Strange as it may seem to modern SEC football fans, Vanderbilt was a traditional southern powerhouse and a perennial contender for the region's mythical championship. The Commodores' so-called rivalry with Kentucky was so lopsided that they won 16 games in the series between the two schools before they lost one. The Wildcats, first win over Vandy was a 21-13 decision that took place on Oct. 7, 1939, before 10,000 fans at Nashville's Dudley Field. The Commodores would win three more before losing again, this time to Bear Bryant's first blue and white squad, in 1946. Vanderbilt, incidentally, still plays its games at Dudley Field, which has a modern capacity of 41,221.

UK's first homecoming football game took place on Nov. 25, 1915, a 6-0 win over Tennessee. Homecoming games, filled with hotel receptions, dinner-dances and reunions, were held on a somewhat hit-and-miss basis in subsequent years. Kentucky has held a homecoming each year since 1946.

Jerry Claiborne's 1983 football team holds the distinction of being the first team in NCAA history to compete in a bowl game after a winless season. The Claiborne era began the previous season with a 0-10-1 record.

The basketball Wildcats have played three triple-overtime games in their history, winning all of them. Kentucky beat Centre 22-20 on February 21, 1918; and Miami of Ohio 43-42 on Dec. 21, 1928. The wildest overtime game in UK history took place on Dec. 7, 1957, in a game that pitted the 1957-58 "Fiddlin' Five" against eastern power Temple. Kentucky won the game—the longest in school history—85-83.

The longest football game in NCAA history took place at Commonwealth Stadium on Nov. 1, 2003. UK lost to Arkansas 71-63 in the seventh overtime of the game, which took four hours and 56 minutes to complete. Wildcat quarterback Jared Lorenzen threw for two touchdowns and rushed for three more in the contest, which saw him go 28 for 49 in passing for 326 yards.

Naming a Stadium

As construction continued on UK's new Stoll Field stadium during the 1923 football season, the Wildcats journeyed to Cincinnati for an October 6 contest against the Bearcats. Kentucky had demolished Marshall 41-0 the previous Saturday, and traveling fans hoped to see another high-scoring contest. They were disappointed until right end Kenneth King picked up a Bearcat fumble in the second quarter and returned it 60 yards for the score. Right halfback Ab Kirwan added a 27-yard touchdown soon afterward to provide the 14-0 margin of victory.

A few minutes before halftime, however, starting Kentucky center Price Innes McLean was hit above the left eye, a blow that staggered him, causing at least some temporary blindness. Refusing to be taken out of the game, the junior center lined up as usual, relying on a teammate to tell him when to hike the ball. "On each play he would line up with his team and automatically charge with the linemen," the *Kernel* reported. "He was unable to remember his signals but with the aid of the guard who played next to him he passed the ball each time until the half closed."

The player walked off the field at halftime and spent the second half pacing along the sideline. He complained of not feeling well, but the consensus among the coaches was that he had a "bruised eye and a headache." After arriving in Lexington on the team train, McLean went to bed and spent the following morning eating breakfast and reading a newspaper.

His ill feeling returned, however, and the UK center was taken to a nearby hospital where it was determined that an immediate operation "was an absolute necessity." Doctors emerged from the operating room that afternoon to report that the procedure had been a success and their patient was resting. At 7:15 p.m., however, McLean died.

The player's 10 teammates were his pallbearers at the funeral the following Tuesday at Lexington Methodist Church, accompanied by every member of the Transylvania football team. UK president Frank L. McVey presided at the service, which also included remarks by Enoch Grehan, representing the UK Athletic Council and faculty, football team captain Dell Ramsey, and presidents of the junior class and student council and McLean's junior engineering class.

In subsequent days, the university received sympathetic telegrams from "individuals in all parts of the country," in addition to schools on the football team's schedule and alumni clubs.

He was eulogized as a man of "sterling qualities," who toiled anonymously for two years on the "Z" or "scrub" team to get his chance to play for his hometown university. It was said that "only the fatal accident that occurred could have prevented him from wearing the varsity "K.""

"Football is a hazardous game," wrote the alumni secretary for the *Kentucky Kernel* campus newspaper. "But to live best and serve most anywhere on the face of the earth is a hazardous life. McLean fell, not a victim to the brutality of the game or the opposing team, but to the law of averages which takes its toll relentlessly from every enterprise in which men engage."

Stoll Field's new facility was named McLean Stadium in the player's memory.

The class of 1925 placed this tablet at McLean Stadium in honor of their fallen classmate.